THE HISTORY OF THE UNITED STATES CIVIL SERVICE

"Few scholars look at how ... presidents have sought greater political control over the civil service and sought to use it as an instrument of executive power. *The History of the US Civil Service: From the Postwar Years to the Twenty-First Century* fills this important gap [by] cogently and succinctly describing the political forces and tensions ... that have arisen among presidents, Congress, and bureaucracy."

David Schultz, *Professor of Political Science,*
Hamline University, USA

The History of the United States Civil Service: From the Postwar Years to the Twenty-First Century provides a broad, comprehensive overview of the US civil service in the postwar period and examines the reforms and changes throughout that time.

The author situates the history of the civil service into a wider context, considering political, social, and cultural changes that occurred and have been influential in the history of American government. The book analyzes the development of administrative reorganizations, administrative reforms, personnel policy, and political thought on public administration. It also underlines continuity and changes in the structures, organization, and personnel management of the federal civil service, and the evolution of the role of presidential control over federal bureaucracy. Taking an essential, but often neglected organization as its focus, the text offers a rich, historical analysis of an important institution in American politics.

This book will be of interest to teachers and students of American political history and the history of government, as well as more specifically, the Presidency, Public Administration, and Administrative Law.

Lorenzo Castellani is Research Fellow and Adjunct Professor in Contemporary History and History of Political Institutions at LUISS Guido Carli of Rome, Italy. He is a political analyst and commentator for national and international media.

THE HISTORY OF THE UNITED STATES CIVIL SERVICE

From the Postwar Years to the Twenty-First Century

Lorenzo Castellani

Routledge
Taylor & Francis Group

NEW YORK AND LONDON

First published 2021
by Routledge
52 Vanderbilt Avenue, New York, NY 10017

and by Routledge
2 Park Square, Milton Park, Abingdon, Oxon, OX14 4RN

Routledge is an imprint of the Taylor & Francis Group, an informa business

Library of Congress Cataloging-in-Publication Data
A catalog record for this title has been requested

ISBN: 978-0-367-54636-6 (hbk)
ISBN: 978-0-367-54541-3 (pbk)
ISBN: 978-1-003-08993-3 (ebk)

Typeset in Bembo
by codeMantra

To my son Niccolò and to my wife Fabrizia

CONTENTS

INTRODUCTION

This book aims to offer an overarching view of the changes that have characterized the federal administration and the U.S. federal civil service since 1945, analyzing the historical evolution of a fundamental institution of the U.S. government, which has tended to be neglected by traditional political history.

Despite this lack of attention to the topic, the history of postwar federal bureaucracy seems particularly significant for its quantitative and functional expansion, for its changing relationship with other political institutions, for its place in the policy-making process, for the continuous efforts by the political actors to reform the executive branch in order to achieve a better political control over federal bureaucracy and/or to make more efficient the machinery of government, and for the increasing relevance of political thought to public administration. For all these reasons, a new and more comprehensive historical account of the postwar federal bureaucracy is needed.

In general terms, there have been numerous publications in the areas of political science and public management that have traced the evolution of federal bureaucracy. These have made important and sometimes fundamental contributions to the field, even from the standpoint of administrative history. Nevertheless, what has so far been written about the postwar federal civil service tends to remain confined within specific disciplines: there is a lack of a wider recognition of the changes in federal civil service. As Paul C. Light noted, "public administration and management scholars have generally focused more on the functional impact of reform than on the history."[1]

This book thus responds to the call for providing a history of the U.S. federal civil service that includes far-reaching analysis, in order to achieve a previously missing synthesis.

Moreover, many individual studies of American public administration have tended to separate the dynamics of administrative reorganization from those of the U.S. federal civil service itself, with the risk of writing a tightly compartmentalized history. The purpose of this study, in contrast, is to analyze the evolution of the U.S. federal civil service while keeping together the history of administrative politics, the structural evolution of the executive branch, and the political thought on public administration. This comprehensive approach is necessary for understanding the ideas and the context which inspired administrative reforms, the institutional ties between the pursuit of political objectives, and the consequent organization of offices, practices, careers, and personnel. As part of this process, it is also necessary to articulate a periodization of a not yet fully explored administrative epoch.

The following text identifies four fundamental periods. First, a period of consolidation and rationalization (1945–1960), in which there was sought, at both the political and theoretical levels, a systemization of the changes that were affirmed during the New Deal and World War II: in the 1930s and early 1940s, the size of the federal government had notably expanded, as had the influence of the White House in organizing executive offices. Next, there followed an epoch of administrative growth and pluralization (1960–1976), which coincided with the realization of Great Society policies, expanding the rights and welfare benefits of federal bureaucrats (as well as those of most American citizens), seeking more socially representative procedures for the hiring of bureaucratic personnel, augmenting diversity among civil servants, and introducing new performance measurements for federal executive agencies, departments, and employees. After the fiasco of the Vietnam War and the Watergate scandal, there ensued an era of crisis and neo-managerialism (1976–2000). The Keynesian paradigm entered into crisis in the mid-1970s, and popular trust in government sharply declined as a result of foreign policy failures, economic slowdown, and domestic scandal. Thus, at the end of the 1970s, a neo-liberal and neo-managerial response was made, aimed at reducing the federal government's economic interventions and at importing managerial techniques from the private sector into the public one: the goal was to give business-like qualities to the federal bureaucracy and its structures. This objective implied the monitoring of administrative performance of agencies and departments, the evaluation of federal civil servants, the contracting-out of numerous activities formerly accomplished by the federal government, and more managerial autonomy for top-level bureaucrats in terms of budget, personnel management, and internal organization. There followed a period of continuity, and of national security (2000–2008), in which the implementation of neo-managerial policies, such as performance management, continued to be implemented. After the trauma of 9/11/2001, however, there was added an increased attention (and increased spending) to national security, with the consequent creation of new agencies and civil service rules and personnel management.

Finally, the book would be incomplete without a synthesis of the principal currents of administrative thought. For this reason, an unusual but potentially useful choice has been made: namely, to give space in the book to the reflections published by the most influential theorists of public administration and its role in the American State. Thus, alongside the institutional and administrative history of federal bureaucracy, the reader will find a history of administrative doctrines, ones which have often influenced public debates and policies.

In this way, the book moves forward within a tripartite arrangement: the evolution of structures and offices in the reorganization of the executive branch; the changes of the U.S. civil service at the levels of personnel policies as well as of the careers, the benefits, and the rights of civil servants themselves; and the currents of thought regarding public administration that emerged and changed through the passing years. All three of these elements are analyzed from the historical viewpoint, concentrating on the period between the end of World War II and recent times.

Filling a Gap

Whoever undertakes research into the history of American institutions, and tries to construct a related bibliography, quickly realizes that there is a scarcity of material on post-World War II federal bureaucracy. For several decades, in fact, there has been a lack of book-length historical studies of American public administration. Scholarship has largely marginalized the importance of "taking history seriously" in public administration research.

The most recent work, and still the most relevant one, is Paul Van Riper's *History of the United States Civil Service*, published in 1958.[2] This author extended the research of his mentor, Leonard D. White, the true founder of American administrative historiography, whose reconstructions, however, stop at the beginning of the twentieth century.[3] Thus, even among American authors, the historical studies of greatest temporal extension essentially end at the years immediately following World War II, with Van Riper's already cited book.

For the era following 1945, one can consult works of public law or political science, but not a single complete historical reconstruction. Even a work of great academic significance—like that of the political scientist Skowronek—goes no further than the 1920s, while that of the jurist Ernst does not reach past the 1940s.[4]

There do exist studies of the textbook and popularizing kind, such as those by Maranto and Schultz, which limit themselves, however, to overviews of the various administrative reforms, thus bypassing, for example, the revealing phenomenon of executive reorganization.[5] In contrast, other works, like those of Arnold and Moe, focus exclusively on administrative reorganization from a presidential perspective, neglecting inherent changes in federal bureaucracy.[6]

More recently there have appeared theoretical and doctrine-oriented works that have retraced the history of American administrative thought such as those by Cook,[7] Rohr,[8] Mosher,[9] and Bertelli and Lynn.[10] Nonetheless, these authors only reconstruct the evolution of the debate between scholars and intellectuals, and of the analysis of the ideologies that have informed administrative reforms. More recently, Joseph Postell has analyzed the history of the American bureaucracy, but mainly from a juridical perspective, while Gary Gerstle and Robert F. Durant have offered a rich and comprehensive view of the American State, but without focusing properly on the federal civil service.[11]

For these reasons, the history of American public administration, especially in the light of the expansion of its importance in both purely quantitative and political terms, appears to be a particularly worthy argument for in-depth treatment by a specialist in the study of American political history.

This volume aims to be agile in its conveying, from an historical perspective, diverse aspects of the federal administration. It relies mainly on secondary or public sources, such as the majority of cited commissions reports and books and academic articles, and only in a more limited way on primary sources from the National Archives and Records Administration, Congressional Records, Government Printing Office, Government Accounting Office, Congressional Quarterly Almanac, and Presidential Libraries. Recurring reference is made to leading thinkers in the administrative field and to the theories that have influenced the reforms of federal bureaucracy during the various epochs considered by this study. This book's main objective is thus to offer a new historical synthesis, as well as to re-frame the principal questions, and to reconstruct the more recent yet less-known period of American administrative history.

A Few Generalizations

In the theoretical context, there exist two prevalent conceptions of bureaucracy. One of them was elaborated by Max Weber, who considers bureaucracy from the cold, rationalistic, and deterministic point of view, and reduces it to an ideal type, traceable in every form of society, whether democratic or authoritarian. This is an ideal form of government for an ever more complex and technological world. In many ways, as Alvin W. Gouldner has written, this is "a punishment-centered bureaucracy..., based on the imposition of rules, and obedience, for its own sake."[12] In the twentieth century, theorists on both the extreme right and extreme left adhered to the Weberian ideal type of bureaucracy, to promote technical efficiency and social planning.[13]

Placed in exact opposition to Weberian theory is that of the supporters of the free-market, and of free enterprise, such as F.A. Hayek and Ludwig von

Mises (Austrian School of Economics), extremely suspicious of administrative efficiency, and advocates of individual liberty. For Mises, rationalized administration would condemn the state of the future to become a "gigantic post office."[14] In a technically complex world, with large-scale economic activities, Mises's proposal, oriented in favor of private initiative and opposed to public sector intervention in social and economic life, envisioned a kind of feudal anarchy, a classist and pre-bureaucratic, pre-modern state.

In pluralistic American democracy, neither the Weberian nor the Austrian conception was able to completely affirm itself. Thanks to its peculiarities, American public administration held to a middle course between the two extremes. However, as Dwight Waldo recognized, in *The Administrative State*, this tendency failed to produce a dominant theory of administrative organization for pluralistic societies.[15]

This fact does not mean that the twentieth-century American administrative system was a compromise between the two prevalent theories; instead it was the result of an integration of them. This is the true meaning of the administrative experiment of the United States.

Thus, it is possible to articulate a few generalizations about the American federal bureaucracy. The first fundamental characteristic of the U.S. civil service is its nonpolitical quality, its being comprised by neutral, nonpartisan employees. These civil servants are chosen through competitive examination and, upon entry into the federal administration, they pledge themselves to renounce political activity. This system of recruiting and hiring in the United States is known as the merit system. The merit system is opposed to patronage, the effective mechanism of public appointments for the highest levels of public administration, and itself characteristic of the American political system. The system of patronage opposes that of merit. While the latter is based on competitive selection, the former functions to nominate people to public office positions based on their loyalty to a party (also known as the spoils system). In the merit system, selection by competency is dominant, while in the patronage system, selection by political affiliation prevails.

In Europe, centralization of power produced professional bureaucracies. This trend established itself between the seventeenth and nineteenth centuries both for the development of the modern state in its military, financial, policing, and territorial structures, and for the sake of responding to the needs of industrial society, more stratified and complex than other contenders. By the mid-nineteenth century, therefore, the various European States had begun to adopt a merit system, in order to choose the men who would serve in administrations. This system was held to be less fragmentary, more stable, and more reliable than that of political appointment. A politically neutral civil service was the European response of a liberal and capitalistic society that sought to bring order to itself.

Moreover, in Europe a monarchical past meant that the democratization of national political systems occurred long after their bureaucratization. Because the legitimate presence and power of bureaucratic organizations were a given by the time democracy came along, the primary democratic task was to control and direct their activities to popular ends. One of the reasons that European political parties developed as programmatic, disciplined organizations was to provide the kind of clear, sustained external direction that bureaucratic agencies need if their organizational goals are to be overcome. The strict internal hierarchy of these agencies, a carryover from pre-democratic days, facilitated this effort: to appoint or control the agency heads was a giant step toward controlling the agency.

In contrast, in the United States the establishment of democratic political institutions preceded the establishment of administrative ones.[16] The latter, which were resisted strenuously in the Continental Congress and scarcely mentioned in the Constitution, have remained somewhat illegitimate in American political culture ever since.[17] From the start, this fact has forced bureaucratic agencies to build independent political bases to provide sustenance to their pursuit of organizational goals, an endeavor encouraged by the constitutional system of divided political control. "The development of political skills," writes Rourke, "was part of the process by which executive agencies adapted to their environment in order to survive in the egalitarian democratic society in which they found themselves."[18]

Due to this historical and theoretical background, the reform of the merit system was activated several decades later than in European States, particularly the English one; in the American system, there remained a coexistence between professional bureaucracy and the patronage system; this American bureaucratic system would then develop its own characteristics.

The reasons were simple. In Europe, necessities nurtured a collective and centralized approach with understated management. Here, in fact, the nation-states competed among each other. The economic system tended to stagnate, or in any case proved to be less productive than the American one. The state did not avoid using forms of economic intervention, and development itself was controlled more by political and administrative power.

In the United States, the ground was free, and boundaries more fluid. A vast, almost boundless physical territory protected the young American republic from direct military competition with other nation-states. Thus there could be affirmed, also as a reaction to the abuses of British public power, a decentralized system of government, and a society founded more on freedom of enterprise and an individualist ethic. Consequently, it is not surprising that nineteenth-century administrative reform movements began with the experiences of local governments and developed only toward the end of the century.

With a constitution that imposed both federalism and the separation of powers, the United States developed a more politicized bureaucracy with its own distinct characteristics. As regards public administration, Americans borrowed models from Europe, but also invented their own system.

Such were the origins of a federal civil service that is both more democratic and more political than its counterparts on the European continent, that reflects the idea of a classless society, and that has forged a more intimate relationship, first with political parties and the U.S. Congress, and then with the presidency, especially after the Progressive Era. In addition, the U.S. civil service has played an important role in the competition between legislative and presidential power. It has shown its unique features in the management of personnel, and through strong cooperation, almost osmosis, with the private sector and civil society. Just as the European political and cultural heritage was absorbed and modified by the United States, so too the institution and reforms of its federal civil service bear the distinct imprint of the institutions and culture of the "new world."

Organization of the Book

The book is organized as follows: Chapter 1 analyzes the increasingly important twenty-first-century debate over the American State, to delineate a more realistic interpretation than the classic one, which has prevailed since the middle of the past century. This passage is a necessary one, in order to understand the context in which to place the history of federal bureaucracy and in which kind of macro-evolution of institutional structures one can locate the specific history of the U.S. civil service. In this chapter, historical analysis is also made of fundamental questions that characterized federal bureaucracy during the eras preceding those assessed in this book. Further analysis is devoted to the administrative traditions and the administrative values of the United States, especially those characteristics which established themselves over time and which form the basis of American public administration. Thus, Chapter 1 sets the scene in which historical events and trends are played out: these will be analyzed in the succeeding chapters.

Chapter 2 undertakes a reconnaissance of the history of the U.S. civil service, from the founding of the Republic to World War II. The chapter mainly provides a summary, but one that serves as a necessary preamble for the following historical analysis.

Chapter 3–5 focus on the administrative epochs that will be analyzed and given periodization. Each chapter is dedicated to a particular phase: Chapter 3 to the period of consolidation and rationalization (1945–1960), Chapter 4 to the phase of growth and pluralization (1960–1976), and Chapter 5 to the crisis of the old order and the neo-managerial rebirth (1976–2000) and to the reinforcement of national security (2000–2008). Finally, the concluding chapter sums up the changes and crucial questions that characterize the historical period covered by the book.

Notes

1 Paul C. Light, *The Tides of Reform. Making Government Work, 1945–1995* (New Haven, CT and London: Yale University Press, 1997), 9.
2 Paul Van Riper, *History of the United States Civil Service* (New York: Row, Peterson, and Co., 1958).
3 Among White's works, especially important ones are his four volumes on the history of the American state: *The Federalists, The Jeffersonians, The Jacksonians, The Republican Era* (New York-London: MacMillan, between 1948 and 1958).
4 Stephen Skowronek, *Building a New American State: The Expansion of National Administrative Capacities, 1877–1920* (Cambridge: Cambridge University Press, 1982); Daniel Ernst, *Tocqueville's Nightmare. The Administrative State Emerges in America, 1900–1940* (Oxford: Oxford University Press, 2014).
5 Robert Maranto and David Schultz, *A Short History of the United States Civil Service* (Lanham, MD: University Press of America, 1991).
6 Peri Arnold, *Making the Managerial Presidency. Comprehensive Reorganization Planning 1905–1996*, 2nd ed. (Lawrence: University Press of Kansas, 1998); Ronald C. Moe, *Administrative Renewal. Reorganization Commissions in Century the 20th* (Lanham, MD: University Press of America, 2003).
7 Brian J. Cook, *Bureaucracy and Self-Government: Reconsidering the Role of Public Administration in American Politics* (Baltimore, MD: Johns Hopkins University Press, 2014).
8 John A. Rohr, *Civil Servants and Their Constitutions* (Lawrence: University Press of Kansas, 2002).
9 Frederick Mosher, *Democracy and the Public Service*, 2nd ed. (Oxford: Oxford University Press, 1982).
10 Anthony Michael Bertelli and Laurence Lynn, *Madison's Managers: Public Administration and the Constitution*, (Baltimore, MD: Johns Hopkins University Press, 2006).
11 See Joseph Postell, *Bureaucracy in America* (Columbia: University of Missouri Press, 2017); Gary Gerstle, *Liberty and Coercion. The Paradox of American Government from the Founding to the Present* (Princeton, NJ: Princeton University Press, 2017); Robert F. Durant, *Building the Compensatory State: An Intellectual History and Theory of American Administrative Reform* (London: Routledge, 2019).
12 Alvin W. Gouldner, *Patterns of Industrial Bureaucracy* (Glencoe, IL: The Free Press, 1954), 24.
13 On Weber's bureaucracy see Peter M. Blau, *Bureaucracy in Modern Society* (New York: Random House, 1956); Brian R. Fry and Jos C. Raadschelders, *Mastering Public Administration: From Max Weber to Dwight Waldo* (Washington, DC: CQ Press, 2013).
14 Ludwig Von Mises, *Bureaucracy* (New Haven, CT: Yale University Press, 1944). On the limited and minimal State envisaged by Hayek see F. A. Hayek, *The Constitution of Liberty* (London: Routledge, 2006; first ed. 1960); F.A. Hayek, *The Road to Serfdom* (London: Routledge, 2014; first ed. 1944).
15 Dwight Waldo, *The Administrative State. A Study of the Political Theory of the American Public Administration* (New Haven, CT: Yale University Press, 1948).
16 The order of American political development (democracy before bureaucracy) also affected the country's political parties. Early American parties, quite understandably, had little of the European concern for curbing and directing bureaucratic power. To them, administrative agencies were sources of bounty (pork and patronage), not places of power in need of control; indeed, Jackson's Democrats fostered the process of bureaucratization for bringing order to the spoils system process. In part, because bureaucracy was looked at this way, parties also had no incentive to develop as programmatic organizations. See Michael Nelson, "A Short, Ironic

History of American National Bureaucracy," *The Journal of Politics* 44, no. 3 (Aug. 1982): 747–778.

17 Michael Nelson, "Holding Bureaucracy Accountable," *Saturday Review* 6, no. 23 (Nov. 24, 1979): 12–17.

18 Francis E. Rourke, *Bureaucracy, Politics, and Public Policy*, 2nd ed. (Boston, MA: Little, Brown, 1976), 73.

Bibliography

Arnold, Peri. *Making the Managerial Presidency. Comprehensive Reorganization Planning 1905–1996*, 2nd ed. Lawrence: University Press of Kansas, 1998.

Bertelli, Anthony Michael, and Laurence Lynn. *Madison's Managers: Public Administration and the Constitution*. Baltimore, MD: Johns Hopkins University Press, 2006.

Blau, Peter M. *Bureaucracy in Modern Society*. New York: Random House, 1956.

Cook, Brian J. *Bureaucracy and Self-Government: Reconsidering the Role of Public Administration in American Politics*. Baltimore, MD: John Hopkins University Press, 2014.

Durant, Robert F. *Building the Compensatory State: An Intellectual History and Theory of American Administrative Reform*. London: Routledge, 2019.

Ernst, Daniel. *Tocqueville's Nightmare: The Administrative State Emerges in America, 1900–1940*. Oxford: Oxford University Press, 2014.

Fry, Brian R., and Jos C. Raadschelders. *Mastering Public Administration: From Max Weber to Dwight Waldo*. Washington, DC: CQ Press, 2013.

Gerstle, Gary. *American Crucible: Race and Nation in the Twentieth Century*. Princeton, NJ: Princeton University Press, 2002.

———. Liberty and Coercion. *The Paradox of American Government from the Founding to the Present*. Princeton, NJ: Princeton University Press, 2017.

Gouldner, Alvin W. *Patterns of Industrial Bureaucracy*. Glencoe, IL: The Free Press, 1954.

Hayek, Friedrich A. *The Road to Serfdom*. London: Routledge, 2014 (first ed. 1944).

———. The Constitution of Liberty. London: Routledge, 2006 (first ed. 1960).

Light, Paul C. *The Tides of Reform. Making Government Work, 1945–1995*. New Haven, CT and London: Yale University Press, 1997.

Maranto, Robert, and David Schultz. *A Short History of the United States Civil Service*. Lanham, MD: University Press of America, 1991.

Moe, Ronald C. *Administrative Renewal. Reorganization Commissions in the Twentieth Century*. Lanham, MD: University Press of America, 2003.

Mosher, Frederick. *Democracy and the Public Service*, 2nd ed. Oxford: Oxford University Press, 1982.

Nelson, Michael. "A Short, Ironic History of American National Bureaucracy." *The Journal of Politics* 44, no. 3 (Aug. 1982): 747–778.

Postell, Joseph. *Bureaucracy in America*. Columbia: University of Missouri Press, 2017.

Raadschelders, Jos C. N. "Administrative History of the United States: Development and State of the Art." *Administration and Society* 32, no. 5 (2000): 499–528.

Rodgers, Daniel T. *Atlantic Crossings: Social Politics in a Progressive Age*. Cambridge, MA: Harvard University Press, 2009.

Rohr, John A. *To run a Constitution. The Legitimacy of Administrative State*. Lawrence: University Press of Kansas, 1986.

———. Civil Servants and Their Constitutions. Lawrence: University Press of Kansas, 2002.

Rosenberg, Hans. *Bureaucracy, Aristocracy, and Autocracy: The Prussian Experience, 1660–1815.* Cambridge, MA: Harvard University Press, 1958.

Rourke, Francis E. *Bureaucracy, Politics, and Public Policy,* 2nd ed. Boston, MA: Little, Brown, 1976.

Schmitt, Carl. *Un giurista davanti a se stesso.* Milan: Neri Pozza, 2005.

Skowronek, Stephen. *Building a New American State: The Expansion of National Administrative Capacities, 1877–1920.* Cambridge: Cambridge University Press, 1982.

Van Riper, Paul. *History of the United States Civil Service.* New York: Row, Peterson, and Co., 1958.

Van Riper, Paul. "The American Administrative State. Wilson and the Founders." In *A Centennial History of the American Administrative State,* edited by R. A. Chandler, 417–431. New York: Free Press, 1987.

Von Mises, Ludwig. *Bureaucracy.* New Haven, CT: Yale University Press, 1944.

Waldo, Dwight. *The Administrative State. A Study of the Political Theory of the American Public Administration.* New Haven, CT: Yale University Press, 1948.

White, L. D. *The Federalists.* New York: MacMillan, 1948.

White, L. D. *The Republican Era, 1869–1901: A Study in Administrative History.* New York: MacMillan, 1958.

1

THE AMERICAN STATE AND ITS ADMINISTRATION

Which American State?

It would be a mistake to confront a portion of the administrative history of the United States without recognizing the development of the American government. The exceptional qualities of this history are reflected in the ways of conceptualizing, constructing, and organizing the country's administration.

In traditional historiography, the United States is considered to be the emblem of a "low-intensity" state. To describe its characteristics, the term "stateless society" has been coined, to indicate a society without strong government, one characterized by a weakly centralized and penetrating state form.[1]

According to this viewpoint, the structure of American democracy was placed above all on principles like those of the protection of private property, of free enterprise, and of the rule of law, of the constitutional checks and balances of federalism, rather than on bureaucratic organization or the centralization of public power and the penetration of government into society, all characteristics generally attributed more to modern European States than to the American republic.[2] This narrative, shaped by such major nineteenth-century thinkers as Tocqueville, Hegel, and Marx, proved to be very resistant over time. For example, as late as the mid-twentieth century, the distinguished German jurist Carl Schmitt underestimated the importance of the state and of its administrative structures for understanding the United States. Once he imprecisely stated, "Italians know what the state is, while the British don't; and not to mention the Americans."[3]

Nevertheless, during recent years, a part of American historical literature has underlined how there occurred a progressive reinforcement of central executive power, especially in the second half of the twentieth century.

Governmental powers have notably increased, in terms of both regulation and control over citizens and their activities. The numbers of federal agencies, departments, and civil servants multiplied by the 1930s and programs and policies managed directly by the federal government increased substantially, in particular by the 1960s. As well as these factors, there need to be recognized governmental powers of surveillance, strengthened during the past two decades to prevent terrorist attacks, and the sizable amount of public money invested in financing expanded military interventionism.[4]

Despite these observations, the dominant perception of the American State has remained the above-cited one, with a classic formulation that strains under the influence of the past, in describing a weak, incomplete, decentralized government, limited in its functions and actions.[5]

This description is not void of historical foundation. In the mid-nineteenth century, the American institutional system was a mosaic which included all those elements that diverged from the European context: a federal structure that assured the holders of local power (states, cities, and counties) complete autonomy with respect to the central government, the principle of the separation of constitutional powers at both the federal and state levels, the system of checks and balances among the institutions expressing diverse powers, the adoption of the principles of self-government, and the rule of law and of judicial review, as fundamental concepts in the structuring of popular sovereignty. Thanks to these characteristics, the American political order showed itself as a system of separated institutions sharing power, in which the principle of popular sovereignty accompanied that of legal limitations on the actions of the government, and the absolute respect for specific areas of the various powers' jurisdiction. In this scenario, administrative action and the means of intervention of public power followed criteria that, while they could be considered irrational from the viewpoint of Weberian logic, acquired sense if appraised in the light of the specific qualities of the U.S. system. In fact, until the third decade of the twentieth century, probably one could not truly speak of the presence of a consolidated bureaucratic system. Still, as we will see, this did not imply an absence of either administrative intervention, on the part of single political authorities, nor an administrative power.

In this vein, analyzing the first century of the American republic, Richard J. Stillman identified the origins of the peculiar development of public administration in a series of elements that have informed "American statelessness."[6] He argued that, precisely because of the lack of explicit constitutional guidelines for administrative systems, one must—in order to understand their characteristics and development—examine the foundational ideas of the American republic, the "Tudor" institutions, the conflictual situations preceding the revolution of the 1770s–1780s, and the myths created around the Constitution.[7] On the basis of these elements, Stillman concluded, one can understand how American government has been, at least until the end of the nineteenth century, a government not of men but of laws, founded on a process of limitation of the executive branch and on the negation of any kind of systematic process for the creation of an effective administrative authority.

This "alternative statehood" had already been observed by Alexis de Tocqueville, certainly the nineteenth century's most acute theoretician of American statelessness, who noted that administrative power in the United States presented neither a centralized nor a hierarchical structure; for this reason, this power was difficult to detect. The power existed, but one did not know where to find those who represented it. According to the French intellectual, there can be glimpsed "the faint traces of an administrative hierarchy," and there was no "center in which there converged the spokes of administrative power."[8] For Tocqueville, the "hypo-administrative" configuration of American democracy could better guarantee protection against despotic degenerations of power, even though this same thinker's alarm regarding the possible degenerations of liberal democracy toward mild despotism could hold true for the United States.

This invisibility of public administration, already noted by early nineteenth-century thinkers, did not, however, mean that there was no uniformity in the work of public employees or that these did not come under forms of political control. Tocqueville, in fact, understood quite well that a dominant concept in the United States was supremacy of the law, which defined administrative action and the activity of civil servants by imposing juridically binding norms that could, above all, make themselves readily respected in courts of law. He wrote,

> In the New England states legislative power extends to a greater number of matters than in Europe. The legislative branch penetrates, in a certain sense, into the very heart of the administration; the law descends, to regulate and minutely execute them, and in this way constrains the secondary organs and their administrators with a series of rigid and rigorously defined obligations.[9]

These trends occurred in the United States because the new country had embraced the Lockean principle that had characterized the English revolution, that is, the protection of the citizen from the actions of an arbitrary government. The very Constitution was born in order to limit and regulate the action of the government with regard to its own structures and individuals, and for this reason administrative intervention was conceived as the mere execution of the will of the only legitimate body for representing the sovereign people, namely, the legislature. Based on these assumptions, public administration thus had to be legally limited, to avoid the danger of excessively arbitrary decisions on the part of civil servants, considered to be detrimental to both the rights of individuals and the principle of the separation of powers. And for these reasons, unlike the case of Continental Europe, at the time Tocqueville was writing there did not exist a special branch of the law, the *droit adminitratif*, to regulate the relationship between citizens and the state.

As explained in the writings of Albert van Dicey, the leading British constitutional lawyer of the nineteenth century, the Anglo-Saxon legal tradition has been marked by the extraneousness of *droit administratif*. In his *Introduction to the Study of the Law of the Constitution*, he wrote that the *droit administratif* rested on ideas that were totally alien to English law: according to administrative law, the relationship between individuals and the state is governed by substantially different principles than those which, in private law, safeguard the rights of citizens with regard to their peers. For English law, questions concerning the application of these principles did not pertain to the jurisdiction of ordinary courts. This essential difference made it impossible to identify administrative law with any branch of English law.[10]

In the Anglo-American world, the ordinary courts were the ones to determine the lawfulness of legislation and, consequently, the legitimacy of acts undertaken by civil servants. Nonetheless, if administrative action came to be defined by the normative production of the legislative body, and by the legal control of the courts, the problem of the recruitment of bureaucrats, at both the federal and state levels, was moved to the background. In fact, the criteria of selection did not have to respond so much to competence and professional qualifications as they did to the principle of representing popular sovereignty. The public employee was understood as a civil servant of the people and the power emanated from them, and not as an intermediary between the will of the government and society at large. Thus, in the United States, the presence of civil servants gained its own legitimization from a democratic process. These officials were representatives, directly elected or nominated by those who were chosen by the people.[11]

This process of legitimization, for European theorists of administrative rationality, was something inconceivable and incompatible with the role of public administration, which was seen as an indivisible element of the organic state and as a branch for executing sovereign will, not for representing common people.[12]

In sum, there emerged the interpretation, which would become a persistent one, that the American State was born and raised, compared to European States, as essentially weak, and in administrative terms, it was considered as acephalous, non-autonomous and ruled by "courts and parties."

However, whereas it seems fair to say that European countries have a strong-state tradition, the notion of a weak U.S. State needs to be clarified. Indeed, recent historical scholarship convincingly demonstrates that the story of a weak U.S. State is a myth.[13] These new research findings emphasize the need for empirical and normative statements regarding U.S. weak-stateness to be differentiated. Referring to Michael Mann's sociological distinction between a despotic and an infrastructural meaning of state power, the historian William

Novak observes that the infrastructural power of the U.S. State has always been extensive.[14]

For these reasons, the weak-state narrative, still persistent today, can hardly be sustained from an empirical perspective. From a theoretical standpoint, however, the United States continues to be viewed as "something of an oxymoron" in a country of alleged weak-stateness. Rather than contend with the proliferation of the administrative state, the U.S. constitutional system of checks and balances was designed to prevent despotic power.[15] As Novak explains, it is this ideational "anti-despotic penchant for balancing power" and for "divided and dispersed organization of governance" that most people have in mind when they talk of the weak U.S. state. In consequence, even though its president, executive branch, legislature, and courts are extremely powerful, the United States continued to be considered as having limited government.[16]

Novak has argued that a more realistic interpretation needs to consider the peripheral and horizontal development of the American State, and consequently the distribution, separation, and delegation of power more than its centralization, rationalization, and integration, since it is the peculiar way in which U.S. power deploys itself.

In the wake of these fundamental considerations, a notable number of scholars seem to have concentrated recent work on a realist-pragmatic historiographical revision of the American State.

For example, Max Edling has reconfigured the history of the American State by focusing on the creation of a strong "fiscal-military" state, developing his analysis around Hannah Arendt's concept, which argues that the true objective of the American Constitution was not that of limiting but creating greater power, stabilizing and constituting an entirely new center of power. A weak state could have been the one constructed under the Articles of Confederation, a government that was quickly superseded in favor of a project of constructing a much more solid state. Jerry Marshaw has reconstructed the development of American administrative law, showing how already during its first century of life, the US saw the growth of both federal bureaucracy and independent commissions of regulation. In the past, historians had attributed this phenomenon only to the period following the institution of the Interstate Commerce Commission, created in 1887 to regulate the railway sector.

Richard John has demonstrated how there is no historical basis for the assumption of an absence of administrative management on the part of the American State in its first years of existence, in the name of laissez-faire. Moreover, starting in the mid-nineteenth century, various state governments moved to regulate their infrastructures of communication, postal services, and telegraph and telephone communications networks. At the center of the history of American public administration, Richard White has placed military and commercial development, as well as the westward expansion, with particular attention to the Native American question. Furthermore, as demonstrated by the studies of social and cultural historians, the state was the leading player in the regulation and promotion of policies related to the removal of indigenous peoples from their lands, to slavery, and to forms of racial, ethnic, and religious segregation. These policies did not result from the politics of laissez-faire, nor from reluctant public power, nor from the tendency toward self-government of American society, but instead they were all questions confronted and managed directly and exclusively by public power.[17]

American historiography has also re-evaluated the process of the formation of fiscal and monetary power. David Moss has revealed the American State's long history of regulatory activism, especially regarding risk insurance, while Michael Dauber has documented the same long history of centralized state interventionism in resolving national emergencies and natural catastrophes. A group of academic scholars formed by Christopher Howard, Jacob Hacker, Jennifer Klein, John Witt, and James Wooten have studied and illuminated the potent redistributive effect of American welfare, especially of public insurance policies.[18] As we will see, this dynamic is fundamental to understanding the growth and development of the federal executive branch and its civil service.

Thus, as one can observe from this brief historiographical survey, a good amount of space exists for a new synthesis freed of the nineteenth-century vision, even if the latter remains fundamental for understanding the rules and canons of the American State. As Novak pointed out,

> the myth of the "weak" American state is such a fiction—a product of both reason and interest, perhaps even need. In an era dominated by both European states and European state theory, the story of an exceptional and weaker version of that state in the United States was predictable, perhaps even necessary. But given the dramatic changes in history, politics, and global statecraft during the last generation, the idea of the American state as weak is no longer reasonable or even interesting. It should be rejected. The extraordinary aggrandizement of power within the American regime demands critical attention and historical explanation.[19]

Thus, the time now seems ripe to overcome the traditional non-historical approach which has characterized the study of the United States' public administration.[20] This new synthesis places the administrative system under a different lens, distinct from the paradigms affirmed in traditional historical discourse on "statelessness," and it gives more centrality to the federal civil service and its historical development.

American Public Administration and the Constitutional Framework. Evolutions and Interpretations of a Complex Institutional Mosaic

Before delving into American administrative history, it is worth making a preliminary analysis of some of its most characteristic aspects. In particular, one must consider what the American Constitution prescribes regarding public administration. In reality—and this would prove to be a recurring problem for twentieth-century reformers—the 1787 Constitution says very little about the organization of the executive branch. There are, however, some provisions for the administration, such as Article II, which states "Executive power shall be vested in a President of the United States of America." The article provides very few explanations, given that a large part of American constitutional doctrine takes the phrase in its literal sense, namely, that the leader of the state is the chief of the executive branch. The constitutionalist Edward Corwin, for example, holds that the phrase cannot be understood in any other way. The extra-constitutional dimension of public administration, therefore, is based on the interpretation of this provision in its founding charter.[21]

This clause, of the attribution of power, has been linked to the third section of Article II, according to which the president "shall take care that the laws be faithfully executed." Nonetheless, even here doubts persist about whether the fact that such prescriptions make the president the chief of the administration and subsume the same under the notion of executive power. According to Corwin, this provision means that the president could take, respecting laws and regulations, all the necessary measures to protect from danger the major interests entrusted by the Constitution to the national government. The "take care" clause, therefore, would be exclusively referred to the implementation and to the respect of laws, and not to administrative organization, through which policies would be put into action.[22] For Herman Pritchett, moreover, this provision aims to emphasize the submission of the American executive powers to ordinary law, in contrast to the ample prerogatives and autonomy which they traditionally have enjoyed in England.[23]

In other words, from the viewpoint of the Constitutional directives, in the United States there does not seem to be any allocation of administrative authority to the office of the presidency apart from—and this responsibility appears to be quite limited, at least at first glance—implementing the laws approved by Congress. A salient fact is that the term "executive," in the late eighteenth-century American political lexicon, indicated the place in which a determined goal was transformed into reality. This did not imply, however, that in order to realize the content of the laws, there had to exist a public administration, composed of professional bureaucrats, under the control of the governmental leader.

Consequently, the constitutional paradox of the United States lies in the fact that while the abovementioned provisions do not afford direct constitutional coverage of public administration, other ones do attribute powers to the president that are tied to the structure of government. For example, Article II confers upon the presidency the power to name civil servants with the "advise and consent" of the Senate. The Senate, however, can also decide if it will or will not confer to the president the power to name officials and heads of departments. Finally, the Chief of State is granted the power to remove heads of departments for opinions related to the tasks of their respective offices.

Essentially, the president can request and obtain the dismissals of these officials, whenever a disagreement emerges with the presidency regarding the area under their jurisdiction. This is the only provision which directly refers to the administrative structure.[24]

In fact, for the American Constitution, Congress is the depository of administrative organization, not the president. It is the primary governing body that formally institutes the mandate for the creation of agencies and for their organization, financing, and discretionary spending capacities. It is legislative power that carries out tasks of delegation and control over administrative organs. All the above holds true, with strict adherence to the literal interpretation of the constitutional text; however, history has shown matters to be far more complex.

Indeed, as the historian Morton Keller has underlined, this negligence of the Constitution for administrative authority can be explained by the fact that the founding charter is the child of a pre-bureaucratic and preindustrial era.[25] Obviously, this does not mean that the Founding Fathers were not concerned with the efficiency and effectiveness of government. In Federalist number 70, Alexander Hamilton wrote, "A feeble Executive implies a feeble execution of the government. A feeble execution is but another phrase for a bad execution; and a government ill executed, whatever it may be in theory, must be, in practice, a bad government."[26]

Still, until the threshold of the nineteenth century, the American administrative system was a rudimentary one: a revealing fact is that in 1806 the total number of federal government employees was 126.[27] Moreover, the first presidents, from Washington to Andrew Jackson, were directly in charge of the federal administration, deviating from the prescriptions of the Constitution with the complicity of Congress, precisely because the administration itself was given limited functions and a small amount of activities. With Jackson, in fact, there ended an era, because after his years in office the presidency retreated from its management of public administration, in favor of the legislative branch. During the 1830s, the political and social scenario significantly changed: the diversity of economic and social interests increased; suffrage for adult male citizens was expanded; the mechanism of patronage, driven by political parties, grew stronger; the size of the administrative system also grew; and big industries as well as mass consumption developed rapidly. The president could no longer be the all-encompassing institution capable of representing the multiple interests of the nation on his own, in an ever more complex socioeconomic panorama. The pressure of these sweeping transformations of the political system determined both an expansion of the federal government's functions and the need to mediate among the various competing interests in Congress. There was a striking increase in the number of public bureaucrats, who were called on to confront the emergence of these new needs: in 1816 there were 4,837 federal employees, and by 1871 there were 51,020.[28]

Nonetheless, the figure of the president continued to be subordinate to Congress, in the context of administrative organization. This was the result of bureaucrats being nominated by political parties, who controlled the legislative assembly. President Hayes, elected in 1876, called this system the "Senators doctrine." According to Hayes, the true center of the system of appointments of civil servants remained the Senate, not the presidency. Therefore, while society and government were rapidly changing, the presidency remained substantially the same. During the course of the nineteenth century, Congress was structured in specialized commissions that permitted it to resolve the conflict between diverse interests and matters of contention, while the president was isolated with respect to his own administration, with only a handful of employees and a pair of secretaries at the White House. As Leonard D. White observed, these presidents were more concerned with Congress than with governmental departments.[29]

All the same, at the end of the nineteenth century the constitutional lacuna in the attribution of administrative authority started to weigh heavily on the government, because of the increased structuring of the executive branch. Until that time, the administration's extra-constitutionality was resolved according to immediate circumstances: as long as political patronage was under control, the running of the administration was carried forward by the presidents themselves. In addition, from the end of the Jacksonian period, Congress had played a preeminent role in the exponential growth of political appointees, both for meeting new needs and responsibilities of the government and for satisfying the demands of the party machines.

Also weighing on this scenario was the general shape of the Constitution, founded on the separation of powers, which did not, however, provide an ideal system for the development of the administrative state. As Judge Louis Brandeis would eventually note, the separation of powers had been adopted not to promote efficiency but to discourage the exercise of arbitrary power.[30] The Constitution foresaw an executive branch of modest dimensions, and the choice of the Founding Fathers no longer seemed capable, by the second half of the nineteenth century, to ensure an efficient administration on a vast scale.

The final 30 years of the nineteenth century forcefully thrust the theme of public administration into the American political system. Power was in fact passed in an increasingly pronounced way to Congress, and to the Senate in particular, where the clientelist interests of the parties were openly declared. The line of responsibility with the presidency was lost, in favor of closer ties with administrative agencies, Congressional commissions, and political factions, rather than subordinating the administration to a hierarchy imposed by the president and responsible toward him. With this system of disorder, the corruption and sinecures multiplied, as denounced by Woodrow Wilson, Frank Goodnow, and other experts on administration.[31] Thus, there began to emerge a current of reformers who aimed to put the administration in order, separating it more clearly from politics and giving its organization the stamp of efficiency, which was bringing success to American private business. The gaps in the Constitution, like the separation of powers, could not be emended. To repair the administrative disorder and undertake this work of rationalization of public power, it was necessary to find a solution that would fill the voids in the constitutional charter. Through a series of reforms, public administration would be reordered and transferred progressively over to presidential authority.[32]

At the end of the nineteenth century, Congress tried to intervene and bring order to the administrative apparatus, but the results proved to be fluctuating. On the one hand, as we shall see, the Pendleton Act of 1883 laid the foundation for a civil service based on the principle of merit, introducing hiring by public competition, but on the other, it became obvious that the Congressional committees were incapable of intervening to guide, correct, and organize the daily operations of the administration.

Notwithstanding the efforts of reform undertaken in these years, there were only scant successes, and for this reason, the role of the presidency became even more crucial at the dawn of the twentieth century. Theodore Roosevelt was the first to institute a commission of experts, appointed to provide recommendations for administrative reorganization.[33] The commission was still too tied to Congress, jealous of its prerogatives, and the commission's directives were largely ignored or evaded, but despite practical failures the first seeds had been sown for defining a new role for the presidency in the management of the executive branch. Gradually the presidential commissions gained greater autonomy from Congress, and the promotion of administrative reforms would become, especially from the time of the New Deal onward, mainly a prerogative of the White House.

There was a shift, then, from a conception of the liberal-empire state, based on the containment of costs and functions of federal bureaucracy, to a more interventionist and centralized one, with a drive toward enacting a more extended vision of administrative organization, in both its forms and its purposes. This shift thus included pragmatic aspirations to achieve new political objectives in a now fully industrialized society, whose managerial class was "nationalized" by the experience of the Civil War and ensuing economic development. Thus, there was also the progressive affirmation of what historians have called the "managerial presidency," to indicate the role of the president in the governance of public administration.[34] This process was reinforced by the creation of a national budget in 1921, the augmentation of the presidential staff, and the plans for comprehensive reorganization formulated in the offices of the White House, beginning with Theodore Roosevelt's presidency.

Finally, as the political scientist Stephen Skowronek has emphasized, between the 1880s and the 1920s there occurred the transition from a state of "courts and parties" to a genuinely administrative state. According to the author of *Building the New American State*, the feeble centralization of the government was pushed aside, during the first century of the American republic, by the power and penetration of the various political parties and the judiciary. Nevertheless, with the growth of industrialization, the pressures on the central government increased, toward the aim of expanding public services necessary for the new socioeconomic panorama, thereby launching the expansion of federal administration.[35] Even though this process was characterized by thrusts and counter-thrusts, between the strong reformatory impetus expressed by several sectors of society and the equally vehement defense of the political patronage system against the institutionalization of professional bureaucracy, a complete transition to an administrative state had been accomplished by the late 1920s. Essential factors in this process included the creation of the "merit system" for the selection of civil servants, as well as the setting up of independent administrative agencies, whose range encompassed legislative, regulatory, and judicial powers. A telling example is that of the Interstate Commerce Commission, created by Congress in 1887 to regulate tariffs on railway transport. On this model of an independent agency, there followed the creations of the Federal Trade Commission (1914), the Federal Communications Commission (1934), and the Security and Exchange Commission (1937). Federal agencies multiplied with the reforms of the New Deal—over 60 of them were founded—and they became a defining element of the organization of the new American administrative state.

In conclusion, it is appropriate to widen the temporal arc, in order to accurately frame the history of the federal bureaucracy. As historian Paul Van Riper has observed, after its first century of existence the American republic already possessed all the characteristics of an administrative state. At the same time, its powers and its reach were notably inferior to those of European nation-states, because of the separation of powers laid down by the Constitution, the youth of a state that had yet to undergo wartime strains and pressures comparable to those across the Atlantic, and the federal structure of its institutions. Not by accident, what Van Riper calls the "first American administrative State" ended with the start of the second industrial revolution and the end of the Civil War.

Between the foundation of the Republic and the 1860s, there had been organizational changes and the size of federal employees increased very much, but the next decades became the real turning point for the construction of the administrative State. Indeed, though the size of the federal government grew through the early and middle decades of the nineteenth century, its functions really did not. The only new department created in this period was that of the Interior in 1849, and it consisted almost entirely of already-existing agencies such as the Patent Office and the Office of Indian Affairs that were grouped together because their previous departmental custodians "had grown tired of them."[36] Of the almost eightfold increase in federal employment between 1816 and 1861, 86% were in the Post Office, which simply had a larger country to serve.[37]

The next 70 years were different. New agencies proliferated, seemingly without following any pattern. By 1887, Woodrow Wilson reasonably could compare American administration to a "lusty child" that "has expanded in nature and grown great in stature, but has also become awkward in movement. The vigor and increase of its life has been altogether out of proportion to its skill in living."[38] The President's Committee on Administrative Management, the Brownlow Commission of 1936, concluded a half-century later that bureaucracy in this period grew like a farm:

> a wing added to the house now, a barn put up later, a shed built at some other time, a silo at one stage, a corn crib at another, until it was spread over the landscape in a haphazard and thoroughly confusing way.[39]

As with most farms, however, there was an underlying order to bureaucracy's apparent chaos. The United States had been changing rapidly, from a rural society, individualist in its values yet rather homogeneous in composition, to one that was urban, industrial, and highly diverse. The rise of a national market economy produced new demands on government for "clientele" agencies that would represent and support society's increasingly distinct economic groups. It also generated a second set of demands for regulation, in part to protect weak, albeit large, groups from more powerful ones.

In sum, the reconstruction of political order after the 1860s war and the necessity of dealing with new needs, interests, economic crises, and worldwide conflicts sparked a long and unstoppable process that, according to the illustrious historian, brought about the development of a "Second American Administrative State."[40] With the New Deal of the Roosevelt presidency, this process reached full maturity, but at the same time propelled the American State toward a third era, characterized by the new hegemonic role of the United States as the leading country of the Western world and by the development of the Welfare State and the national security apparatus. It is this third epoch, dubbed by Morton Keller the post-World War II "imperial bureaucracy," that still calls for exploration by historians. As Keller accentuates, the studies of this most recent phase of the life of the American State are themselves still in a developmental phase.[41]

Administrative Values and Traditions of the United States

Before getting to the heart of federal civil service history, it is worth tracing the "enduring patterns" of the American administrative system. Administrative traditions help us to assess the main characteristics of the public administration in terms of structure and organization, while administrative values show us the development of the main trends that shaped American public administration in relationship with the other powers. In both cases, different traditions and values are always simultaneously present in the body of the administrative system, even when there exists a cyclical predominance of some traditions and values over the others, depending on the historical period.

Administrative Traditions

Every administrative system presents, in the course of its historical development, its own unique elements, its recurrent political-institutional behaviors that constitute the very form of the given system, and long-term generalizations that serve as identifying marks of a specific institutional development. In the case of administrative history, these "enduring patterns" typically take the name of administrative traditions.[42] Painter and Peters wrote that "an administrative tradition is a more or less enduring pattern in the style and substance of public administration in a particular country or group of countries."[43]

Thus, before directly entering the story of the federal bureaucracy, it is opportune to make an ulterior historical contextualization of American public administration, for the sake of locating and tracing these administrative traditions. At first glance, the search for these "enduring patterns" might appear to be an excessive attempt at formulaic modeling, at making an artificial construction of Weberian ideal types. Nevertheless, it will be useful to propose a few generalizations before moving on to a more precise and in-depth treatment of the subject.

An especially important contribution to the question has been made by the public management expert Donald Kettl, who has identified four traditions in American public administration: the Hamiltonian, the Jeffersonian, the Madisonian, and the Wilsonian.[44] The Hamiltonian tradition gave pre-eminence to the executive branch, and the central role of the latter, dressed in the division of powers. Hamilton's idea was to have a strong and preeminent president, supported by a federal administration organized in a hierarchical fashion (top-down). In this context, a federal government with more ample spaces to exercise its powers and the edification of a centralized chain of command came to be fundamental for the direction of the United States.

In contrast, the Jeffersonian approach was centered on legislative power and is present even today in the interpretation of important contemporary scholars. For Jefferson, administrative organization rises from below, from local and states' communities, and the greater part of administrative power must rest and pivot on these entities (bottom-up). The principal political value was not—as it was for Hamilton—authority, but rather the Anglo-Saxon one of accountability, understood as the institutional mechanism for controlling the acts of public power. The principal instrument with which this value gained expression was popular participation: as a result, citizens would be represented by governmental institutions.

James Madison, the architect of the balance among constitutional powers, expressed different concerns. He mainly concentrated his attention on containing the partisan conflicts that threatened to tear apart the nascent Republic. Consequently, Madison focused primarily on issues of institutional engineering and on constructing a system based on the separation and balance of powers. In this way, the most important political value was that of the capacity to tie the actions of the leader and of the parties to the institutions, and constitutional law was the means of achieving this binding together. This implied an existent, legitimized federal executive power, in contrast to Jefferson's minimalist vision, even if Madison's model limited the executive's relationship with other public powers.

Finally, at the end of the nineteenth century, there developed what Kettl calls the Wilsonian tradition, which in fact had been anticipated by the reform of the civil service accomplished with the Pendleton Act of 1883. As recognized above, Wilson believed in the central rôle of bureaucracy in managing the complexities of the emergent interests of democratic and industrial society. A society that had grown demographically, territorially, and economically out of all previous proportions had to be brought back into order through an increased role for the federal administration. The chief tenets of the Wilsonian vision were the hierarchy among the various administrative levels, a meritocracy in hiring and promotion, and the neutrality of civil servants regarding politics. In this sense, he was inspired by the German bureaucratic model, characterized by a unitary, hierarchical, competent, and powerful central bureaucracy.[45] Much like Madison, Wilson sought to avoid partisanship and the administrative precariousness induced by the spoils system that had been practiced in ever more unscrupulous ways since the 1830s. Until the end of the nineteenth century, the political parties and the courts, beyond the presidency, were the true factory of the American State, but as the new century began, executive power had to embark on an additional route of development, based on a technocracy composed of a professional bureaucratic corps. This prefigured a new role for the executive branch, also with respect to the new economic potentates (trust and monopolies), directed at balancing the power of great private enterprises, and to provide citizens much more extensive and efficient services. This project could only be achieved through a depoliticization of public administration because, as Wilson wrote in 1887, public administration had a technical meaning:

> It is the object of administrative study to discover, first, what government can properly and successfully do, and, secondly, how it can do these proper things with the utmost possible efficiency and at the least possible cost either of money or of energy.[46]

To sum up, as in the German administrative model, bureaucratic organizations had to be independent and not subject to the influence and the decisions of politics. In essence, Wilson argued that freeing bureaucrats from the interference of politics could increase the efficiency of the administration, which themselves would be freer to import models and practices from other countries and, especially, from the private sector. At the same time, politics freed from administration could more easily supervise it and ensure political scrutiny. In fact, Wilson himself wrote a book in 1885 entitled *Congressional Government*, in which he underlined the necessity to reinforce political and legislative control over a more independent public administration and in which organization would be aimed mainly at the implementation of public policies, more than at their elaboration, and at the provision of means more than at the definition of objectives.[47] To the traditions of the Founding Fathers, therefore, there was added a more technical and modern one, which reserved for the administration a purely implementation and organizational role in managing resources, in order to reach the goals set by politics; introduced the figure of the career bureaucrat into the American political system; and characterized it with political neutrality and professional competence.

As we will see in the following historical analysis, these four administrative traditions, albeit in an asynchronous manner, together emerge during the entire course of American history. They are always coexistent, precisely because they are incorporated into the Constitution and the American political tradition.

Moreover, these traditions have produced centuries of debate and conflict in American public administration. Where should power be centered? What is the relationship between the executive branch and the other institutions? The different traditions have resulted in very different answers to these questions. The conflicts are likely to continue for as long as American democracy exists, because the American approach to bureaucracy embodies two important sets of trade-offs: (1) about how bureaucracy ought to work—bottom up or top down—and (2) about how bureaucracy ought to be integrated into American republican government—whether bureaucracy is central or peripheral. Americans have struggled for more than 200 years to resolve these "riddles of power," and they have proven singularly unsuccessful in doing so. They probably will not be able to solve the enigma in the future, because these different traditions lie at the heart of the possible forms that American institutions, and consequently American public administration, might assume through time.

Administrative Values

According to Herbert Kaufman, "an examination of the administrative institutions of this country suggests that they have been organized and operated in pursuit successively of three values, here designated representativeness, neutral competence, and executive leadership."[48]

While each of the above values has dominated the others at different points in history, no one value has totally suppressed any of the other values. Each of the values has been pursued simultaneously. Shifts from one value to another generally appear to have occurred as a consequence of the difficulties encountered in the period preceding the change. Continued conflict is expected to widen the gulf between supporters of different schools, as each group espouses values that strengthen their preferred institution. Representativeness held the most promise in the post-colonial period, and it was hailed as a way to keep executive power in check. In the words of Kaufman,

> the earliest stress was placed on representativeness in government, the quest for which clearly had its roots in the colonial period, when colonial assemblies were struggling with royal governors for control of political life in the New World and "No taxation without representation" was a slogan that expressed one of the principal interests and anxieties of the colonists. The legislatures thus became the champions of the indigenous population, or at least of the ruling elements in the colonies, against what was regarded in many quarters as executive oppression.[49]

It was manifested in the widespread perception of the legislature as the champion of the citizens and limited powers of executives (such as the governors or local representatives /mayors). Up to the end of the Civil War, it was through the legislatures that government policy was formulated and legitimated. The emphasis on representativeness was manifested in the form of an increasing number of official positions filled by balloting.

Legislative supremacy, however, opened the way for entrenched legislatures, who proved for being particularly vulnerable to the corrupting influence of the industrial system, particularly to the aim of creating powerful monopolies and trusts. Kaufman argued that "corruption beset legislatures from county boards and city councils right up to Congress itself, and the venality and incompetence of many public officers and employers were common knowledge."[50] This also opened the way to political bosses, who managed the parties and public power in a clientelistic way, spreading corruption, particularly at local and state levels.

This situation led, particularly among the urban and intellectual classes, to disillusionment with the existing government machinery, and reformers began the quest for neutral competence in government officials. As a reaction to this perception of widespread corruption and clientelism,

> at every level, reformers began to cast around for new governmental machinery that would provide a high level of responsible government service while avoiding the high costs of unalloyed representative mechanisms. Thus began the quest for neutral competence in government officials, a quest which has continued to the present day.[51]

The core value of this search was the ability to do the work of government expertly and to do it according to explicit, objective standards rather than to personal or party or other obligations and loyalties. The slogan of the neutral competence school became "take administration out of politics." This new school of administrative thought produced the politics-administration dichotomy, according to which politics and administration are separable processes that should be assigned to distinct organs. Its mechanisms were independent boards and commissions and the merit system. It gathered momentum after the creation of the Interstate Commerce Commission (1887) and the passage of the Pendleton Act (1883), which led to the taking of power for hiring from the hands of executive heads (political appointees) and lodging it with experts, who could at least screen out all those who could not pass some sort of test.

Agencies, at every level, differed from each other in details, but had the same underlying structure: their members were appointed for overlapping terms supposedly on the basis of their reputations for general ability and character, and their specialized knowledge. They were granted wide discretion and secure tenures, and they were expected to formulate policy on nonpolitical premises. For these strengths, Kaufman underlined the resiliency of the criterion of neutral competence within the American administrative system:

> The quest for neutral competence, though it began about a century ago, has never waned. The training of civil servants became steadily more formal and systematic as time passed; courses, departments, and even schools of administration appeared in universities. Organization and methods analysis became a profession in itself.[52]

The weaknesses of government, resulting from the work of both the representativeness and neutral competence schools, gave impetus to the supporters of a third value: executive leadership.[53]

The earlier values, and the mechanisms to which they gave rise, created a thrust toward fragmentation of government, as officials went about their business without reference to each other or other organs of government.

There was lack of coordination, with conflict over turfs and gaps in the provision of service and supervision, and special interest groups often succeeded in capturing control of government agencies. This impetus toward fragmentation could not be countered by legislative bodies or the courts. These were the forces that led many reformers to argue that chief executives would have to be strengthened to take charge of the machinery.

Moreover, World War I, the economic depression, the second global conflict and the rising of the United States as the Western world's leading country increased the incentive to look for a more unitary executive and a clearer chain of command. In this context, the Office of the Chief Executive became the hope for a good number of political observers and practitioners, because it was the only means of achieving the end sought.

In the federal government, the movement toward strengthening chief executives took the form of struggles between presidents and Congress for control of policy. One of the first signs was the new emphasis on the executive budget, as a central point where total expenditures could be reviewed and competing claims balanced against each other.

At the federal level, there were occasional adjustments and readjustments in the machinery of government in the early part of the century, and the president was even invested with broad powers of reorganization during the emergencies of World War I and the depression. But it was not until the mushrooming agencies of the New Deal strained that machinery to its limits that the practices and supporting dogmas of the reorganizers made their appearance in strength in Washington. Few clearer statements of the executive leadership's value than the Report of the President's Committee on Administrative Management in 1937 have ever been published. With its recommendations on pulling the administrative functions of the independent regulatory commissions back under the president's supervision, on drawing the government corporations back into the hierarchy, on bringing personnel management under close direction by the president, on strengthening the White House staff, on taking the General Accounting Office out of the pre-auditing field and returning this operation to the executive branch, the Committee offered the classic presentation of the reorganizational aspects of the executive leadership school.

A third sign of this quest for executive leadership is the increase in the size of executive staff. The symbol is the Executive Office of the President, established by Franklin Delano Roosevelt in 1939, with its hundreds of specialists providing the president with advice on every aspect of policy, reviewing legislative proposals to work out the presidential attitude, studying administrative management from the president's point of view, planning, researching, furnishing legal counsel, serving as a source of informational alternatives supplementary to the formal hierarchy, and studded with "the president's men," responsible and loyal to him and him alone.

This new framework, based on the increase of the executive staff, helped to give the chief executive the means with which to direct the heads of agencies and to formulate programs and press them into operation; it has helped make the president a real center of political power.

On a theoretical basis, one of the main reasons for the rise of the executive leadership paradigm was the necessity to eliminate the fragmentation resulting from acceptance of the idea of the separability of politics and administration. Gradually, therefore, the politics–administration dichotomy fell out of favor in public administration, and the doctrine of the continuity of the policy-formulating process, better suited to the aims of executive leadership, began to replace it. Before long, the traditional orthodoxy became old-fashioned and found few defenders. By every measure, then, the years from 1910 to 1950 were characterized by the increasing quest for executive leadership to assume a place of pre-eminence in administrative thought and action.

Finally, while each of the above values has dominated the others at different points in history, no one value has totally suppressed any of the other values. Each of the values has been pursued simultaneously. Shifts from one value to another generally appear to have occurred as a consequence of the difficulties encountered in the period preceding the change. Continued conflict is expected to widen the gulf between supporters of different schools, as each group espouses values that strengthen their preferred institution.

In conclusion, it is worth stating that at no point was any single one of these values pursued to the complete exclusion of one or both of the others; evidence of interest in all three can be found at any stage of American administrative history. The defense of any one of them was often framed in terms of the simultaneous advancement of the others. The story is thus one of changing balance among the values, not of total displacement.

Notes

1 The outlines of this vision of the American nation-state, which enabled it to endure for such a long period of time, were laid out in the fundamental contributions by major nineteenth-century thinkers like Alexis de Tocqueville, Karl Marx, and G. W. F. Hegel. See G. W. F. Hegel, *Lectures on the Philosophy of History* (New York: Wordbridge Publishing, 2011); Karl Marx, *Critique of Hegel's Philosophy of Right* (Cambridge: Cambridge University Press, 1970); G. A. Kelly, "Hegel's America," *Philosophy and Public Affairs* 2 (1972): 2–36; Alexis de Tocqueville, *Democracy in America*, trans. J. P. Mayer (New York: Harper & Row, 1988). For a broader approach to the question of a stateless society, see Kenneth Dyson, *The State Tradition in Western Europe* (ECPR Press Classics, 2010; first ed. 1980).

2 On the theme of the *stateless society*, see the works by Eric Foner, *The Story of American Freedom* (New York: W.W. Norton & Company, 1999); Melvin I. Urofsky and Paul Finkelman, *A March of Liberty: A Constitutional History of the United States* (Oxford and New York: Oxford University Press, 2001); David H. Fischer, *Liberty and Freedom: A Visual History of America's Founding Ideas* (Oxford and New York: Oxford University Press, 2004); Richard Hofstadter, "History and the Social Sciences," in *The Varieties of History: From Voltaire to the Present*, ed. Fritz Stern (New York: Vintage, 1956), 359–370.

3 See Carl Schmitt, *Un giurista davanti a se stesso* (Milan: Neri Pozza, 2005), 53. Translated by the author.

4 See Michael Mann, *The Sources of Social Power*, vol. 4 (Oxford: Oxford University Press, 2011).

5 On these adjectives see Theda Skocpol, *Social Policy in the United States* (Princeton, NJ: Princeton University Press, 1995); Stephen Skowronek, *Building a New American State: The Expansion of National Administrative Capacities, 1877–1920* (Cambridge: Cambridge University Press, 1982); Barry D. Karl, *The Uneasy State: The United States from 1915 to 1945* (Chicago, University of Chicago Press, 1983); Bruce S. Jansson, *The Reluctant Welfare State: A History of American Social Welfare Policies* (Belmont, CA: Brooks Cole, 1988); Jacob S. Hacker, *The Divided Welfare State: The Battle over Public and Private Social Benefits in the United States* (Cambridge: Cambridge University Press, 2002).

6 Richard J. Stillman II, "The Peculiar 'Stateless' Origin of American Public Administration and the Consequences for Government Today," *Public Administration Review* 50, no. 2 (1990): 156–167.

7 On this point, see Don K. Price, *Unwritten Constitution: Science, Religion and Political Responsibility* (Baton Rouge: Louisiana State University Press, 1983); John A. Rohr, *To Run a Constitution. The Legitimacy of the Administrative State* (Lawrence: University Press of Kansas, 1986).

8 de Tocqueville, *Democracy,* 394

9 de Tocqueville, *Democracy,* 395.

10 Albert van Dicey, *Introduction to the Study of the Law of the Constitution* (New York: Liberty Fund, 1982; first ed. 1902), 388.

11 On bureaucratic representation, see Herbert Kaufman, "Emerging Conflicts in the Doctrines of Public Administration," *American Political Science Review* 50, no. 4 (1956): 1057–1073.

12 On this point, see, for example, Hans Rosenberg, *Bureaucracy, Aristocracy, and Autocracy: The Prussian Experience, 1660–1815* (Cambridge, MA: Harvard University Press, 1958).

13 See the bibliography provided by Karen Orren and Stephen Skowronek, *The Search for American Political Development* (Cambridge: Cambridge University Press, 2004); D. King and R. C. Lieberman, "Ironies of State Building: A Comparative Perspective on the American State," *World Politics* 6, no. 3 (2009): 547–588; P. Baldwin, "Beyond Weak and Strong: Rethinking the State in Comparative Policy History," *Journal of Policy History* 17 (Nov. 2005): 12–33; James T. Sparrow, William J. Novak, and Stephen W. Sawyer, eds., *Boundaries of the State in US History* (Chicago, IL: University of Chicago Press, 2015); and Morton Keller, *America's Three Regimes: A New Political History* (Oxford: Oxford University Press, 2007).

14 Michael Mann, "The Autonomous Power of the State; Its Origins, Mechanisms and Results," in *States in History,* ed. John A. Hall (Oxford: Basil Blackwell, 1986), 109–136.

15 Peri Arnold, *Making the Managerial Presidency. Comprehensive Reorganization Planning 1905–1996,* 2nd ed. (Lawrence: University Press of Kansas, 1998), 10.

16 William J. Novak, "The Myth of the "Weak" American State," *The American Historical Review* 113, no. 3 (2008): 763.

17 Max Edling, *A Revolution in Favor of Government: Origins of the U.S. Constitution and the Making of the American State* (Cambridge: Cambridge University Press, 2003); Jerry L. Mashaw, "Recovering American Administrative Law: Federalist Foundations, 1787–1803," *Yale Law Journal* 115 (2006): 1256–1344; R. R. John, *Spreading the News: The American Postal System from Franklin to Morse* (Cambridge, MA: Harvard University Press, 1995); Gary Gerstle, *American Crucible: Race and Nation in the Twentieth Century* (Princeton, NJ: Princeton University Press, 2002); S. Barringer Gordon, *The Mormon Question: Polygamy and Constitutional Conflict in Nineteenth-Century America* (Chapel Hill, NC: North Carolina University Press, 2002); Barbara Young Welke, *Recasting American Liberty: Gender, Race, Law, and the Railroad Revolution* (Cambridge: Cambridge University Press, 2001).

18 On this subject, see David A. Moss, *When All Else Fails: Government as the Ultimate Risk Manager* (Cambridge, MA: Harvard University Press, 2002); Christopher Howard, *The Hidden Welfare State: Tax Expenditures and Social Policy in the United States* (Princeton, NJ: Princeton University Press, 1997); Hacker, *The Divided Welfare State;* Jennifer Klein, *For All These Rights: Business, Labor, and the Shaping of America's Public-Private Welfare State* (Princeton, NJ: Princeton University Press, 2003); Michael B. Katz, *The Price of Citizenship: Redefining the American Welfare State* (Cambridge: Cambridge University Press, 2001); Edward D. Berkowitz, *America's Welfare State: From Roosevelt to Reagan* (Baltimore, MD: The John Hopkins University Press, 1991); Daniel P. Carpenter, *The Forging of Bureaucratic Autonomy: Reputations, Networks, and Policy Innovation in Executive Agencies, 1862–1928* (Princeton, NJ: Princeton University Press, 2001); Bartholomew H. Sparrow, *From the Outside In: World War II and the American State* (Princeton, NJ: Princeton University Press, 1996).

19 Novak, "The Myth," 772.

20 See Michael W. Spicer, "Public Administration, the History of Ideas, and the Reinventing Government Movement," *Public Administration Review* 64, no. 3 (2004): 53–62; Jos C. N. Raadschelders, "Administrative History of the United States: Development and State of the Art," *Administration and Society* 32, no. 5 (2000): 499–528.

21 Edward S. Corwin, *The President: Office and Powers* (New York: New York University Press, 1957), 12.

22 Edward S. Corwin, *The Constitution and What It Means Today* (Princeton, NJ: Princeton University Press, 1974).

23 C. Herman Pritchett, *The American Constitution* (New York: McGraw Hill, 1959), 309–310.

24 On this point, see Louis Fisher, *The Constitution Between Friends* (New York: St. Martin's Press, 1978), 50–81; Leonard White, *The Federalists* (New York: MacMillan, 1948), 20–25.

25 For Keller, Franklin Delano Roosevelt's Presidency ushered in a "populist-bureaucratic regime." See Keller, *America's Three Regimes.*

26 Alexander Hamilton, John Jay, James Madison, *The Federalists* (New York: Modern Library, 1937), 455.

27 Noble E. Cunningham, *The Process of Government under Jefferson* (Princeton, NJ: Princeton University Press, 1978), 325–326.

28 U.S. Bureau of the Census, *Statistical History of the United States* (New York: Basic Books, 1976), 1102.

29 Leonard D. White, *The Republican Era, 1869–1901: A Study in Administrative History* (New York: MacMillan, 1958).

30 In Myers vs US 272 US 52, 1926.

31 Woodrow Wilson, "The Study of Administration," *Political Science Quarterly* 2, no. 2 (1887): 197–222; Frank Goodnow, *Politics and Administration: A Study in Government* (New York: Macmillan, 1900).

32 M. J. C. Vile, *Constitutionalism and the Separations of Powers* (Oxford: The Clarendon Press, 1967), 266–267.

33 This was the Keep Commission (1905–1909), which took its name from its president, Charles Hallam Keep, an Assistant Secretary of the Treasury.

34 Arnold, *Making the Managerial Presidency.*

35 On this point, see Skowronek, *Building the New American State.*

36 Lawrence C. Dodd and Richard L. Schott, *Congress and the Administrative State* (New York: John Wiley & Sons, 1979), 20.

37 James Q. Wilson, "The Rise of the Bureaucratic State," in *The American Commonwealth*, eds. Nathan Glazer and Irving Kristol (New York: Basic Books), 81.

38 Wilson, "The Study," 203.

39 M. Nelson, "A Short, Ironic History of American National Bureaucracy," *The Journal of Politics* 44, no. 3 (Aug. 1982): 768.

40 Paul Van Riper, "The American Administrative State. Wilson and the Founders," in *A Centennial History of the American Administrative State*, ed. R. A. Chandler (New York: Free Press, 1987), 3–36.

41 Keller, *America's Three Regimes.*

42 For an overview of "administrative traditions," see Martin Painter and B. Guy Peters, *Tradition and Public Administration* (Basingstoke: Palgrave Macmillan, 2010).

43 Painter and Peters, *Tradition and Public,* 6.

44 See Donald Kettl, *The Transformation of Governance: Public Administration for the Twenty-First Century,* (Baltimore, MD: The John Hopkins University Press, 2015), especially Chapter 2.

45 On the relationship and cultural influence between Germany and the USA in the late nineteenth century, see Daniel T. Rodgers, *Atlantic Crossings: Social Politics in a*

Progressive Age (Cambridge, MA: Harvard University Press, 2009); also F. Sager, C. Rosser, C. Mavrot, and P. Y. Hurni, *A Transatlantic History of Public Administration* (Cheltenham: Edward Elgar Press, 2019).
46 Wilson, "The Study," 199.
47 Woodrow Wilson, *Congressional Government: A Study in American Politics* (New York: Firework Press, 1924).
48 Kaufman, "Emerging Conflicts," 1057–1073.
49 Kaufman, "Emerging Conflicts," 1058.
50 Kaufman, "Emerging Conflicts," 1059.
51 Kaufman, "Emerging Conflicts," 1061.
52 Kaufman, "Emerging Conflicts," 1061.
53 Kaufman pointed out that

> Just as the excessive emphasis on representativeness brought with it bitterly disappointing difficulties unforeseen by its advocates, so too the great stress on neutral competence proved to be a mixed blessing. And just as the failures of the machinery established with an eye primarily to representativeness helped produce the reaction toward neutral competence, so too the weaknesses of the governmental arrangements devised by the latter school-or, more accurately, the weaknesses of government resulting from the work of both schools-gave impetus to the supporters of a third value: executive leadership.
>
> ("Emerging Conflicts," 1061–1062)

Bibliography

Arnold, Peri. *Making the Managerial Presidency. Comprehensive Reorganization Planning 1905–1996*, 2nd ed. Lawrence: University Press of Kansas, 1998.

Baldwin, P. "Beyond Weak and Strong: Rethinking the State in Comparative Policy History." *Journal of Policy History* 17 (Nov. 2005): 12–33.

Barringer Gordon, S. *The Mormon Question: Polygamy and Constitutional Conflict in Nineteenth-Century America*. Chapel Hill: North Carolina University Press, 2002.

Berkowitz, Edward D. *America's Welfare State: From Roosevelt to Reagan*. Baltimore, MD: John Hopkins University Press, 1991.

Carpenter, Daniel P. *The Forging of Bureaucratic Autonomy: Reputations, Networks, and Policy Innovation in Executive Agencies, 1862–1928*. Princeton, NJ: Princeton University Press, 2001.

Corwin, Edward S. *The President: Office and Powers*. New York: New York University Press, 1957.

———. *The Constitution and What It Means Today*. Princeton, NJ: Princeton University Press, 1974.

Cunningham, Noble E. *The Process of Government under Jefferson*. Princeton NJ: Princeton University Press, 1978.

Dicey, Albert van. *Introduction to the Study of the Law of the Constitution*. New York: Liberty Fund, 1982 (first ed. 1902).

Dodd, Lawrence C., and Richard L. Schott. *Congress and the Administrative State*. New York: John Wiley & Sons, 1979.

Dyson, Kenneth. *State Tradition in Western Europe*. Colchester, Whinoe Park: ECPR Press Classics, 2010 (first ed. 1980).

Edling, Max. *A Revolution in Favor of Government: Origins of the U.S. Constitution and the Making of the American State*. Cambridge: Cambridge University Press, 2003.

Fischer, David H. *Liberty and Freedom: A Visual History of America's Founding Ideas.* Oxford: Oxford University Press, 2004.

Fisher, Louis. *The Constitution between Friends.* New York: St. Martin's Press, 1978.

Foner, Eric. *The Story of American Freedom.* New York: W.W. Norton & Company, 1999.

Gerstle, Gary. *American Crucible: Race and Nation in the Twentieth Century.* Princeton, NJ: Princeton University Press, 2002.

———. *Liberty and Coercion. The Paradox of American Government from the Founding to the Present.* Princeton, NJ: Princeton University Press, 2017.

Hacker, Jacob S. *The Divided Welfare State: The Battle over Public and Private Social Benefits in the United States.* Cambridge: Cambridge University Press, 2002.

Hamilton, Alexander, John Jay, and James Madison. *The Federalists.* New York: Modern Library, 1937.

Hegel, G. W. F. *Lectures on the Philosophy of History.* New York: Wordbridge Publishing, 2011.

Hofstadter, Richard. "History and the Social Sciences." In *The Varieties of History: From Voltaire to the Present*, edited by F. Stern, 359–370. New York: Vintage, 1956.

Howard, Christopher. *The Hidden Welfare State: Tax Expenditures and Social Policy in the United States.* Princeton, NJ: Princeton University Press, 1997.

Jansson, Bruce S. *The Reluctant Welfare State: A History of American Social Welfare Policies.* Belmont, CA: Wadsworth, 1988.

John, Richard R. *Spreading the News: The American Postal System from Franklin to Morse.* Cambridge, MA: Harvard University Press, 1995.

Karl, Barry D. *The Uneasy State: The United States from 1915 to 1945.* Chicago, IL: University of Chicago Press, 1983.

Katz, Michael B. *The Price of Citizenship: Redefining the American Welfare State.* Cambridge: Cambridge University Press, 2001.

Kaufman, Herbert. "Emerging Conflicts in the Doctrines of Public Administration." *American Political Science Review* 50, no. 4 (1956): 1057–1073.

Keller, Morton. *America's Three Regimes: A New Political History.* Oxford: Oxford University Press, 2007.

Kelly, G. A. "Hegel's America." *Philosophy and Public Affairs* 2 (1972): 2–36.

Kettl, Donald. *The Transformation of Governance: Public Administration for the Twenty-First Century.* Baltimore, MD: John Hopkins University Press, 2015.

King, Desmond, and Robert C. Lieberman. "Ironies of State Building: A Comparative Perspective on the American State." *World Politics* 6, no. 3 (2009): 547–588.

Klein, Jennifer. *For All These Rights: Business, Labor, and the Shaping of America's Public-Private Welfare State.* Princeton, NJ: Princeton University Press, 2003.

Light, Paul C. *The Tides of Reform. Making Government Work, 1945–1995.* New Haven, CT and London: Yale University Press, 1997.

Mann, Michael. *The Sources of Social Power*, vol. 4. Oxford: Oxford University Press, 2011.

Maranto, Robert, and David Schultz. *A Short History of the United States Civil Service.* Lanham, MD: University Press of America, 1991.

Marx, Karl. *Critique of Hegel's Philosophy of Right.* Cambridge: Cambridge University Press, 1970.

Mashaw, Jerry L. "Recovering American Administrative Law: Federalist Foundations, 1787–1801." *Yale Law Journal* 115 (2006): 1256–1344.

Moe, Ronald C. *Administrative Renewal. Reorganization Commissions in the Twentieth Century.* Lanham, MD: University Press of America, 2003.

Mosher, Frederick. *Democracy and the Public Service,* 2nd ed. Oxford: Oxford University Press, 1982.

Moss, David A. *When All Else Fails: Government as the Ultimate Risk Manager.* Cambridge, MA: Harvard University Press, 2002.

Nelson, Michael. "A Short, Ironic History of American National Bureaucracy." *The Journal of Politics* 44, no. 3 (Aug. 1982): 747–778.

Orren, Karen, and Stephen Skowronek. *The Search for American Political Development.* Cambridge: Cambridge University Press, 2004.

Painter, Martin, and B. Guy Peters. *Tradition and Public Administration.* Basingstoke: Palgrave Macmillan, 2010.

Postell, Joseph. *Bureaucracy in America.* Columbia: University of Missouri Press, 2017.

Price, Don K. *Unwritten Constitution: Science, Religion and Political Responsibility.* Baton Rouge: Louisiana State University Press, 1983.

Pritchett, C. Herman. *The American Constitution.* New York: McGraw-Hill, 1959.

Raadschelders, Jos C. N. "Administrative History of the United States: Development and State of the Art." *Administration and Society* 32, no. 5 (2000): 499–528.

Rodgers, Daniel T. *Atlantic Crossings: Social Politics in a Progressive Age.* Cambridge, MA: Harvard University Press, 2009.

Rohr, John A. *To Run a Constitution. The Legitimacy of Administrative State.* Lawrence: University Press of Kansas, 1986.

———. *Civil Servants and Their Constitutions.* Lawrence: University Press of Kansas, 2002.

Rourke, Francis E. *Bureaucracy, Politics, and Public Policy,* 2nd ed. Boston, MA: Little, Brown, 1976.

Sager, F., C. Rosser, C. Mavrot, and P. Y. Hurni. *A Transatlantic History of Public Administration.* Cheltenham: Edward Elgar Press, 2019.

Skocpol, Theda. *Social Policy in the United States.* Princeton, NJ: Princeton University Press, 1995.

Skowronek, Stephen. *Building a New American State: The Expansion of National Administrative Capacities, 1877–1920.* Cambridge: Cambridge University Press, 1982.

Sparrow, Bartholomew H. *From the Outside In: World War II and the American State.* Princeton, NJ: Princeton University Press, 1996.

Spicer, Michael W. "Public Administration, the History of Ideas, and the Reinventing Government Movement." *Public Administration Review* 64, no. 3 (2004): 353–362.

Stillman II, Richard. "The Peculiar 'Stateless' Origin of American Public Administration and the Consequences for Government Today." *Public Administration Review* 50, no. 2 (1990): 156–167.

Tocqueville, Alexis de. *Democracy in America,* trans. J. P. Mayer. New York: Harper & Row, 1988.

Urofsky, Melvin I., and Paul Finkelman. *A March of Liberty: A Constitutional History of the United States.* Oxford: Oxford University Press, 2001.

U.S. Bureau of the Census. *Statistical History of the United States.* New York: Basic Books, 1976.

Van Riper, Paul. *History of the United States Civil Service.* New York: Row, Peterson, and Co., 1958.

Van Riper, Paul. "The American Administrative State. Wilson and the Founders." In *A Centennial History of the American Administrative State,* edited by R. A. Chandler, 417–431. New York: Free Press, 1987.

Vile, M. J. C. *Constitutionalism and the Separations of Powers*. Oxford: Clarendon Press, 1967.

Waldo, Dwight. *The Administrative State. A Study of the Political Theory of the American Public Administration*. New Haven, CT: Yale University Press, 1948.

White, L. D. *The Federalists*. New York: MacMillan, 1948.

White, L. D. *The Republican Era, 1869–1901: A Study in Administrative History*. New York: MacMillan, 1958.

Wilson, James Q. "The Rise of the Bureaucratic State." In *The American Commonwealth*, edited by Nathan Glazer and Irving Kristol, 79–96. New York: Basic Books, 1976.

Wilson, Woodrow. *Congressional Government: A Study in American Politics*. New York: Firework Press, 1924.

Young Welke, Barbara. *Recasting American Liberty: Gender, Race, Law, and the Railroad Revolution*. Cambridge: Cambridge University Press, 2001.

2

FROM THE FOUNDATION OF THE REPUBLIC TO WWII

A Brief Overview of the U.S. Civil Service History

A Periodization of the U.S. Civil Service History

Although this book mainly focuses on the post-World War II years through the 1990s, it is useful to provide a wider perspective on administrative development, starting with the origins of the American Republic.

As emphasized before, when one grapples with the history of American administration and public policy, it seems impossible to follow the classic periodization of political history. Inspired by Frederick Mosher's classification, we can identify five phases in U.S. administrative history, between the foundation of the Republic to World War II, as follows: "government by gentlemen" (1789–1829), "government by the common man" (1829–1883), "government by the good" (1883–1906), "government by the efficient" (1906–1932),[1] and "government of emergency" (1932–1945).

Government by Gentlemen (1789–1929)

During its first phase, the life of the Republic was thoroughly shaped by the political objectives at the basis of the Revolution, such as self-government, the protection of individual freedoms, states' rights, and the rule of law.

Thus, the first president, George Washington, worked in a context still heavily influenced by the Declaration of Independence, whose principles of liberty and equality provided the intellectual framework for the self-limitation of presidential and governing powers. In fact, Congress represented much less than the majority of white male adults, and the government and its offices were reserved for an extremely small élite. American society was still characterized by its pre-industrial British heritage.

A large portion of the American "aristocracy" was formed by prominent landholders and, to a lesser extent, by manufacturing entrepreneurs. In short, society was markedly stratified and divided among the wealthy, the middle class, the poor, and slaves. Even if nine out of ten Americans during this era lived by agriculture, ownership of the land was concentrated in the hands of only a few citizens. These rich landowners, who represented a tiny fraction of the rural populace, were at the heart of the "aristocracy" which governed the United States during these years. They were a hereditary landowning "haute bourgeoisie" who lived—in economic, social, political, and cultural terms—in a very different way than did low- to middle-ranking farmers, who were mainly holders of modest tracts or renters. In addition to this division, another one developed amidst the metropolitan centers and rural areas. In the cities, in fact, there began to prosper a second élite, composed of merchants and professionals. Among the latter there were also many sons of the leading landowners, who moved to the major cities in order to practice the professions of highest prestige. These professions were indeed considered to be privileges, since doctors, lawyers, professors, and military officials comprised no more than 2% of all workers in 1800.[2]

The great landowners, notwithstanding the progressive loosening of the ties of democratic suffrage, continued to dominate politics, economy, and society for this entire period, holding the vast leading portion of legislative and executive positions. Essentially, continuity was maintained between colonial and early nineteenth-century society, given that a precise social and economic block continued to exert political power.

In this scenario, George Washington and his immediate successors were able to devote special attention to their choice of the most capable men for occupying specific governmental offices. The first president employed, as a single criterion of selection, "fitness of character," in other words the capacity of a given individual to hold a given administrative post. The leaders of the executive branch considered this system to be a meritocratic one, albeit in a sense different from that in use today. In fact, the merits of potential administrators were evaluated according to a man's family background, his education, the honor and esteem attached to his profession, and his degree of loyalty vis-à-vis the new government. Moreover, appointments were made according to a criterion aimed at maintaining a balance of geographical representation. After Washington's presidency, and even more after that of Jefferson, political parties began to develop, and in the naming of civil servants growing importance was given to party allegiance, and loyalty to political leadership. Nonetheless, this development did not make a serious dent in the composition of the administrative élite, which continued to match that of society in general.

Federal administration personnel tended to be divided into two groups. Those who held the highest positions, and who covered public duties, were chiefly concerned with taking political decisions; they had extensive responsibilities, in both the political and executive contexts. Among them were members of the Presidential Cabinet and their assistants, the territorial governors, and the heads of the budgetary and census offices. These officials were named by the president or, in some cases, by Cabinet members, and they constituted the élite of executive power, with strong political influence.

The second group was formed by employees of the customs, the inspections office, the postal service, and many other departments. They were much more numerous, but also much less influential in affecting government policies. In addition, they did not for the most part work in Washington, as the first group did, but instead they were distributed across the entire national territory. According to Mosher's estimate, in 1800, only 150 out of 3,000 employees were residents in the capital.[3] These workers, moreover, came from a different social background than that of the top-level managers. While the latter belonged to the landowning and commercial aristocracy, the former hailed from the middle-upper class. To qualify for service in the lower branches of the administration, at least competent literacy was required, as was a professional apprenticeship, as a lawyer or doctor, or as an accountant or skilled artisan. Besides, with their not having any legal protection nor social benefits, it was taken for granted that those who were part of the "low-middle level" bureaucracy could hold on to their posts for life, with guarantees. In this case, the principle of rotation (the spoils system) was never really applied to this category, and it was reserved only for the top-level positions.

In the first group, on the other hand, mobility was prevalent. The most reliable source on appointments' mobility is the statistical comparison made by Sidney Aronson among the John Adams, Thomas Jefferson, and Andrew Jackson presidencies. Aronson has revealed that out of 87 appointments made by President Adams, 60 of them assigned the office to men who had never before held administrative positions. In the case of Thomas Jefferson, the rate was 73 out of 92, while in Jackson's presidency there were 95 out of 108, meaning that almost 90% of incumbent civil servants were replaced by new ones. Still, Aronson's numbers show that during the passage from the first to the fourth presidency, even if a large majority of administrators still came from the great landowning families, there was a progressive rise in the percentage of merchants and professionals. In general, however, in the three presidencies of Adams, Jefferson, and Jackson, more than 90% of top-ranking civil servants remained members of the urban and territorial *upper class*.[4] Nevertheless, this establishment would not keep such a dominant place as it had maintained in the first 40 years of the U.S. Republic.

Government by the Common Man (1829–1883)

Andrew Jackson's victory in the 1828 presidential election has become regarded as a crucial turning point in the history of American government and administration. The populist president did in fact carry with him into office a strongly democratized conception of government, imbued with egalitarianism and moralism. Consequently, there emerged the necessity to make extensive use of the spoils system, and the recourse to the criterion of political loyalty, more than the meritocratic one, in the definition of middle- and high-level administrative appointments. These changes derived from those of the political system, in which the parties, precisely with the 1828 election, had launched a new approach to seeking a consensus, structuring themselves on the territory, and organizing electoral propaganda.

President Jackson's ideas about the spoils system, however, remained controversial. In his inaugural address, he cited the necessity of

> reform, which will require particularly the correction of those abuses that have brought the patronage of the Federal Government into conflict with the freedom of elections, and the counteraction of those causes which have disturbed the rightful course of appointment and have placed or continued power in unfaithful or incompetent hands.[5]

And he promised to choose diligent and talented men, who would ensure capable and loyal cooperation. In other words, Jackson, in continuity with his predecessors, sought a compromise between meritocratic selection and political fidelity.

Nevertheless, a few months after making this speech, he presented to Congress a method for the rotation of appointments which excluded the meritocratic criterion. Jackson dismissed the idea of permanent public posts, namely, that a governmental office could become the "property" of the person named to occupy it as a civil servant.[6] This did not mean that incompetent individuals were nominated, or that policies of pure clientelism had to be enacted, but there was a complete rejection of the idea that the United States needed a professional bureaucracy. Jackson himself named, once more, people linked to the world of the establishment, and his project of democratizing public service was a substantial failure, since the pool of qualified candidates for appointments was still quite restricted.

All government and top-level bureaucratic positions were assumed by sons of the American *haute bourgeoisie*, descendants of the agricultural and manufacturing oligarchy. The same turnover of appointments, accomplished by Jackson upon his entering the White House, was not much greater than either that of the preceding or the following presidency. Jackson's egalitarian philosophy, however, became a fundamental guide for contemporary and future politicians, not only at the federal level but also at the state level. The spoils system spread more and more widely, not always with positive consequences: after every election, there ensued a chaotic period in which the president or the governor had to decide the naming and distribution of appointments; amidst the populace, the idea was reinforced that the U.S. public administration was over-politicized and technically incompetent; conflicts increased between the executive and legislative branches regarding public appointments; and there was a rising flood of requests and pressures for obtaining offices, made by those who were employed in electoral campaigns.[7] At the same time, there took hold the idea that ample political patronage was a practice of true democracy, capable of boosting the common man's access to public offices, and that the efficiency of the governmental machine also depended on the political loyalty that high-level bureaucracy felt for the president.

Thus, if Jackson did not succeed in breaking out of the Washington establishment's tight circle with regard to the naming of public officials, he did lay the groundwork for what would happen with his successors. In this sense, the upper class of the great landowners would be superseded by the "common man,"[8] in the taking of seats at governmental desks. The new middle class, generated by industrial progress and by territorial expansion, for the first time looked into the windows of federal government. Without a doubt, this dynamic made for a more representative bureaucracy than that of the past, which had greater responsibility regarding the electorate. Still, the administration, with the spreading of the spoils system and the assuming of dilettante administrators hailing from the entire country, lost its skill and expertise in managing policies and in organizing offices. In this process, public offices became an exchange commodity, and practices of corruption and favoritism grew more diffuse. This situation would become so blatant and severe that by the final two decades of the nineteenth century, a reaction burst forth, which opened the way toward a reform opposed to the Jacksonian government's "democratizing" philosophy and directed toward professionalizing public administration.

In the business sector, moreover, a transformation developed at the same pace with the administrative one. The new bourgeoisie expected freer access to the financial market and to public appointments. This impetus, also due to the process of democratization promoted by Jackson, on the one hand, culminated with the approval by the states of the general incorporation acts that liberalized the corporations and, on the other, opened the season of the spoils system for government appointments.

The progress of the industrial revolution brought a marked change in politics, since the numbers of new entrepreneurs, professional and commercial individuals were increasing, and adding themselves to the landowning aristocracy in their desire to participate in and influence public affairs. The oligarchy of prominent landowners which had always managed public matters now found itself constrained to share—through political patronage—a rising number of administrative positions with the new bourgeoisie.[9]

All the same, turbulence marked the unfolding of this process. In fact, after the end of Jackson's presidency, there began a period of political instability, due in large part to the economic crisis of 1837, that drastically reduced President Van Buren's reform plans. The Whigs returned to the White House in 1840 and, though they had strongly criticized the Jacksonian spoils system methods when they were the opposition party, once they came into power, they replicated the same style and methods, with *en masse* rotations of civil servants based on political loyalty. This scenario would be repeated in 1848, when the Democrat Zachary Taylor won the elections, and replaced more than 30% of current civil servants with loyal members of his own party.[10] The continued presence of the Democrats in the White House with James Buchanan's election in 1856 did not change the handling of political appointments, since civil servants named by the previous president were supplanted by ones from the same party. The same thing happened with the accession of Franklin Pierce, another Democrat elected as president. This political instability, united with the extremely strong recourse to spoils, was not, however, without innovations. Many candidates were evaluated by the Presidential Cabinet following the criterion of organizational efficiency, and the candidacies and promotions themselves were based on written exams or on more informal methods for assessing the capacities of political appointees. In 1853, Congress passed the first law which introduced an obligatory exam for the hiring of several categories of the lowest ranking federal employees. In these same years, there was also introduced a schema for salary levels and for a classification based on responsibilities and duties.[11] In 1861, the country split into two and started a Civil War, after the election to the presidency of the Republican Abraham Lincoln. Paradoxically, in order to manage the conflict, Lincoln was a president who made extended use of political patronage in his administration, notwithstanding his message of the "moralization" of politics, which aimed to reduce the turning to the spoils system. Of the 1,639 federal administrative positions at his disposal, the Republican President used 1,457, replacing a vast number of governmental employees.[12] During the conflict, the nominees for a single office changed two or even three times. With this method, Lincoln made sure that he could offer compensation to seal pacts of political loyalty with members of his own party, and then of the National Union, moves that were important for maintaining power in the most delicate phase in the history of the United States.

As the historian Carl Fish observed, "If Lincoln had made appointments by merit only, the war might have been shortened; on the other hand, he might not have preserved a united North to carry on the war."[13] Moreover, the Civil War created the preconditions for the birth of a "national class" and of a more solid federal government that, together with extraordinary industrial development, would lay the foundations for the development of an ordered, centralized bureaucracy based on the principles of responsibility and merit.[14]

Government by the Good (1883–1906)

1883 is a crucial date for the history of the U.S. federal civil service, because in this year the Pendleton Act was passed. This law was important not only because it broke with the egalitarian philosophy of the Jacksonian spoils system but also because it constructed an administrative system that differed radically from that of the first century of U.S. history. The reformers' initiative was overtly inspired by the *Northcote-Trevelyan Report* of 1854, implemented by the British government to reorganize administration according to meritocratic principles and to guarantee the middle classes their access to professional bureaucracy.

During the same period, in Washington DC, the idea was ripening of a reform capable of "opening" public service to the best qualified individuals, reaffirming and regulating the meritocratic principle as a response both to societal changes and to the corruption and inefficiency produced by the spoils system. The reform introduced the use of exams, which determined the level of requisite qualification for being named to a given public office, even if initially this was limited to the lowest branches of the federal bureaucracy (clerical positions).[15]

The Pendleton Act of 1883 was the culmination of one of the most vigorous political reform campaigns in American history. The bipartisan reform movement had taken root immediately after the end of the war of secession, when a window of opportunity was opened for a meritocratic reform of public administration. By this point, the spoils system no longer served to unite the country, as had happened during Abraham Lincoln's administration, when it was widely used to hold the Unionists together. With the return of peace, the system now showed all its weaknesses, especially in the area of corruption.[16] In 1871, President Grant made a first attempt to create a new civil service and to establish a Civil Service Commission (CSC), but he lacked a Congressional majority. Still, the theme remained at the center of the political agenda for the entire second half of the 1870s and the first years of the 1880s. The enthusiasm and commitment for reform were motivated and supported by strongly moralistic ideals, shared by many members of the American intellectual world of the time. The same reform campaign was articulated in Manichean terms: right vs. wrong, good vs. evil.

This approach brought three effects: first, the beginning of a discourse regarding public administration that used messianic terms, treating the sector as one in need of thorough cleaning up, for the sake of good government; second, as Van Riper underlined, the quest for efficiency yielded to the necessity of introducing a meritocratic and less corrupt system; and third, the reformist approach was characterized by a fundamentally negative anthropology, which aimed to eradicate the evil that inherently afflicted American institutions.[17]

In reality, there did not exist the kind of revolutionary and penetrating thought that the reformers offered the public to believe in at first sight. The practical mission was simply to imitate the British model, substituting the spoils system with the introduction of a public competition, to determine the candidates best-qualified to hold certain public appointments. Nonetheless, while taking inspiration from the Northcote-Trevelyan Report, and from the principle of public competition, the American system maintained its own specific and peculiar characteristics.

The idea of bureaucratic neutrality gained acceptance, promising a stable and continuous administration free from political pressures and obligations. This choice, however, became inserted into the American tradition through two major differences. The first concerned the modality of the competition: while the English required testing of academic preparation, of the quality of writing and capacity for analysis, the Americans preferred a "practical in character" competition, i.e. one based on assessment of prerequisites, and of the practical skills needed to hold a determined position.

From these facts, one can perceive a fundamental difference between the American and European approaches. In fact, while the European States had fostered a professional bureaucracy generally anchored on classical and juridical studies, the United States sought after more in-depth specialization, which would perfectly cohere with the tasks that one was expected to carry out. What interested Americans were the abilities and proficiencies for best accomplishing the intrinsic possibilities of a specific position. This process improved the preparation of bureaucrats in a given area, but it also made the system less flexible and open to change. The second difference, on the other hand, resided in the fact that the English envisaged a single competition for starting a career in the civil service at the lowest level, before advancing by rigidly arranged steps, while the Americans allowed for a fast-stream entrance, that is, even at higher levels of an administrative career. This choice stemmed from the pragmatism of American culture, which favored the participation of experts at any level of public administration, thus quickly opening a stronger connection with the private sector. In addition, in the United States connective channels with the universities were lacking: in fact, there did not exist the official kind of recruiting found in the English system, which depended on Oxford and Cambridge graduates, nor in the French system, reliant on the *grandes écoles*, whose alumni could choose to enter the public sector and pursue an almost regimented and automatic career, leading to the apex of the bureaucracy. Therefore, the selection of civil servants mainly involved the "practical" middle class of the professions and of commerce, more than the intellectual élite. Indeed, in 1905 the CSC's Twenty-Second Report declared that "the great defect in the Federal service to-day is the lack of opportunity for ambitious, well-educated young men."[18]

Finally, there existed a third and even more profound difference. The 1883 reform did not complete the process of forming a true, full-fledged administrative élite. It did not provide for the commissioning of permanent secretaries, high-ranking bureaucrats deployed to manage the ministries, as in the United Kingdom. In fact, despite the regularizing of the bureaucratic career and the principle of meritocratic selection, all the top-level bureaucratic appointments were still made according to the old system of spoils and political loyalty. In other words, while in the United Kingdom the high bureaucracy formulated and implemented policies, in the United States any political and discretionary choice was left to the president, to his own political appointees, and, naturally, to the Congress. Appointees continued to occupy the highest spheres of the administration, without ever having to undergo a public competition and without any guarantee of tenure. In addition, the Pendleton Act applied only to the federal bureaucracy and to a few predetermined types of position.

The reform thus left the problem of the relationship between politics and administration partially unresolved. The American political tradition did not seriously consider the possibility of a "permanent government," in which discretionary choices could be left to a nonelected professional bureaucratic corps, without a recognizable public face. What was acceptable for the American tradition was only the separation between politics and administration, meaning that political choices would be left to those who had been elected or to those whom the elected officials had nominated; meanwhile, the implementation of choices, i.e. the organization and the means to realize these choices, remained the prerogative of the new bureaucracy instituted by the Pendleton Act.

This arrangement, which clearly emerged from the 1880s debate over reforms, would persist through the first 30 years of the twentieth century and would become the object of fundamental speculation by the most important American theoreticians of public administration.

Woodrow Wilson, the future president and a renowned political scientist, was one of the most ardent supporters of the 1883 reform of civil service, and afterward he became the president of the National Civil Service Reform League, the most important association of public administration reformists born in the 1870s. In 1887, he published a long article entitled "The Study of Administration," in which he thoroughly theorized the doctrine of the separation between politics and administration.[19] After praising the reform, and stressing the need to depoliticize bureaucracy, Wilson argues that "administration lies outside the proper sphere of *politics* [Wilson's italics]. Administrative questions are not political questions. Although politics sets the tasks for administration, it should not be suffered to manipulate its offices."[20] Thus, in underlining the neutrality of administration, Wilson introduces a fundamental concept for the administrative future of the United States, namely that

> the field of administration is a field of business. It is removed from the hurry and strife of politics; it at most points stands apart from the debatable ground of constitutional study. It is a part of political life only as the methods of the counting-house are a part of the life of society; only as machinery is part of the manufactured product.[21]

Public administration becomes understood as completely separate from politics, and the bureaucracy is seen as neutral, a technical body informed and guided by the principles of merit. The executive branch is simply "machinery," an instrumental device for implementing political decisions. In the Wilsonian conception, the administrative system is an instrument fully independent from political affinities, a meritocratic institution "in the service" of politics.

The work of the jurist Frank J. Goodnow, entitled *Politics and Administration*,[22] follows the same trajectory. He also underlines how politics and administration should be separated, in order to guarantee the efficient functioning of government. Goodnow's position aimed to legitimize the study of public administration as an autonomous discipline, and he advocated for the creation of a professional bureaucracy, hierarchically organized and dedicated to policy implementation.

These ideas, theorized after the reform, were already there in nutshell form. The late nineteenth-century reformers believed that administration needed to be cleansed of the excess of political appointments, and that the federal civil service had to operate above and beyond the political arena. A plural corps, composed of representatives of all political parties, needed to be installed, in order to supervise the activity of a depoliticized administration, so that no leader or single party could undermine its neutrality. From the 1883 Pendleton Act there was born the CSC, which represented both an embryonic model for the establishment, during the following years, of independent regulating agencies and committees, and for the authority responsible for issuing guidelines for managing and organizing public employees on a nationwide basis. The members of the commission were named by the president prior to approval by the Senate, and the commission could not make appointments for public offices: this measure prevented violating the constitutional prerogatives of the president and kept the commission's political powers in check. It could only choose, for the highest administrative offices, a shortlist of three candidates, based on a public competition, from which the winning candidate would be named, using the classic selection mechanism described above. This "rule of three" was adopted by the commission in 1888, then officially regulated by an Act of Congress in 1944 (Veteran's Preference Act), and it remained in force until the abolition of the commission itself in 1978, as a result of the Civil Service Reform Act.

Born to give long-term support to presidential appointments, the commission gradually attained more independence, until it became a bona fide guarantor of the neutrality of public administration, resisting pressure from the parties, the president, and Congress. It became not only an instrument for organizing the merit system but a complete and trusted guardian of the independent prerogatives of the civil service. This model was so successful that already at the end of the nineteenth century, it was replicated at the states' level.

The commission's work produced two long-lasting effects. First, it closely linked civil servants with morality, a legacy of nineteenth-century reformers. Second, it brought a separation between personnel management and general administration, that is, between the dynamics of civil servants' recruitment and career advancement, on the one hand, and their activities of policy-making, namely their functions and their role in the decision-making process, on the other.[23]

Over the course of time the merit system progressively expanded. This process was already launched by President Arthur (1881–1885), who had extended the new regulation of the civil service—following the Pendleton Act—to 12% of the total number of federal administration employees.[24]

This was a step forward, albeit only a modest one, since the Republican President was concerned about possibly losing the next election, and he aimed to save the administrative posts of numerous appointees named by the Republicans who had governed for 24 years. In 1885, the Democrat Grover Cleveland took office as president: he would more vigorously support the implementation of reform, extending to 25% the number of civil servants chosen by public competition. Between Cleveland's two mandates came that of Harrison (1889–1993), who added only 5% to the number of positions governed by the principle of merit. Much more vigorous action was taken during Cleveland's second mandate (1893–1897), which brought the extension of the Pendleton Act to almost 50% of the federal government's workforce. A step backward came with the election of the Republican William McKinley (1897–1901), who chose to re-classify—exhuming Jacksonian positions influenced by the growth of populism—several thousand positions, returning them under the spoils system.[25] He did not destroy the progress made by his predecessors with the principle of merit—indeed, he was the first president to limit his own authority to remove civil servants—but he did not increase the number of positions selected by competition.

This situation was in fact a serious problem, since the expansion of the West was still in action, and the federal government could only certify the growth of the territory and establish its borders. The tasks carried out by central power were minimal, such as defense or the postal service. Meanwhile, the liberalization of charters to set up corporations and the revolution in the transportation sector had catalyzed a massive economic transformation. According to Les Hannah, the number of corporations increased tenfold during this period, passing from 30,000 in 1860 to 300,000 in 1915.[26] Thanks to these measures, businesses evolved toward national dimensions.

Thus, while the economy developed at high speed, it generated new interests and demands, and society was transformed, moving toward national dimensions; public institutions, however, did not change at the same pace.

As Skowronek has emphasized, an authentic "void in governance" characterized the country during this era. After the Civil War, the parties and the law courts entered this void, and they set themselves up as the true spinal cord of American power, though they risked not being able to sustain the country's economic and territorial expansion. The political parties were the genuine command centers of the epoch, and they provided coordination at both the national and local levels.[27] Alongside this hegemony over public affairs, there developed the influence of the law courts, the single effective counterweight to the "partisan machines." With their decisions and sentences, they contributed to performing a social function of regulation and to reaffirming common sense.

In addition, the dismantling of the wartime administration had contributed to reinforcing the weight of judicial power. The Supreme Court itself had increased its influence, by determining new principles that would go on to condition administrative actions. Troubled by the politicians' corruption and incompetence, judges transformed themselves into champions of *laissez-faire* and defenders of businesses, considering it a part of necessary progress to lessen the control over market activities by the power of the parties, which was held to be perverse and invasive.

In reaction to this state of affairs, a powerful reformist current began to emerge in the 1870s and 1880s. The problem of railways regulation was a ripe field for putting into practice these new ideas about the role of the state in society. At the economic level, the railroad tracks were the foundation for the commercial and industrial development of an immense country. Thanks precisely to its vast extension, this infrastructure was already unmanageable at the state level, despite the law's predisposition for this.[28] In social matters, the same two decades had also seen a rise in the grievances of farmers, called on to put pressure on companies to limit and regulate the transport tariffs on grain products, and to constrain them to end discriminatory tariffs. There thus existed many elements for making this sector become a large-scale reform experiment.[29]

A turning point was marked by the approval of the Interstate Commerce Act in 1887, an emblematic provision for a new conception of public management and the development of the administrative state. The law determined a definite number of rules for limiting the tariff-charging practices of companies, in particular prohibiting abuses and discriminations. Above all, the law created a special independent authority called the Interstate Commerce Commission (ICC), charged with supervising the enactment of these measures and, more generally, with regulating the sector. This brought a rupture with the "classic" conception of the role of administration in America, and in fact the choice was a hard-fought one. Congress had engaged in long debate over the need to create an autonomous agency, or rather to entrust this task to the already existing federal administration. The absolute necessity of removing from partisan politics such a strategic sector for the country appeared to be the main concern of congressmen. In their eyes, there was a need to "nationalize" the question of the railways and to "de-politicize" it as well, but this implied a recognition that the administration of the time could not guarantee the nation's common interest. In another sense, it meant that Congress would show its distrust in the capacity of the executive branch to adequately protect the common interest. If the political element and that of distrust toward the parties lay at the heart of the decision to appeal to an independent authority, there were at least three other elements that influenced the choice.[30] First, the necessity of forming an authority endowed with a high level of expertise. This was urgent, because the demands related to tariff-imposing, to the rules of competition, and to the establishment of security norms required a series of specific expertises and management skills which the federal service lacked. There was a need for incremental, flexible, and reactive regulations, in contrast to the rigidity of traditional bureaucratic management. In addition, it was necessary to build a structure that could enact arbitration. This last point concerned the companies, but it was especially necessary to protect a multitude of diverse customers from the privileges of the major corporations, in order to stabilize a balance of power that was structurally unequal in practice. Therefore, the objective was to act in such a way that all interests were equally held in consideration. For this reason, the usual boundaries among political, administrative, legislative, and judicial power became reshuffled in an unprecedented way.

Critical voices were raised, especially against the weakening of the separation of powers and the merging of the role of the law with practical administration. Still, the arguments in favor of the establishment of an independent commission clearly prevailed and, even if the law of 1887 did not expressly include the term "independence," it was around this notion that the new system pivoted. This was founded upon a principle of the bipartisan composition of the new institution. Of the five committees comprising the ICC, no more than three could be led by the same party. Appointed by the president for a six years' mandate, with the approval of the Senate, the ICC members could be removed only for reasons of corruption or negligence. This meant that the commission was an institution designed to remain beyond the influence of the governing party. The autonomy of the ICC was consequently reinforced, and its powers extended even further.[31]

After 1889, the election of Benjamin Harrison to the U.S. presidency pushed Congress to reinforce the independence of the new institution, given that the new resident of the White House had been the lawyer for railroad companies, a fact which increased the diffidence of senators and representatives toward the chief executive and his advisors. Political independence thus became inseparable from a functional autonomy vis-à-vis the executive branch. The ICC also thus became the model for later independent regulatory committees, which would multiply in the following decades, taking the names of "commission" or of "agency."[32] These were the result of a process of depoliticization related to decisions regarding cases of particular complexity or ones considered too delicate to be left exclusively to the readiness of one of the constitutional organs.

Thus, the establishment of the ICC in 1887 laid the foundation for the development of the administrative state.

To this initiative, there was added Congress's approval in 1890 of the Sherman Act, the antitrust law that sought to break the power of monopolies and to slow the processes of fusion and acquisition that jeopardized free competition. This was a body of norms that paved the way for the creation, in 1914, of the Federal Trade Commission, one of the United States' most important and powerful independent regulatory commissions.

The federal government therefore sought to react to a new economic gigantism which risked undermining the competitiveness of the country and the autonomy of politics. In this historical phase, the state was called on to make laws regarding private property, contracts, managerial conduct, and business interests, in the name of public well-being and security.[33] Moreover, the regulatory function had already been nationalized, through the establishment of independent authorities and by the new federal laws, like the Sherman Act. The central bureaucracy, professionalized and rationalized in the organization of personnel and of structures, was consequently called to carry out, beyond the traditional practices of government, this new function of bridging between public and private interests.

Government by the Efficient (1906–1932)

The separation of politics from administration, theorized by Frank J. Goodnow and Woodrow Wilson, and put into practice through the extension of the merit principle to an ever-larger part of the civil service, prepared the ground for the following season, distinguished by the idea that a neutral and meritocratic bureaucracy was the starting point for directing the system toward efficiency.

The passage from the nineteenth to the twentieth century was rich with political and cultural transformations. In particular, new scientific and technological discoveries linked to extraordinary industrial development had changed American society. The entrepreneur and frontier fortune-hunter were being superseded by managers; local industry and commerce were evolving into gigantic industrial instillations and great multistate infrastructures; the organization of parties and of nationwide newspapers and magazines was taking over from local politics and media. Social complexity grew exponentially, both in the performing of services and activities and in the dimensions in which these were distributed.

As a result, the historian Robert Wiebe has noted that if the nineteenth-century middle class had found its self-legitimization in the concept of "character," that of the early twentieth century found it in the concept of "expertise." It was the expert, supported by science, who came to embody a new era composed of numerous specialized elements within a systematically organized entirety, where nothing could have functioned without attentive scientific preparation. Americans believed that disinterested scientific expertise, accompanied by practical application, was the key to the well-being of society.[34]

In the nineteenth century, therefore, science—as understood by the middle and intellectual classes—always required a specializing method of thinking, which only a few individuals had the capability of putting toward the service of many.[35]

This vision launched a vast process of restructuration of political life and released new energies and demands that, at the beginning of the twentieth century, converged in the progressive movement, a cross-parties political and intellectual movement that formulated a new mission for federal government.[36] The latter was now seen to have the responsibility of promoting education, the rehabilitation of the weak and dispossessed, the protection of women, and the provision of new forms of social assistance. Inequalities were to be counterbalanced by the public sector, and government must arbitrate economic disputes, especially with respect to the great corporations, for actions developed at the turn of the century and often organized in trusts and monopolies.

Despite the clarity of several positions, progressive thought struggled to attain its own homogeneity. A few intellectuals, like Lippmann and Dewey, concentrated on the difficulty of guiding the knowledge and attitudes of public opinion in a vast democracy; others, like Veblen and Croly, aspired to construct a technocratic system, with efficient planning, to govern growing socioeconomic complexity; still others, like Brandeis, dedicated themselves above all to protecting fair competition and small- to medium-sized businesses from trusts and monopolies. As the historian Robert Higgs has noted, the opinions of the progressive intellectual world were replete with gray areas, often with incompatible visions, but all these thinkers did share a common objective: to strengthen the federal government's leadership of American society at the political, cultural, and economic levels.[37] All of them considered it necessary to develop a more centralized public system that would resolve democratic, social, and economic aporias brought by the new century's burgeoning transformations.

In addition, new and growing inequalities raised questions about the functioning of civil society and the role of politics in it. The progressives' ideas sought to create alert and informed public opinion, and for this purpose they advocated democratic renovation. The objective was to forge a close and constant relationship between government and the citizenry, for example, by using direct democracy: popular legislative initiatives, referendums, and the possibility of removing public servants from office. On the eve of World War I, 20 states passed laws based on popular initiatives, and 23 on referendums. Primaries for choosing political candidates became more frequent, and in 1913 the Seventeenth Amendment provided for common voters' direct election of senators, instead of by state legislatures.

The progressives deployed two strategies: on the one hand, the attempt to democratize public life through popular vigilance over the "vested interests," in particular those of the great industries and their trusts and cartels, and, on the other, the construction of a new technocracy, founded on the criteria of skill and expertise.

This inclination aroused impatience toward ignorant and apathetic citizens, hostility toward local, party-impacted questions, and, vice versa, appreciation for efficient administrative solutions to the major problems of public life. For this reason, the progressives aimed for specialization, both for institutions and their leaders and for their own use of language, since it allowed them to exclude unprepared citizens from the political struggle. The less that the people understood them, the greater would be the entrustment given to the technocratic resolution of problems. Thus, if on the one hand the progressives had made governments more conscious of citizens' social needs, on the other, they made bureaucrats less open to hearing their voices. Neither can it be forgotten that the dawn of the twentieth century brought the development of *scientific management*, characterized by a neo-positivist approach promoting society's total commitment to working for economic growth and technological modernization. This rationalistic approach cultivated faith in science and scientific methods for addressing organizational matters. In this scenario, efficiency became a key concept, linked to a manicheistic model which cast a neutral and efficient administration as good, and a politically biased and inefficient one as evil. Consequently, Frederick Taylor's principles of scientific management were quickly imported into the public sector where, as has been seen, the terrain had been prepared by ideas for the depoliticization and professionalization of bureaucracy, which were affirmed on the institutional level at the end of the nineteenth century.

Under the cultural influence of the progressives, two myths regarding administration developed during the first years of the twentieth century: political neutrality and efficiency. A given public administration could only achieve goodness by pursuing these two principles: the first promoting merit and the second scientific management. The latter was born at the end of the nineteenth century, with a packet of methods designed to improve the efficiency of growing American industrial production. In a few years this approach gained so much scientific and "philosophical" influence that its paradigm was adopted by industry, and likewise by any organization in the private and public sectors.

The managerial doctrine, therefore, also encompassed public administration, which would be rendered more business-like, or better, to which would be applied the same organizational techniques of private enterprise. The movement for managerial reform of administration found its initial impetus in the cities, since most of the scandals linked to the public sector originated in rural areas. This was also the case because the influence of local government in this era considerably outweighed that of the federal government. A revealing fact is that 60% of U.S. public spending was carried out by local governments. Besides, the cities managed a series of public services (sanitation, transport, aqueducts) that were visibly operative, and thus more easily assimilated into the private sector. It was in the sphere of local public services that the first experiments were made with the techniques of scientific management. Which specific principles were applied by this first wave of managerialism? Rationality in the management of resources; careful planning to attain clearly defined objectives; specialization of employees, ways, means, and products; quantitative measurement of operations; the pursuit of the "one best way", i.e. of work, of materials, and of the best instrumentation of a given activity; and the standardization of all similar activities performed by the public sector.[38] In other words, the managerial credo imposed a maximization of the product for a given input or the minimization of costs for a certain result.

In this context, it was the presidency of Theodore Roosevelt that would nurture one of the most representative administrations for both progressive reformism and the diffusion of the principle of merit. Roosevelt reorganized the government's diverse departments following the principles of scientific management, imposed more severe regulations on the work of public employees, and put more distance between civil servants and their collaboration with congressional committees. Roosevelt saw cooperation between bureaucrats and congressmen as potentially dangerous, because from his viewpoint it could undermine presidential authority. In fact, through the congressional committees there passed the pressures of lobbies formed by the great industrial groups: their members sought to steer the ministerial policy-making process toward the protection of their own corporate interests.

Public pressure to break these lobbying relations thus cohered perfectly with Roosevelt's strategy to combat the giant American industrial groups and cartels. By the end of his second mandate, the merit system accounted for around 60% of federal employees, even if the president had deftly opted for a territorial strategy. Roosevelt had applied the principle of public competition, on a massive scale, to the recruiting of federal employees who worked in solidly Republican areas, while he left increased space to spoils system appointments in electoral zones on the bubble between his own party and that of the Democrats. In addition, in 1905 the president established the Keep Committee "to place the conduct of the executive business of the Government in all its branches on the most economical and effective basis in the light of the best modern business practice."[39] The commission recommended the creation of a public pension system, the centralization of public administration expenditures, and a series of minor changes in administrative methods for the sake of improved efficiency.[40] This was the executive branch's first major effort to reorganize administration.

Roosevelt's successor, Howard Taft, took a more conservative approach to presidential appointments, preferring radical conservatives over candidates influenced by progressive ideas, with the aim of maintaining Republican party unity. Nonetheless, he extended the merit principle to government attorneys, raising to 70% the number of federal administration positions under the jurisdiction of the Pendleton Act.[41]

Of much greater importance, however, was Taft's contribution to the process of administrative reorganization. The president invited Frederick Cleveland, one of the era's leading scholars of public administration, to design new policies and innovative systems for governmental activity and subsequently entrusted him with forming an *ad hoc* committee. This committee was led by Cleveland himself, together with Frank Goodnow. They resumed the use of the ideas expressed by the Keep Committee, and they extended them, proposing to submit to public competition all positions that were not tied to policy-making decisions, to reorganize agencies on the basis of the objectives that the executive branch wished to pursue, and, most importantly, to create a federal budget.[42]

While the first of these recommendations was followed by the president and, as has been noted, easily implemented, the other two were hotly contested. Both civil servants themselves and the congressional committees were opposed to reorganization and to the establishment of an "executive budget."

Both entities felt themselves threatened by the reforms that would have increased the power of the presidency, with respect to bureaucracy and legislative power. Taft disregarded the Congress and asked a number of financial officials to prepare the budget, but only a handful accepted his invitation, and the project floundered.[43]

Moreover, by the 1910s the paradigm of scientific management made its entry into the American educational system. First at the University of Wisconsin, then at other institutions, courses, degrees, and schools of public administration were developed, centered on the methods and techniques of business administration.[44] These programs provided civil servants with training for the institutionalizing of scientific management and for developing administrative principles based on rationality, planning, specialization, quantitative assessment, standardization, and, obviously, the political neutrality of the civil service.

Woodrow Wilson's presidency, begun in 1913, represented the apex of progressive democracy, since the liberal, reformist academy directly entered the oval office. Strong pressures were exerted on the president by his own Democratic party, which for 16 years had not held executive power (since Cleveland's presidency), to increase the number of offices governed by the spoils system. Nevertheless, Wilson, whose theoretical publications had fervently supported the principle of merit and the separation of politics from administration, managed to resist, and he accepted an increase of political appointments only in the Department of State, which had to confront World War I.

Wilson created new administrative agencies excluded from the principle of merit, exploiting the emergency of global conflict, but at the same time without questioning the selection by public competition for the central corps of the federal administration. Another interesting element of this epoch involved salary levels and the demand for employment positions in the public sector. The latter remained elevated until 1914, but with the arrival of an economic depression the interest of politically active Americans for positions in the federal administration significantly dropped. This decline occurred because federal salaries were not particularly high, and positions run by political patronage were on the decrease, thanks to the progressive extension of the merit system. Therefore, considering that political appointments were now few and far between, the government had little incentive to raise federal salaries in order to gain consent.

Meanwhile, the same managerial methods used in the private sector were being introduced into the public one, but to the reinforcement of quality control and office hierarchies imposed by the reforms there did not correspond to salaries equivalent to those of private industry. The situation improved during and especially after World War I, when there was a vast surge of unionization, which led to better wage guarantees and conditions. The war also brought a new wave of experts from the private sector, especially scientists and engineers, who were directly hired without having to pass a public examination and screening process. This was the case because, despite the movement to professionalize bureaucracy, the public sector remained short of personnel in many areas, especially compared to the great variety of specialists found in the industrial sector. This disparity held true both for training systems and for the private sector's marked advantage in paying higher salaries. The necessity of confronting the global conflict resulted in a rapid increase in public personnel, thanks to the passage of professionals from the private and industrial worlds into government offices, which then drew benefits from the imported proficiencies and organizational methods.[45]

This effort was financially sustainable because the patriotism imposed by the war encouraged many experts to accept their positions without pays (the "dollar a year" practice).[46] This interpenetration between the public and private worlds would not disappear with the conclusion of the war, but would condition organization, techniques, and recruiting in postwar administration. All the power of the nation, composed of technological know-how, industries, men, and machines, converged in the federal apparatus to support military actions.

Thanks to this transfer of technicians from the private to public sector, during World War I there was even more diffusion of a "quasi-scientific" mentality of public organization, since the army would become the great laboratory for the experimentation of managerial methods. The army was the first major institution which utilized the schema of personnel classification, the introduction of vocational tests, and the distribution of assignments based on them.[47] The system worked well, and it was replicated in administrative agencies during the 1920s and 1930s.

During the 1920s, with the return of the Republicans to government, President William Harding sought to weaken the merit system and created new posts in his administration for appointing politically loyal civil servants. Nevertheless, apart from suppressing a few dozen positions subject to public competition, Harding's actions did not destroy the already consolidated merit system. The changes were carried out only according to the logic of more effectively implementing different policies than those of the Wilson years. In this phase, the search for technical skills and capacities was strong enough to influence even the partisan-shaded positions, for which the presidents of the progressive era sought to choose men both highly qualified and politically aligned. This pattern occurred during the presidency of Calvin Coolidge, who did not modify the proportions between the spoils and merit systems. Herbert Hoover, in contrast, increased the number of positions chosen by public competition, arriving at 80% of the total of federal employees. Moreover, of the remaining 20%, only a small fraction remained of the narrowly political stamp, since most of them were formed by political sympathizers with certified professional and technical abilities.[48]

During this period, the quest for efficiency guided the reorganization of governmental offices.

The presidency played a more decisive role of centralization and coordination, the 1923 Classification Act rationalized the retributive system, and the duplication of functions was abolished: these were then brought together, in a more homogeneous way, in the departments and agencies. The reorganization did not reduce public spending, nor did it aim to oppose the World War I period expansion of the federal government, but rather it simply sought to render more efficacious and efficient a federal government that had been notably expanded and modernized.

It was no accident, then, that these ideas became especially effective at the level of public personnel management. In fact, it was no longer enough to have a preparation related to the duties and responsibilities of one's own assigned role, but the work positions themselves had to be differentiated from each other, divided into classes and sub-classes, and successively standardized in their organization and operational qualities. This was the foundation on which the positions of the civil service were divided into classes. The hiring competitions also changed, becoming much more precise and standardized, depending on the level and kind of position that the candidate aspired to hold. In this case as well, it no longer sufficed to have practical and generically theoretical preparation, accompanied by political neutrality and honesty. The need was for a team of specialists who could maximize their own employment mission.

To enact this idea, training programs were launched, reserved for the development of proficiency and of the ability to occupy positions of advanced technical skills. In 1930 an efficiency rating was introduced. This was an evaluation of the efficiency achieved by the upper levels of the civil service, and it supervised the work of administrative officials, determining their promotions according to more decidedly meritocratic criteria.[49]

Another important reform associated with administrative reorganization was the establishment of the executive budget, ratified by the Budget and Accounting Act of 1921. As Taft had already stressed, the weight of the public sector was far too extensive to leave to Congress alone the management of the budget, encumbered even more by the deficit accumulated during the wartime endeavor. In 1920, the United States was the only Western country that did not yet have a budget presented by its executive leaders. The time was ripe for a step forward. With this law, the president and his offices became the institutions assigned to develop and coordinate the federal budget, that then would be debated, amended, and approved by Congress.

The provision launched both the Bureau of the Budget (BOB), which managed and supervised the budget accountability on the presidential front, and the General Accounting Office (GAO), which checked the viability of public accounts for the White House's congressional counterpart. The new budgeting system was also the fruit of two processes originating with the idea of progressive democracy: (1) an augmented function for the government and the presidency in administering the necessary policies for governing an industrialized society and (2) enhanced supervision and managerial direction of the activities of the executive branch itself.

The influx of scientific management led to the birth of the bureaus of municipal research, which worked to reform local governments, rendering them more rational, efficient, and less corrupt. The first of these, the New York Bureau of Municipal Research, was founded in 1906. These offices were not created by the government, nor could they be considered public institutions, but at the same time they could not be assimilated with private consulting companies. The bureaus were philanthropic institutions sponsored by a single individual or by an association of philanthropists and derived their influence from the very fact of their being external to public administration and their being considered independent from any government. They were born from the ideological premise that any citizen had the right, but especially the duty, to know exactly what the government was doing and in what way. The movement of these institutions invoked the citizenry's sense of responsibility and of their practical participation in the governance of their city and their nation.

Essentially, these were organizations that had a precise political mission and, at the same time, were distanced from the managerial movement of the private sector. The first leaders of the bureaus primarily sought for the insertion of efficiency into the public sector, but in succeeding years the movement campaigned for the democratization of that same sector.[50] The published works of many bureau leaders, such as Frederick Cleveland, Luther Gulick, and Charles Beard, demonstrate their intellectual drive to reconcile the increase of efficiency with that of participation. This experiment showed, moreover, how public administration lent itself to an interdisciplinary theoretical-practical elaboration, given that the activists of these associations were mainly engineers and economists, who were venturing into the field of political theory.[51]

Finally, a leading role was played by the CSC, authorized to select and direct civil servants and their organization. Above all, the commission aimed to safeguard professional and technical specialization, isolating civil servants from politics and interest groups who could threaten their professionalism. The CSC, endowed with independent powers by the law, worked to protect the autonomy and to promote the professionalization of public officials.[52] This was without doubt a successful operation, confirmed by the fact that during the first three decades of the twentieth century the profession of civil service became a respected one, which required solid basic instruction and progressive specialization.

The Government of Emergency: From the New Deal to World War II

On October 29, 1929 the New York Stock Exchange collapsed and lost 40% of its estimated value. The consequences were devastating: gross national product lost 50%; manufacturing enterprises fell from 133,000 to just over 72,000; real salaries dropped by 30%; and unemployment, depending on the region, rose to 25 to 40%, with more than 15 million Americans out of work.[53]

An economic upheaval of these proportions could not but have a major impact on the role of the state in American society. Until the moment of the Crash, American political culture did not assign to the government any responsibility for intervening in the economy, nor the task of preparing measures for combatting poverty and unemployment. In the 1920s, the theory of *laissez-faire*, according to which the government had to keep to a minimum its interventions of regulation and assistance in the capitalist system, was still prevalent among the American governing class.

The Republican Herbert Hoover, elected president in 1928, deemed the American capitalist system superior to any other for both the production of wealth and the protection of liberty. For this reason, despite the crisis, he never decided to substantially alter the relationship between the state and the marketplace. Thus, he chose not to intervene directly with governmental programs but to exert pressure on the world of industry to avoid cuts to production and layoffs of workers. Hoover's idea was that the Great Depression was particularly aggravated by unionism and absenteeism, which had exploited the economic downturn to demand further rights for workers and their organizations. He pressed for the creation of "trade associations," which he had already promoted as the Secretary of Commerce several years earlier, with the purpose of reducing unfair competition and stabilizing the industrial system. The president urged the great industrialists to control prices, to increase salaries, to rationalize the organization of large-scale enterprises, to develop cooperation, to reinforce industrial research, and to redistribute investments.[54] He also tried to spur volunteer and private organizations to undertake relief and assistance works for the poor. Still, in this scenario the federal government only assumed the role of coordinator, and while seeking to facilitate the resolution of the crisis, it did not step in with legislative and administrative actions. Only at the end of his mandate, after he had vainly attempted to instill optimism in the industrial community, did the president decide to create the *Reconstruction Finance Corporation* (RFC), a program of public intervention for stimulating investments, saving the banks, and launching the reconstruction of the industrial sector. By this point, however, popular support for Hoover had become attenuated, and his actions were considered ineffective and insufficient.[55] The president had failed to restore faith among investors and in the action of institutional coordination aimed at reviving the economy. He, together with a large part of the American élite, regarded any concerted government intervention in the economy as an affront to the Constitution and to basic economic principles and as an expedient that would take an even heavier toll in the long run. The electorate, meanwhile, could wait no longer. At the end of Hoover's term of office, a quarter of the workforce was unemployed, poverty had spread far and wide, and corporate profits were negative for the second straight year. A change of leadership and the government model loomed on the horizon.

As a result of Hoover's prudence in managing public affairs, at first the Depression did not have a major impact on public administration. The merit system and organization by rank were not reformed, and staffing cuts were not enacted, despite attempts to halt the expansion of the deficit. In 1929, civil servants in the employ of the federal government numbered 579,559. By 1933, this figure had risen to 603,587.[56]

This equilibrium, dependent on the administration's neutrality, was destined to change with the 1932 election of Franklin Delano Roosevelt as president. After 50 years of the expansion of the principle of merit, through the selection of civil servants by competitive public examination, the Roosevelt era opened a phase that witnessed the return of a more extensive use of the spoils system.

With his New Deal programs, Roosevelt created numerous new institutions, dozens of agencies and offices, and in this extraordinary expansion of the public sector the president opened thousands of new positions in the Federal Administration: to these positions were appointed men who were politically tied to the head of government and his party. In this transformation of governance, Roosevelt faced on the one hand the need to create new administrative agencies to manage the New Deal, and on the other hand the pressure to satisfy the demands of his Democratic colleagues who, excluded from government since the Wilson presidency, laid claims for positions and offices. Roosevelt himself did not trust the men named by his Republican predecessors, and consequently he further augmented the newly expanded civil service with a series of appointments to fill both new posts and ones left vacant by the non-confirmation of old bureaucrats. Between 1933 and 1934, the president created more than 60 administrative agencies whose mission was to develop the policies of the New Deal. Many of the new post holders were appointed through patronage.[57] The number of civil servants in the central government exploded, passing from 603,000 to almost 900,000 by the end of 1936. The positions assigned by public competition passed from over 80% of the total, in the Hoover years, to less than 60% after Roosevelt's first mandate.[58] A secure calculation sets the total figure at around 400,000, for the presidential appointments in the federal administration's offices, a true full-fledged army of non-professional bureaucrats named on the basis of their political loyalty. Recruitment, in fact, was reserved for those who sympathized with the president's ideas, while those who continued to believe in *laissez-faire* and individualism were excluded from governmental positions. The new arrivals were convinced, like Roosevelt, that there was no turning back from a solid cooperation between government and the world of business. This is clear proof of how the first New Deal was more than a mere political strategy, but an authentic transformational turn, in political and cultural terms, in the relationship between citizens and the state, with the latter called to play the active leading role in providing assistance and security to the former.[59] In this dynamic, the president's need to rapidly resolve the emergency of the economic crisis played its fundamental part in successfully widening the federal government's interventionism.

A roadblock, however, toward the realization of the New Deal was placed by the Supreme Court, whose rulings expressed the judges' skepticism regarding the constitutionality of new administrative agencies and their regulatory powers, as well as the delegating of legislative powers to private entrepreneurial groups, for regulating standards and practices indicated by the world of business.[60]

During 1935–1936, with a series of judicial decisions, the Supreme Court determined that a vast number of the New Deal's programs were unconstitutional, and these verdicts drained the recently created agencies of their powers. All the same, in 1936 the incumbent president won a landslide victory in the election and then proposed a law to change the rules of election and permanence on the benches of the Supreme Court. This law would have permitted Roosevelt to remove the most elderly and conservative judges. Congress, however, opposed the president's plan. Nevertheless, under these political pressures the Court approved the new reforms package, known as the "Second New Deal," which re-proposed similar policies to those of the First New Deal, though now oriented more toward the social assistance of citizens than economic interventionism. The Court changed its own ideological orientation, and the attendant underlying juridical arguments, and let go of its previous arguments in favor of *laissez-faire*, based on a strictly literal interpretation of the Constitution.

The Rooseveltian philosophy of government's role in the American economy had by 1937 overcome even the filter of the judicial institutions. It was an epochal step for the history of the federal government. As noted by the constitutional expert Edward Corwin,

> the change which the views of a dominant section of the American people regarding the purpose of government underwent during this period was nothing short of revolutionary, and it was accompanied in due course by a corresponding change of attitude toward constitutional values.[61]

After this shift, any economic regulation on the federal government's part would be free from the bonds of the Constitution.

With the definitive approval of Roosevelt's program, the administrative state began to take definitive shape.[62] In the course of the economic emergency, and the ensuing military one, power became centralized in the federal government and extended its functions into society and the economy. Some commentators noted that in this historical cycle the public sphere prevailed over the private one, and in many ways this was the case. As Van Riper wrote, the Roosevelt era was probably the interval of maximum prestige and influence for the federal bureaucracy, while Arthur Schlesinger Jr. underlined the prevalence of public interests, due to the new interventionism of the government, with respect to the market and the private sector.[63]

Consequently, after the approval of the Second New Deal and with the first gusts of war in 1938, the dimensions of public administration increased still further, arriving at nearly one and a half million employees. This exponential growth, together with the need to consolidate the New Deal and its institutional creations, posed a series of problems for Roosevelt, deriving first from the colossal size of the administration and the necessity to coordinate its rampant growth. Then there were the pressures exerted by Congress, in particular by the opposition, which reproved the president for having destroyed the progress made by the merit system and for having exposed the administration, with an excessive use of the spoils system, to politicization and the risks of corruption.

In order to confront these difficulties, Roosevelt sought to impose thorough reorganization on the executive branch and federal bureaucracy. Starting in 1936, the president started to arrange for enhanced coordination of the administrative agencies and hired Louis Brownlow, an important academician whose intellectual roots were founded in the progressive thought of the 1920s and 1930s: Roosevelt gave Brownlow two years to complete a study of the comprehensive reorganization of the executive branch. Through his consultations with Brownlow, the president became convinced that reorganizing the government could be productive in the political context as well, and he extended his advisor's mandate to the formation of a committee whose members would include two other leading scholars, Charles Merriam and Luther Gulick.[64]

The Committee's report was drafted at the beginning of Roosevelt's second mandate, and it opened by specifying that its mission was to create an executive administration capable of fulfilling vigorous action and leadership,[65] and that in order to succeed the president would need help.[66] The report carried the weight of the past, in particular that of the scientific management developed during the first 20 years of the century. This ideological nucleus was burdened further by the imperatives to expand the public apparatus and to reinforce presidential powers. With Roosevelt's presidency, in fact, the interpretation of the powers of the U.S. president was inverted: in the past, these powers were considered to be only those foreseen by the Constitution, but with Roosevelt there began the consideration that the limit to presidential power was only what was explicitly prohibited by the Constitution. Thus, there was a change from a restrictive to an extensive conception, with respect to the power of the chief executive.[67]

This shift was also reflected in the Brownlow Report, which made important recommendations to the government. These included the expansion of the White House staff; increased presidential control over administrative agencies, in particular the Bureau of the Budget; the extension of the merit system of all positions that were not involved in discretional policy choices; raised public salary levels to attract top-level talent; the reorganization of over 100 existing agencies within enlarged departments, and with even more finalized functions; and a study of the budget and the procedures to monitor it, in order to better manage spending.[68]

In essence, the Brownlow Committee aimed to construct a more hierarchical and executive-centric administrative system, with the White House and the president and his staff at the top. The report declared that "the president needs help," which could be provided by the reorganization of the state's apparatus along more modern and orderly lines. In addition, for the first time there was the affirmation of the idea that the president was directly responsible for the organization of the executive branch.

Roosevelt's project was clear: strengthened national administrative capacities. The historian Barry Karl has viewed Franklin Delano Roosevelt's administrative reform efforts between 1937 and 1939 as a systematic effort to establish a modern bureaucratic state in American politics, a project to develop the managerial capacity characteristic of modern states elsewhere, but still absent in the United States of that period, due to the extraordinary antipathy to administrative centralization in this country.[69]

Initially, the policy recommendations articulated by the Brownlow Committee had trouble in affirming themselves. The opposition raised by the Democratic senator Harry Byrd and his supporters managed to bury the reform law based on the recommendations of the Committee's report.

Only in 1939, with the war in Europe about to erupt and a still flawed economic recovery, did Congress pass the Reorganization Act, which permitted the president to increase his staff at the White House and to reorganize, within limits, the governmental machinery. Roosevelt used this permission to found the Bureau of the Budget, with other less important agencies, giving it functions of planning and creating the new Executive Office of the President, designed to strengthen and develop the three management arms of the president, that is, the ones dealing with the budget, planning, and personnel.[70]

The Reorganization Act authorized the president to appoint six administrative assistants, creating the White House Office. The Executive Order 8248 on September 8, 1939, established these assistants as personal aides of the president, charged with the task of gathering, condensing, and summarizing information. This provision materialized the recommendation to "help the President" made by the Brownlow Report, and it set the premises for the flourishing of the White House staff in the following decades.

Moreover, in its report, the Brownlow Committee spoke of "managerial" agencies that would aid the chief executive in managing the vast and complicated administrative machine of the federal government and placed the personnel agency in this category. The Committee stated that "personnel administration lies at the very core of administrative management." It further stated that

> Personnel management is an essential element of executive management. To set it apart or to organize it in a manner unsuited to serve the needs of the Chief Executive and the executive establishments is to render it impotent and ineffective.[71]

To some, this was a revolutionary concept. To others, it was merely a return to sound management principles and to the intent of the Civil Service Act and the provisions of the Constitution.[72]

The Congress failed to accept these suggestions, which would have implied the downsizing or even the abolition of the CSC but did authorize the president to appoint six administrative assistants and to reorganize a part of the executive branch by issuing executive orders to transfer, consolidate, or abolish agencies. The Congress specifically exempted the CSC from this general reorganization authority. Nevertheless, in his message to the Congress transmitting Reorganization Plan No. I, the President placed the Congress on notice that he would take appropriate action to include within the Executive Office of the President at least a part of the personnel functions that were essential for good management of federal affairs.[73]

Reorganization Plan No. I and No. II were approved by Congress. No reference was made to the President's declaration of purpose regarding personnel matters. There was thus an implied approval of the action which the president proposed to take. This action was followed, on September 8, 1939, by the issuance of Executive Order No. 8248, establishing the Liaison Office for Personnel Management (LOPM) as the fourth of the six divisions set up within the Executive Office of the President. Section II, 4 of the order contained the following statement:

> In accordance with the statement of purpose made in the Message to Congress of April 25, 1939, accompanying Reorganization Plan No. I, one of the Administrative Assistants to the President, authorized in the Reorganization Act of 1939, shall be designated by the President as Liaison Officer for Personnel Management and shall be in charge of the Liaison Office for Personnel Management. The functions of this office shall be: (a) To assist the President in the better execution of the duties imposed upon him by the Provisions of the Constitution and the laws with respect to personnel management, especially the Civil Service Act of 1883, as amended, and the rules promulgated by the President under authority of that Act. (b) To assist the President in maintaining closer contact with all agencies dealing with personnel matters insofar as they affect or tend to determine the personnel management policies of the Executive branch of the Government.

The president subsequently appointed one of his administrative assistants to serve as Liaison Officer for Personnel Management.

The LOPM periodically met with Civil Service Commissioners to discuss and consider the personnel policies of the executive branch and the problems with which the CSC could face as the central personnel agency of the federal government. The president delegated to the Liaison Officer for Personnel Management authority to decide, on his behalf, those problems which the Liaison Officer considers of concern to the chief executive. Thus, many policy matters were quickly clarified without immediate presentation to the president and without the delay attendant upon a meeting of the commission with the busy chief executive. The Liaison Officer, of course, subsequently reported to and discussed with the president the matters that had thus been considered. The Liaison Officer for Personnel Management also maintained close contact with the executive departments, independent establishments, and other agencies of the federal government to discuss with their heads or their representatives the personnel problems with which they were faced. Similarly, appropriate relationships were maintained with the Council of Personnel Administration, made up largely of the directors of personnel of the federal agencies. In this manner, the chief executive was informed of personnel problems faced by the agencies of the government and took an active part in determining major policies regarding them. Many of these problems were outside the jurisdiction and scope of activities of the CSC, but they were of direct concern to the chief executive. When they did relate to the commission's work, the Liaison Officer discussed them with the commission.

In conclusion, when considering personnel matters or personnel policies, the president sought the assistance of the Liaison Officer for Personnel Management. The president referred all proposals regarding personnel matters to the Liaison Officer, to bring together all pertinent facts and viewpoints, to determine that appropriate consideration has been given to the overall management aspects of the problem, and to furnish advice. The president had indicated that he would not act on any personnel matters, except those regarding policy-determining posts, without obtaining the advice and recommendation of the Liaison Officer for Personnel Management.

If, on the one hand, however, the president aimed to achieve better control of personnel management, on the other hand, the time was ripe for expanding the merit system, after several years of broad use of the spoils system. Indeed, since 1934 the opposition had continually attacked Roosevelt for having sabotaged the principle of competitive selection and for having abused his powers of appointment. Now that New Deal reforms were complete, the president confirmed the extension of public competition to 90% of available positions in the federal administration. This meant that a large number of previously appointed civil servants would have to face a competitive procedure to maintain their positions. This move worked well for Roosevelt who, on the eve of the global conflict, could expand the posts allotted for public competition with the goal of regularizing a considerable part of civil servants who were ideologically close to the government. The extension was gradual and enacted through an executive order, and the Ramspeck Acts of 1938, 1940, and 1943, which regularized around 200,000 civil servants, requesting those who had been recruited without a competition to pass a test to confirm their place in the administration. To this move was added the departments' more fully supervising management of personnel, and a more rigid vigilance on the practices of officials, arranged to put in practice the recommendations of the Brownlow Committee.[74]

This governmental control over federal officials acquired further reinforcement from the Hatch Act of 1939, which sought to limit these employees' political activities.[75] Federal workers were prohibited from running for public office, participating in electoral campaigns, or dedicating themselves to raising funds for a party or candidate. Penalties were fixed by the CSC, and they ran from a simple fine to job termination. On two occasions, recourse was made to the Supreme Court, to denounce the unconstitutionality of the Hatch Acts, for violation of the First Amendment protection of free speech for federal employees. Both times the judges determined that the laws on public employment were admissible and constitutional. The guideline prevailed, to avoid excessive politicization of the administration, and a counterproductive return to old-style political patronage. The federal administration, in fact, had to remain neutral, in order to avoid distractions from its principal tasks, namely to devote itself with the spirit of public service to the implementation of any decision made by any presidency. To this scruple were added national security concerns: amidst the war, the goal was to keep to a minimum the possibility of foreign intelligence agents infiltrating federal government offices. An expansion of political appointments could indeed have multiplied the opportunities for infiltrators to succeed in entering the ranks of the administration. Therefore, though they were periodically opposed, the Hatch Acts continued to be protected by presidential vetoes, as well as by the civil servants themselves. Their revocation never occurred, at least for the duration of the Cold War. Thus, the strict refusal to politicize the bureaucracy remained a policy fixture until the 1990s.[76]

In conclusion, the New Deal era had numerous institutional legacies. At the practical level, the most evident of these were (1) the federal government's increased interventionism in social and economic fields, (2) a plethora of new laws designed to rationalize and streamline competition, (3) a wide range of federal subsidies, (4) the centralization of the federal government's regulation and supervision of bureaucracy, and (5) the multiplication of administrative agencies.

Above all, there was the cultural and intellectual legacy. A new system of values emerged, which then became a basis for the postwar mixed economy: these values implied that the government could serve as a fundamental means for realizing the aspirations of private citizens, such as obtaining work, an income, or specific services. The government was legitimized as capable of appropriating citizens' private resources, in a much more extended way than in earlier times, in order to attain collective goals and objectives. As Franklin Delano Roosevelt stated in the Commonwealth Club address, delivered during the electoral campaign of 1932, the task of modern government was "to assist the development of an economic declaration of rights, an economic constitutional order."[77] The traditional emphasis in American politics on individual self-reliance should therefore give way to a new understanding of individualism, by which government acted as a regulating and unifying agency, guaranteeing individuals' protection from the uncertainties of the market. This implied even a political shift, as Milkis pointed out,

> whereas the two party system was created to protect interests in society against the government, the "modern" presidency and administrative agencies that emerged during the 1930s were molded to use government as an instrument for the attainment of positive public ends.[78]

This paradigm shift, as we shall see, would have an enormous impact on the structure and functions of public administration during the following decades. First, however, the federal government, the president, and his civil servants had to confront a more difficult challenge, that of World War II.

World War II

The United States' entrance into World War II posed two fundamental challenges to the federal administration. On the one hand, there was the need to mobilize *en masse* and to undertake ample, high-speed recruiting of new civil servants among the civil population; on the other, there was the need to reorganize the civil service, in order to adapt it to military demands. During the period from 1940 to 1945, personnel administration in the federal government had to readjust not only to the new legislation and executive orders of the New Deal era but also to the massive urgency of the total war.

According to Van Riper, at the dawn of World War II the CSC faced five major problems: defining its wartime role and securing commensurate funds and personnel, procuring and initially allocating civilian manpower in a period of manpower shortage, providing for proper manpower and utilization control, controlling decentralization of authority over personnel practices and procedures, and assuring administrative responsibility and loyalty during a period of bitter ideological conflict.[79]

The transition of the government toward a wartime setup started in 1939, when Roosevelt created a War Resources Board, which had the task of studying economic mobilization in case of war. To this were added a series of new governmental bodies dedicated to the planning and coordination of the American industrial system, in readiness for the conflict: the National Defense Advisory Commission (May 29, 1940), the Office of the Administrator of Export Control (July 2, 1940, then transformed into the Board of Economic Warfare in December, 1941), the Office of Production Management (January 7, 1941), the Office of Price Administration and Civilian Supply (April 11, 1941), and the Supply Priorities and Allocations Board (August 28, 1941). None of these offices held vast powers of administrative independence or of particularly influential leadership. All of them were created by the executive action of the president, who prudently kept for himself all the prerogatives linked to maintaining power in such politically sensitive sectors. These administrative bodies were filled with professional bureaucrats and experts with direct ties to the president. They had primarily organizational powers, such as setting priorities in the selection and use of military materials, the coordination of wartime programs, the rationing of resources, and the monitoring of salaries, prices, and production to meet the demands of the military machine and simultaneously provide for the survival of the civil population.[80]

In addition, the First War Powers Act of December 18, 1941 gave to these organizations, departments, and administrative agencies the freedom to negotiate with private contractors for military production, thus deviating from prior regulations of procedures, performance, and modifications provided by traditional competitive bidding. The Second War Powers Act of March 27, 1942 strengthened the role of the ICC in managing highways and railways infrastructures and gave the president free rein to allocate any useful resource to the war effort, in the way he saw best fit. In January 1942, Roosevelt created a new institution of coordination, the War Production Board (WPB), which he entrusted to Donald M. Nelson, former director of the Sears Corporation.[81] The Board's mission was to "exercise general direction over the war procurement and production programs," and to "determine the policies, plans, procedures, and methods of the several Federal departments, establishments, and agencies, in respect to war procurement and production."[82] Between 1942 and the end of 1945, when the Civilian Production Administration was transformed, the WPB administered 183 billion dollars, spent on armaments and military supplies.[83] In less than three years, from 1939 to the beginning of 1942, the entire extraordinary power of the United States was vigorously deployed, through a notable quantitative and functional reinforcement of the federal government.

By 1940, the CSC developed new examinations for junior managers, in order to introduce rapidly college trained personnel into the civil organization. Recruiting was speeded up. The mechanization of basic records was undertaken on a large scale. The commission was organized in 13 district offices and 500 local boards, and 150 special rating boards at large industrial establishments were set up to decentralize recruitment and organization. A Coordinator and Director of Training position was created to overlook the training process of the new recruits, a Division of Personnel Supervision and Management to aid line administrators, and a Division of Information to assist the general public. Moreover, with Executive Order 8257 of September 1939, President Roosevelt had, at the commission's proposal, permitted the relaxation of competitive requirements subject to the commission's approval.[84] By June 1940 the implementation of the commission's recruiting methods was becoming increasingly positive: eligible employees were supplied upon 24-hour notice, and a coding system was applied to the qualifications of several hundred thousand current federal government employees in order to streamline transfer procedures. Executive, scientific, and technical recruiting plans were all under way. In 1942, with the Executive Order 9063 of 1942, the hiring procedure was further simplified. Under the new regulation, the commission proclaimed competitive examination only when the supply was ahead of the demand. In the case of noncompetitive examinations, a simple determination of minimum qualifications was to be made and age limits were imposed for most positions. The new regulations relaxed certain procedures, but they tightened others. Indeed, all government agencies were required to supply the commission with personnel estimates for advance planning. Their own plans for the recruitment of personnel were to be coordinated with those of the commission. Separate departmental programs were to continue only with the authorization of the commission, and all programs for publicizing personnel requirements were to be cleared with it as well.[85] All in all, as Van Riper summarized, "the overall effect of the regulations was to consolidate the Commission's position as the director of the manpower activities of the federal government."[86]

The impact of the war and the consequent commission's internal overhaul was huge. The numbers of the state's mobilization speak for themselves. Although the federal administration was already numerically far superior to that of 1917, when America entered World War I, its size grew astronomically in just a few dozen months. Between 1941 and 1942, the federal government passed from 1,437,682 to 2,296,384 employees, and in 1945 it reached the record number of 3,816,310 public workers.[87] The turnover was very high in the civil service during the war: from June 1, 1939 to June 30, 1945 about nine million placements were made within the federal bureaucracy.[88]

The New Deal had already overloaded the CSC through the multiplication of agencies, but with the war its burden dramatically increased. Nevertheless, the commission did not request Congress for any change of rules, nor for any suspension of public competitions for posts. What did happen was a simplification of recruiting procedures for expediting the hiring of civilians in the ranks of the administration, the establishment of a system of direct invitations to experts for occupying positions of high technical specialization, and the delegation of several powers to administrative agencies, to facilitate the organizational system of newly hired employees.[89]

While the commission's approach preserved the merit system, and the rules adopted during the preceding years, it also stiffened its operation. In fact, 95% of positions continued to be subject to public hiring competitions and to the statutory rules of the civil service, making it more difficult for public employees to be transferred or relocated, for the sake of meeting demands for personnel in certain determined areas. Another element of this rigidity resulted from the specialization and professionalization that public administration had undertaken during the preceding two decades and that, in the course of the war, did not allow renouncing lengthy training processes for new hires, who often lacked the necessary skills and knowledge for holding the positions they had been assigned. On top of this phenomenon, there was the occupational dynamic imparted by the war. The best trained and most specialized young men were in fact employed in military operations or in private sector jobs supporting wartime activities. The Federal Civil Service had to call on undereducated women and black men, who in 1945, respectively, represented 40% and 12% of the total workforce.[90] These individuals, however, had been engaged in other, often unskilled occupations before the war, and consequently they needed a training period before their potential could be developed and put to best effect.

Especially important activity in this period was carried out by numerous businessmen and private sector managers employed by the government, confirming once more how the wartime emergency fostered further osmosis between the public and private worlds. Initially they took part as temporary civil servants of the federal government. At the same time, however, given that their economic positions partook of classic liberalism, these businessmen were little inclined to expand the government's interventions and to let it control industrial procedures. They nonetheless quickly realized that, without comprehensive control of an entire industrial sector, the government would not readily reach its production level objectives and consequently bring the war to a victorious outcome. Paradoxically, those who arrived in the government with the greatest faith in the market often became the most dedicated planners of governmental interventions.[91] The principles of the government's enlarged social control, and of a capitalism also administered by a visible public presence, had already made inroads among the élite during the 1930s, in confronting the economic depression. These concepts gained further reinforcement during the war, when managers and entrepreneurs had the opportunity to build closer relationships with the nation's professional bureaucracy.

As Otis Graham has observed, "The 'positive state' idea was not really debatable. Businessmen themselves were responsible for much of the expansion of governmental power of the 1930s. In any event, the war firmly cemented the government's compensatory role in the minds of a crucial segment of the public. Thousands upon thousands of businessmen and lawyers who still harbored a suspicion of government came to Washington to help staff the war mobilization."[92] The idea of industrial planning on the part of the federal government, which until ten years earlier would have been inconceivable in the United States, began to convince a good portion of the American establishment. In 1943 the National Association of Manufacturers created a planning committee for re-conversion, and the vice-president of General Motors openly supported the cause of national planning.[93] Declarations of this kind were published by the associations of various industrial and commercial sectors during the first postwar years. In this version, planning did not carry collectivist or socialist implications, but indicated the need for entrusting the government with a new coordinating role, in order to sustain economic and industrial development and to invest public resources toward reaching and maintaining full occupation. This was indeed a sweeping paradigm shift markedly reducing the separation between the government and private economic protagonists. Beyond the rhetoric of anti-statism propaganda, used especially by the Republicans, no one in the political and economic worlds continued to question public interventionism in the socio-economic context. The debate now was focused only on how governmental interventions were to be structured, organized, and carried out. A return to the governing dimensions and functions of the early twentieth century was already excluded from any realistic government program. The politics of re-scaling the role of the government remained an element of nostalgic propaganda but unworkable in practice, as the future political choices of Truman and especially of Eisenhower would eventually demonstrate.

Despite this new vital and intellectual boost, public administration had to face problems related to both economic centralization and the coordination of the federal bureaucracy with military offices, which insisted in having a say in the management of resources. The centralization of the administration's functions was realized with the presidential signing of an executive order, which in 1942 established the War Manpower Commission (WMC), charged with coordinating federal administration personnel. In this case, the CSC was put into a subordinate position to the WMC. Still, the latter's powers were never absolute and always coordinated with the CSC, and the opposing voices intervened only sporadically to criticize the use of powers. The WMC served as a control room, with respect to the delegation of functions that the CSC had made toward administrative agencies. These followed the directives of the WMC to undertake recruiting procedures, the running of competitions, and the classification of positions.

In this context, the merit system and the CSC received unconditional support by President Roosevelt. All the executive orders followed the commission's suggestion and finally, with the War Service Regulations, the delegation of authority was complete. Former Commissioner and scholar Leonard D. White reported that

> members of the United States Civil Service Commission, dealing with Franklin Roosevelt in the White House on matters which required his attention, were deeply impressed with his extraordinary grasp of principle and detail. (...) He approved the basic War Service Regulations effective March 16, 1942. He integrated the work of the Civil Service Commission with that of the Manpower Commission. He endorsed the decision of the Civil Service Commission itself to turn over the initial conduct of defense and war civil service matters to the minority member of the Commission, again confirming his preference for a single head of the central personnel office.[94]

Moreover, political control over civil servants was established and confirmed, with particular attention toward those who might express Communist or Nazi-Fascist sympathies. The commission was responsible for monitoring public opinion, and between 1943 and 1945 almost 350,000 government employees were investigated for their political views. At this time, however, real threats to divergent public opinions were few, and the results of the investigations did not reveal particular problems of political loyalty to the American government. After the war, legislation and the courts set very tight limits on the exclusion from public administration for a person's political opinions.[95]

Finally, the federal government's budget underwent enormous expansion. Before official participation in the war in 1940, the government spent ten billion dollars to obtain goods and services, but by 1945 the same kind of expenditure reached 95 billion dollars. Meanwhile, the gross national product grew by 100 billion dollars to 213 billion, of which 40% was destined to military activities.[96] The permanent national emergency triggered by the worldwide conflict brought about the political and economic preconditions for what would be called "the military-industrial complex," underlining the links among the expansion of governmental spending, the growth of the military apparatus, and the involvement of the industrial sector in weapons and defense systems.[97] This type of combination, as had been witnessed in the case of the New Deal, favored the evolution of the system in a mixed economy, especially in certain sectors, that was probably the most long-lasting legacy of the 1930s and 1940s.[98]

In conclusion, during the period of the New Deal and World War II, several fundamental transformations of American administration occurred. The presidency of Franklin Delano Roosevelt demonstrated that the meritocratic principle could be played like an accordion, and that it was possible to expand presidential power into the area of appointments. The spoils system, which had been reduced to about 10% of the total number of positions in the federal administration during the preceding decades, returned to reach almost 40% of civil servants by the end of the New Deal. This increase brought specialists and academics ideologically close to the Democratic party to occupy governmental positions, and it also involved a displacement of the principle of public hiring competition. All the same, in the years following the New Deal, the accordion of the federal bureaucracy returned to moving in the opposite direction, bringing the merit system back to its previous levels.[99]

In this process, the weight of the scientific management developed in the early years of the twentieth century was felt, which had fully permeated the culture of high-level bureaucrats and the academic world within the orbit of power. This technocratic system was boosted still further by the administrative agencies founded by the New Deal, and it was assigned to the implementation of policies via a more professionalized recruiting system. The Brownlow Committee and its report of 1937 were the embodiment of these transformations, summing up the need both to valorize presidential leadership and to select competent and neutral civil servants.

Finally, the war caused a rearrangement of the federal bureaucracy in the service of the global conflict, with the creation of new institutions and agencies, substantial growth in the number of public employees, and the emergence of coordination problems between agencies and departments. Moreover, there emerged the "military-industrial complex," that contributed to the massive expansion of federal spending and created a connecting point among the military apparatus, governmental officials, and large corporations. This connection promoted the maintenance of a mixed economy, based on free competition among businesses, as well as on intervention in public regulation, especially in certain sectors.[100]

In conclusion, according to the historian Gladys Kammerer, there were five major achievements for the civil service during World War II: the survival of merit system principles through adaptability and flexibility of the personnel system, success in recruitment for staffing the expanded federal civil service, progress in the development of training programs, realization of the importance of employees relations in the public service, and a new recognition of the personnel administration itself.[101] The 1945 Annual Report of the CSC added to these points also the emergence of the commission as the government's central personnel agency, the reliance on direct recruitment, the recognition of the need for improvement in supervision, the extension of retirement coverage, and the increased emphasis on internal management improvement.[102]

Essentially, the Roosevelt era produced long-lasting organizational and ideological transformations. The perception of the role in society of both the government and the president changed, since Roosevelt himself and his operative circumstances made it acceptable for the government to intervene in social and welfare affairs. Stemming from the progressive movement of the 1910s and 1920s, a new administrative ideology attained its fulfillment, in seeking for a "government of managers" and the separation of politics from administration. What remained at the end of the war was, in substantial terms, a political system that had at its apex a leader, the president, who was supported by an expanding federal government in his direction of a broadened administration. This federal administration was itself governed by the criteria of efficiency, neutrality, and expertise. Postwar politics was organized around the White House, which issued policy directives and decisions that needed to be developed by the federal bureaucracy.[103]

There thus was reached a political-administrative symmetry, which was partially the culmination of the progressive ideology of the early twentieth century, and partially the offspring of historical circumstances caused by the 1929 economic crisis and World War II. Nonetheless, even an apparently rational system, hierarchical and ordered in its ways such as the one that emerged in the wake of the Brownlow Report, could not evade the growing complexity of the postwar democratic system of government and of the many attendant social transformations of the United States. In the years lying ahead, there would be the need for further consolidation.

Notes

1 Frederick Mosher, *Democracy and the Public Service*, 2nd ed. (Oxford: Oxford University Press, 1982).
2 Sidney H. Aronson, *Status and Kinship in the Higher Civil Service* (Cambridge, MA: Harvard University Press, 1964), 35.
3 Mosher, *Democracy*, 61.
4 Aronson, *Status and Kinship*, 64.
5 J. D. Richardson, (ed.), *Messages and Papers of the Presidents*, Vol. II (Washington, DC: Bureau of National Literature and Art, 1903), 438.
6 The idea of allodial property derived from the practices already employed in the British civil service, where until 1855 public offices were sold to the aristocracy and upper-middle class. See Michael Coolican, *No Tradesmen and No Women: The Origins of the British Civil Service* (London: Biteback, 2018).
7 As noted by Leonard D. White, *The Jacksonians* (New York: MacMillan, 1954).

8 Applied to the Jacksonian epoch, the term "common man" means a middle-class individual, the "self-made man" who all by himself has achieved his own social ascent. See Arnaldo Testi, *La formazione degli Stati Uniti*, Chapter Four (Bologna: Il Mulino, 2003).

9 On this point, see Robert H. Wiebe, *The Search for Order 1877–1920* (New York: Hill and Wang, 1980).

10 Patricia Ingraham, *The Foundation of Merit: Public Service in American Democracy* (Baltimore, MD: Johns Hopkins University Press, 1985), 23.

11 Ari Arthur Hoogenboom, *Outlawing the Spoils* (Urbana: University of Illinois Press, 1961), 6.

12 Paul Van Riper, *History of the United States Civil Service* (Evanston, IL: Row Peterson, 1958), 43.

13 Carl R. Fish, *The Civil Service and the Patronage* (New York: Longmans, Green and Co., 1905), quoted by Van Riper, *History*, 43.

14 See Wiebe, *The Search*.

15 As explained by D. B. Caton, *Civil Service in Great Britain. A History of Abuses and Reforms and their Bearings upon American Politics* (New York: Harper and Brothers, 1880).

16 The problem of the spoils system was deeply felt, so much so that it was a leading theme of public debate. Among the leaders of reform were Carl Schurz, George William Curtis, Doman Eaton, Richard Henry Dana, and Thomas Jenckes. In the generation following the Pendleton Act, there were the future Presidents Theodore Roosevelt and Woodrow Wilson.

17 Van Riper, *History*, 85; also see Dwight Waldo, *The Administrative State* (New York: The Ronald Press, 1948), 192.

18 Civil Service Commission, *Twenty-Second Report* (Washington, DC: National Archives and Records Administration, 1905), 23.

19 Woodrow Wilson, "The Study of Administration," *Political Science Quarterly* 2, no. 2 (June 1887): 197–222.

20 Wilson, "The Study," 210.

21 Wilson, "The Study," 209–210.

22 Frank Goodnow, *Politics and Administration* (New York: MacMillan, 1900).

23 Mosher, *Democracy*, 72.

24 Robert Maranto and David Schultz, *A Short History of the US Civil Service* (Washington, DC: University Press of America, 1991).

25 This data is taken from Maranto and Schultz, *A Short History*. Regarding the populist affirmation, one can cite the foundation of the People's Party in 1892 and its electoral growth during the following years, accompanied by its influence over public debate through its accusations of the corruption of the capitalist and political élites.

26 Les Hannah, "Corporations in the US and in Europe, 1790–1860," *Business History* 56, no. 6 (2014): 865–899.

27 Stephen Skowronek, *Building a New American State. The Expansion of National Administrative Capacities 1877–1920* (Cambridge: Cambridge University Press, 1982).

28 See Robert E. Cushman, *The Independent Regulatory Commissions*, 2nd ed. (Oxford: Oxford University Press, 1972), 20–34.

29 On this point, see Charles Francis Adams, *Railroads: Their Origins and Problems* (New York: Putnam's, 1886), which clearly expresses the viewpoint of the entrepreneurial groups of the sector.

30 As noted by Louis Fisher, *The Politics of Shared Powers: Congress and The Executive* (Washington, DC: Congressional Quarterly Press, 1981), 147–148.

31 On this process of reinforcement of the commission's independence, see Martha V. Gottron, ed., *Regulation: Process and Politics* (Washington, DC: Congressional Quarterly, 1982).

32 For example, the Federal Reserve was given a Board of Governors in 1913; the Federal Trade Commission was founded in 1914.

33 In this case, Ernest Freund talked of a State with "enlarged police power," in order to underline how the new regulations had a primarily controlling and sanctioning function, with respect to private companies and entrepreneurial activities in particular. See Ernest Freund, *The Police Power: Public Policy and Constitutional Rights* (Chicago: Callaghan and Company, 1904).

34 Wiebe, *The Search,* 222.

35 Wiebe, *The Search,* 223.

36 The historian Hamby describes the Progressive Movement as a "political movement that addresses ideas, impulses, and issues stemming from modernization of American society. Emerging at the end of the nineteenth century, it established much of the tone of American politics throughout the first half of the century." See Alonzo L. Hamby, "Progressivism: A Century of Change and Rebirth," in *Progressivism and the New Democracy*, eds. Sidney M. Milkis and Jerome M. Mileur (Amherst: University of Massachusetts Press, 1999), 40.

37 Robert Higgs, *Crisis and Leviathan. Critical Episodes in the Growth of American Government* (Oxford: Oxford University Press, 1987).

38 Mosher, *Democracy,* 75.

39 Elting E. Morison, ed., *Letters of Theodore Roosevelt*, Vol. IV (Cambridge: Cambridge University Press, 1951–54), 1201.

40 On this point, see R. D. White, "Executive Reorganization, Theodore Roosevelt and the Keep Commission," *Administrative Theory and Praxis* 24, no. 3 (2002): 507–518.

41 Maranto and Schultz, *A Short History*, 77.

42 Peri A. Arnold, *Making the Managerial Presidency* (Lawrence: University Press of Kansas, 1986), 76.

43 Most federal bureaucrats did not wish to take the risk of acting in supposed violation of the Constitution, which expressly did not foresee the drafting of a budget on the part of the presidency.

44 Alice B. Stone and Donald B. Stone, "Early Development of Education in Public Administration," in *American Public Administration: Past, Present, Future*, ed. Frederick Mosher (Tuscaloosa: University of Alabama Press, 1975), 11–48.

45 For an appraisal of bureaucratic growth during the World War, see Gary Gerstle, *Liberty and Coercion. The Paradox of American Government from the Founding to the Present* (Princeton, NJ: Princeton University Press, 2015).

46 Skowronek, *Building a New American State*, 200–203.

47 Van Riper, *History*, 252.

48 Maranto and Schultz, *A Short History,* 80.

49 Arnold, *Making*, 64–82.

50 William J. Novak, "Public-Private Governance. A Historical Introduction," in *Government by Contract. Outsourcing and American Democracy*, eds. Jody Freeman and Martha Minow (Cambridge, MA: Harvard University Press, 2009), 23–40.

51 The concept of the "Associational State", as the contribution of the third sector to American institutional architecture, has been most fully elaborated by the historian Brian Balogh. See Brian Balogh, *The Associational State: American Governance in the Twentieth Century* (Philadelphia: University of Pennsylvania Press, 2015).

52 See Pamela S. Tolbert and Lynne G. Zucker, "Institutional Sources of Change in the Formal Structure of Organizations: The Diffusion of Civil Service Reform, 1880–1935," *Administrative Science Quarterly* 28 (1983): 22–39.

53 Joseph G. Rayback, *A History of American Labor* (New York: Free Press, 1966), 320–321.

54 On Hoover's political and economic conception of the State, see Otis Graham, *Toward a Planned Society. From Roosevelt to Nixon* (Oxford: Oxford University Press, 1976).

55 Arthur J. Schlesinger, *The Crisis of the Old Order* (Boston, MA: Houghton Mifflin Company, 1957).

56 Van Riper, *History,* 312.

57 William E. Leuchtenburg, *Franklin D. Roosevelt and the New Deal* (New York: Harper & Row, 1963), 52–60.

58 Maranto and Schultz, *A Short History,* 89.

59 For a reconstruction of the socio-cultural implications of the New Deal, see David T. Rodgers, *Atlantic Crossings: Social Politics in a Progressive Age* (Cambridge, MA: Harvard University Press, 2009).

60 Schultz and Maranto, *A Short History,* 91.

61 Edward S. Corwin, *Total War and the* Constitution (New York: Knopf, 1947), 170.

62 Leuchtenburg, *Franklin D. Roosevelt,* 63.

63 Arthur Schlesinger Jr., *The Cycles of American History* (Boston, MA: Houghton Mifflin, 1986), Chapter 1.

64 Arnold, *Making,* 127.

65 Louis Brownlow, Charles Merriam and Luther Gulick, "Report on the President's Committee on Administrative Management," in *Classics of the American Presidency,* ed. Harry A. Bailey (Oak Park, IL: Moore Publishers, 1980).

66 Brownlow, Merriam, and Gulick, "Report," 1.

67 Arnold, *Making,* 81–118.

68 Arnold, *Making,* 129.

69 Barry Karl, *The Uneasy State: The United States from 1915 to 1945* (Chicago, IL: University of Chicago Press, 1983).

70 Arnold, *Making,* 114.

71 President's Committee on Administrative Management, *Report with Special Studies* (Washington, DC: U.S. Government Printing Office, 1937), 7–14 and 59–133.

72 On this debate, see Mordecai Lee, *A Presidential Civil Service: FDR's Liaison Office for Personnel Management* (Tuscaloosa: University of Alabama Press, 2016).

73 According to Lee, *Presidential Civil Service,* 76: "FDR had wanted to terminate the independent, autonomous, and bipartisan three-member CSC and replace it with a civil service administrator who would function in the HR sphere comparable to the president's budget director. After more than two years of fierce political battle, Congress had prohibited FDR from doing so by banning use of his new reorganization powers to make any modifications whatsoever in the CSC. Given this seemingly fixed statutory environment, a central perspective for this inquiry is what, if anything, LOPM was able to accomplish to come closer to FDR's personnel management goals while the CSC continued to exist and operate in an unchanged legal environment."

74 Van Riper, *History,* 332–334.

75 Hatch Acts, located in 5 US Code 7324 (1988). The original version refers to the Act of August 2, 1939, chap. 410, 53 Stat. 1147, and the Act of July 19, 1940, chap. 640, 54 Stat. 767.

76 Their repeal did not come until the Clinton presidency.

77 Franklin D. Roosevelt, *Public Papers and Addresses* (New York: Random House, 1938–1950), 1: 752.

78 Sidney M. Milkis, *The President and the Parties* (Oxford: Oxford University Press, 1993), 24.

79 Van Riper, *History,* 366.

80 See Higgs, *Crisis and Leviathan,* Chapter 7, 123–155.

81 The WPB was created by President Roosevelt with the Executive Order 9024, on January 16, 1942. Besides its chairman, the Board's members were the Secretary of War, the Secretary of the Navy, the Secretary of Agriculture, the Army General responsible for military acquisitions, the director of the Office of Price Administration, the Federal Loan Administrator, the President of the Board of Economic

Warfare, and the President's special advisor of Defense. There also existed 12 territorial offices, whose staff were comprised primarily by federal civil servants.

82 Samuel P. Huntington, *Soldier and the State* (Cambridge, MA: Harvard University Press, 1957), 340.

83 Civilian Production Administration, *Industrial Mobilization for War. History of the War Production Board and the Predecessor Agencies* (Washington, DC: Government Printing Office, 1947), 960–961.

84 However, persons appointed under this authority could not receive a permanent classified status.

85 See A. S. Flemming, "Emergency Aspects of Civil Service," *Public Administration Review* 1 (Autumn 1940): 25.

86 Van Riper, *History,* 371.

87 As noted by Van Riper, *History,* 374.

88 USCSC, 62 Report, 1945, 37, quoted by Van Riper, *History,* 374.

89 See Maranto and Schultz, 1991, *A Short History of the US Civil Service,* 97.

90 Department of Labor, Bureau of Statistics, 1947.

91 As noted by Graham, *Toward a Planned Society,* 80.

92 Graham, *Toward a Planned Society,* 81.

93 Graham, *Toward a Planned Society,* 83.

94 Leonard D. White, "Franklin Roosevelt and the Public Service," *Public Personnel Review* 6 (July 1945): 143.

95 Van Riper, *History,* 396.

96 Graham, *Toward a Planned Society,* 72.

97 On this point see Higgs, *Crisis and Leviathan,* 194–195.

98 The process of state-making found continuity in what came to be defined as the National Security State, born between the 1940s and the 1950s. A new expansion of the federal government, in both its expenditures and its public personnel, worked to construct the military-industrial complex that would serve to compete with the Soviet Union. On this point, see Michael J. Hogan, *A Cross of Iron: Harry S. Truman and the Origins of the National Security State* (Cambridge: Cambridge University Press, 2010).

99 On this point, see Arnold, *Making.*

100 For a more detailed definition of the military-industrial complex, see Higgs, *Crisis and Leviathan,* Chapters 8 and 9.

101 Gladys M. Kammerer, *Impact of War on Federal Personnel Administration: 1939–1945* (Lexington: University Press of Kentucky, 2014).

102 United States Civil Service Commission, *62 Annual Report* (Washington DC: GPO, 1944–1945).

103 The reinforcement of the presidency meant that the "fitness of character" of the individual elected to the White House became all the more important, to obtain the results that the administration had set for itself, as demonstrated by Richard Neustadt, *Presidential Power and the Modern Presidents* (New York: Free Press, 1991). Morton Keller has considered the period starting with Franklin Delano Roosevelt's presidency as the populist and Caesarist era of American political history.

Bibliography

Adams, Charles Francis. *Railroads: Their Origins and Problems.* New York: Putnam's, 1886.

Arnold, Peri A. *Making the Managerial Presidency.* Lawrence: University Press of Kansas, 1986.

Aronson, Sidney H. *Status and Kinship in the Higher Civil Service.* Cambridge, MA: Harvard University Press, 1964.

Balogh, Brian. *The Associational State: American Governance in the Twentieth Century.* Philadelphia: University of Pennsylvania Press, 2015.

Brownlow, Louis, Charles Merriam, and Luther Gulick. "Report on the President's Committee on Administrative Management." In *Classics of the American Presidency*, edited by H. A. Bailey. Oak Park, IL: Moore Publishers, 1980.

Caton, D. B. *Civil Service in Great Britain. A History of Abuses and Reforms and their Bearings upon American Politics.* New York: Harper and Brothers, 1880.

Civil Service Commission. *Twenty-Second Report.* Washington, DC: National Archives and Record Administration, 1905.

Civilian Production Administration. *Industrial Mobilization for War. History of the War Production Board and the Predecessor Agencies.* Washington, DC: Government Printing Office, 1947.

Coolican, Michael. *No Tradesmen and No Women: The Origins of the British Civil Service.* London: Biteback, 2018.

Corwin, Edward S. *Total War and the Constitution.* New York: Knopf, 1947.

Cushman, Robert E. *The Independent Regulatory Commission*, 2nd ed. Oxford: Oxford University Press, 1972.

Fish, Carl R. *The Civil Service and the Patronage.* New York: Longmans, Green and Co., 1905.

Fisher, Louis. *The Politics of Shared Powers: Congress and the Executive.* Washington, DC: Congressional Quarterly Press, 1981.

Flemming, A. S. "Emergency Aspects of Civil Service." *Public Administration Review* 1, no. 1 (Autumn 1940): 25–31.

Freund, Ernest. *The Police Power: Public Policy and Constitutional Rights.* Chicago, IL: Callaghan and Company, 1904.

Gerstle, Gary. *Liberty and Coercion. The Paradox of American Government from the Founding to the Present.* Princeton, NJ: Princeton University Press, 2017.

Goodnow, Frank. *Politics and Administration.* New York: MacMillan, 1900.

Gottron, Martha V., ed. *Regulation: Process and Politics.* Washington, DC: Congressional Quarterly, 1982.

Graham, Otis. *Toward a Planned Society. From Roosevelt to Nixon.* Oxford: Oxford University Press, 1976.

Hamby, Alonzo L. "Progressivism: A Century of Change and Rebirth." In *Progressivism and the New Democracy*, edited by Sidney M. Milkis and Jerome M. Mileur, 40–80. Amherst: University of Massachusetts Press, 1999.

Higgs, Robert. *Crisis and Leviathan. Critical Episodes in the Growth of American Government.* Oxford: Oxford University Press, 1987.

Hogan, Michael J. *A Cross of Iron: Harry S. Truman and the Origins of the National Security State, 1945–1954.* Cambridge: Cambridge University Press, 1998.

Hoogenboom, Ari Arthur. *Outlawing the Spoils.* Urbana: University of Illinois Press, 1961.

Huntington, Samuel T. *Soldier and the State*, Cambridge, MA: Harvard University Press, 1957.

Ingraham, Patricia W. *The Foundation of Merit: Public Service in American Democracy.* Baltimore, MD: Johns Hopkins University Press, 1985.

Kammerer Gladys Marie, *Impact of War on Federal Personnel Administration: 1939–1945*, Lexington: University Press of Kentucky, 2014.

Karl, Barry. *The American Uneasy State: The United States from 1915 to 1945.* Chicago, IL: University of Chicago Press, 1983.

Lee, Mordecai. *A Presidential Civil Service: FDR's Liaison Office for Personnel Management.* Tuscaloosa: University of Alabama Press, 2016.

Leuchtenburg, William E. *Franklin D. Roosevelt and the New Deal.* New York: Harper & Row, 1963.

Maranto, Robert, and David Schultz. *A Short History of the US Civil Service.* Washington, DC: University Press of America, 1991.

Milkis, Sidney M. *The President and the Parties.* Oxford: Oxford University Press, 1993.

Morison, Etling E., ed. *Letters of Theodore Roosevelt*, Vol. IV. Cambridge, Cambridge University Press, 1951–1954.

Mosher, Frederick. *Democracy and the Public Service*, 2nd ed. Oxford: Oxford University Press, 1982.

Nathan, Richard. *The Administrative Presidency.* New York: John Wiley and Sons, 1983.

Neustadt, Richard E. *Presidential Power and the Modern Presidents.* New York: Free Press, 1991.

Novak, William J. "Public-Private Governance. A Historical Introduction." In *Government by Contract. Outsourcing and American Democracy*, edited by J. Freeman and M. Minow, 23–40. Cambridge, MA: Harvard University Press, 2009.

Rayback, Joseph G. *A History of American Labor.* New York: Free Press, 1966.

Richardson, J. D., ed. *Messages and Papers of the Presidents*, Vol. II. Washington, DC: Bureau of National Literature and Art, 1903.

Rodgers, David T. *Atlantic Crossings. Social Politics in a Progressive Age.* Cambridge, MA: Harvard University Press, 2009.

Roosevelt, Franklin D. *Public Papers and Addresses.* New York: Random House, 1938–1950.

Schlesinger, Jr., Arthur. *The Crisis of the Old Order.* Boston, MA: Houghton Mifflin Company, 1957.

———. *The Cycles of American History.* Boston, MA: Houghton Mifflin, 1986.

Skowronek, Stephen. *Building a New American State. The Expansion of National Administrative Capacities 1877–1920.* Cambridge: Cambridge University Press, 1982.

Stone, Alice B., and Donald B. Stone. "Early Development of Education in Public Administration." In *American Public Administration: Past, Present, Future*, edited by Frederick Mosher, 11–48. Tuscaloosa: University of Alabama Press, 1975.

Testi, Arnaldo. *La formazione degli Stati Uniti.* Bologna: Il Mulino, 2003.

Tolbert Pamela S., and Lynne G. Zucker. "Institutional Sources of Change in the Formal Structure of Organizations: The Diffusion of Civil Service Reform, 1880–1935." *Administrative Science Quarterly* 28 (1983): 22–39.

Van Riper, Paul. *History of the United States Civil Service.* Evanston, IL: Row Peterson, 1958.

Waldo, Dwight. *The Administrative State.* New York: The Ronald Press, 1948.

White, Leonard D. "Franklin Roosevelt and the Public Service." *Public Personnel Review* 6 (July 1945), 139–146.

———. *The Jacksonians.* New York: MacMillan, 1954.

———. "Executive Reorganization, Theodore Roosevelt and the Keep Commission." *Administrative Theory and Praxis* 24, no. 3 (2002): 507–518.

Wiebe, Robert H. *The Search for Order, 1877–1920.* New York: Hill and Wang, 1980.

Wilson, Woodrow. "The Study of Administration." *Political Science Quarterly* 2, no. 2 (1887): 197–222.

3

FROM THE POSTWAR PERIOD TO THE 1960S

The Role of Federal Bureaucracy between Administrative Reorganization and Development of the Welfare State

The New Postwar Order. A Theoretical Perspective

Soon after the end of World War II, the New Dealers tried to convince the public that their wartime sacrifices were for the sake of a new social order. President Roosevelt outlined the postwar agenda of modern liberalism in his 1944 State of the Union, where he explained that rights articulated in the Declaration of Independence and protected by the Constitution, "our rights to life and liberty," had become "inadequate to assure us equality in the pursuit of happiness." Thus, "a second Bill of Rights" was needed to provide economic security. Among the new economic rights were the right to a job, the right to adequate farm prices, the right to a decent home, and the right to a good education. The task of the New Deal administrative state was to secure these rights. These new "economic rights," added to the ones of the Founders, were entitlements that the government would provide to every American citizen.[1]

In this context of expanded federal governmental management, the political scientist Dwight Waldo outlined the vision of the new order in his 1948 book, *The Administrative State.* He described the philosophy and values behind what he called "the heavenly city of the twentieth-century administrators." The last vestiges of authority and religion had disappeared from politics. Planning had become the new faith.

> Once it is realized that there is no natural harmony of nature, no divine or other purpose hidden beneath the flux and chaos of present planlessness, it becomes immoral to let poverty, ignorance, pestilence, and war continue if they can be obliterated by a plan.

Planning was based on scientific naturalism or materialism; it viewed human happiness in hedonistic terms, as Waldo argued, "The Good Life is chiefly a matter of the possession or employment of tangible things." The civil servants' job was to provide as many of these things to as many people as possible. The equal distribution of material goods was the chief ingredient of their sense of justice. Liberty and democracy had to support equality and be administered for its sake. Public administration, in Waldo's words, expected to "engineer for Heaven an earthly locus."[2]

At the administrative level, the case for the "unitary executive" made by the Brownlow Report of 1937, which argued for a centralization of presidential control over the bureaucracy, remained the dominant stream of administrative thought up to the 1960s. Public administration was still seen as "the management of men and materials in the accomplishment of the purposes of the state."[3] In White's view, the state was "an important means by which the program of social amelioration is effected." "In every direction," he noted, "the task of the modern state is enlarging" and "the range of public administration is being extended."[4] For Luther Gulick, administrative organization was about translating "the central purpose or objective of an enterprise ... into reality."[5] It was about

> the development of intelligent singleness of purpose in the minds and wills of those who are working together as a group, so that each worker will of his own accord fit his task into the whole with skill and enthusiasm.[6]

Gulick argued that this sense of a "singleness of purpose" should extend far beyond the walls of government agencies and into the minds of the citizenry and its political leadership. As he observed when reflecting on the lessons learned from World War II,

> truly effective action in administration arises from singleness of purpose and clarity of policy, ardently believed in both by the leaders and by the public in all parts of the country and in all strata of society.... When a nation drives forward with unity of purpose, then administration can accomplish the impossible.[7]

Gulick clearly believed that an increasingly broad range of human action in communities should be brought perhaps slowly, but inevitably, under the domain of some type of conscious and planned coordination. He saw no limits to the effort mankind is prepared to make to render life more secure and abundant through socially enforced coordination, and no need to accept the view that there are fixed limits of coordination beyond which mankind can never go.[8] These writers also voiced a deeply held faith in the potential of social science to direct public policy and administration. To achieve an efficient coordination and planning, it was necessary to design a more managerial, technocratic, and scientific system of government.

In this vein, Herbert Simon set the tone for what then become the thought of postwar mainstream public administration, as well as the emerging new policy sciences, when he wrote that the central concern for administrative theory should be "the rationality of decisions—that is their appropriateness for the accomplishment of specified goals."[9] For him, it is simply a particular type of "organization," whose task is "to bring the organizational components of its parts ... into conformity with the objectives of the organization as a whole."[10] Furthermore, public administrators, like business administrators, are to "take as their ethical premises the objectives that have been set for the organization."[11]

From his perspective, a practical science of administration should consist of "those propositions as to how men would behave if they wished their activity to result in the greatest attainment of administrative objectives with scarce means,"[12] and efficiency should be "a guiding criterion in administrative decision-making."[13] A public administrator, for Simon, needs "to maximize the attainment of the governmental objectives ... by efficient employment of the limited resources ... available to him."[14] Indeed, for Simon, organizations are "fundamental ... to the achievement of human rationality in any broad sense," and "the rational individual is, and must be, an organized and institutionalized individual."[15]

Sheldon Wolin has observed, from the perspective of Simon and like-minded theorists, how organization becomes "the grand device for transforming human irrationalities into rational behavior."[16] The continuing power of Simon's vision within the field of public administration has manifested itself in a variety of ways. In the long run, it can be seen in the preoccupation of scholars over the 1950s and 1960s with a seemingly endless variety of rationalist decision-making techniques such as program budgeting, management by objectives, policy analysis, systems analysis, management science, and strategic planning.

This set of ideas and theories had a remarkable impact on the minds of the administrative reformers of the 1940s and the 1950s, who tried to put order, to rationalize, and to complete the achievements of the administrative state reached during the New Deal and World War II.

Consolidating the Administrative State: The Truman Presidency

At the end of World War II, in December 1945, the new president Harry Truman signed the law that determined the course of American institutions as they passed from the context of war to that of peace. The text granted the president a two-year period to reorganize the executive branch, subject to the eventual veto of Congress, whenever the proposals of the White House went beyond their proper prerogatives.[17] Truman sought to centralize the presidency even further and to reorganize the federal administration after the American victory in the global conflict. Truman's Bureau of Budget proposed three reforms to Congress, the first two of which rendered permanent several changes made during the war, centralized the agencies of public construction works under the Housing and Home Finance Agency, and reorganized the departments. The first two plans met with resistance from Congress, but they succeeded in surviving. The third reform, which aimed to transfer welfare policies under the control of the Federal Security Administration, was defeated by the congressional majority.[18]

After the re-conversion of the government, Truman developed two lines of reform: one dedicated to military service and intelligence, and the other to public administration. The military one aimed to reduce and revise the organization of the armed forces, with the objective of reducing defense expenditures. The reform materialized as the National Security Act of 1947. The law suppressed the War Department and the Department of the Navy, creating in their place the National Military Establishment, with the Secretary of Defense as its head. The executive departments of the army, navy, and air force became concentrated at a level below this principal one. In addition, in order to confront the Cold War, the National Security Council, the National Security Resources Board, the Central Intelligence Agency, the Munitions Board, and the Research and Development Board were created.[19]

Moreover, Congress helped Truman, although for the most part unintentionally, to institutionalize the presidential bureaucracy. Congressional statutes, for example, established the Council for Economic Advisers (CEA) in 1946, to aid the president in the formulation of fiscal policy, while the legislative body appropriated funds for a larger staff to assist him. At the federal bureaucracy level, the transition back to normal operations was produced by an Executive Order 9691 issued by President Truman in February 1946, which authorized Temporary Civil Service Regulations to suspend the War Service Regulations. The temporary regulations, which went into effect from March 7, 1946, to April 30, 1947, permitted federal agencies to make temporary appointments, while the commission devoted its resources to the establishment of registers leading to permanent appointment. During this period, reductions in force continued, with war service and temporary appointees being displaced. New civil service rules, issued under Executive Order 9830 of February 24, 1947, replaced the temporary regulations. An attempt was made to continue, in the new rules, the best practices developed during the war. The policy of delegating authority to agencies to act in individual personnel matters without prior Civil Service Commission approval—such as individual promotions, reassignments, and transfers—was confirmed and extended. These actions, however, were subject to commission standards. The executive order also reaffirmed the commission's role as the government's central personnel agency; it outlined the general responsibilities of the commission and all Federal agencies in the field of personnel management, and it established the new commission's inspection program. Moreover, during the war the merit principle was derogated to deal with the urgency of the conflict. Most of the federal employees have been hired without an open competition procedure. It therefore became necessary, after the war, to hold open competitive examinations for the positions occupied by employees without competitive status. This examining process was necessary, even though reduction in forces was going on at the same time, resulting in an overall drop in the size of the workforce of more than a million. At the end of the war, the number of federal civil servants selected through competitive exams was only 33% of the total. All the others had been re-examined, in a series of examinations open to the general public as well. If the employees earned a sufficiently high score on the registers, their appointments were converted to probational. If not, they were replaced by eligible candidates at the top of the registers. Between July 1946 and July 1949, the commission announced 104,413 examinations and processed more than 4.7 million applications, which resulted in 1,348,470 placements. These results testified to the basic efficiency of the Civil Service Commission and the machinery it supervised. In July 1949, the civil servants with permanent status (examination passed) rose to 84% of the total, from the 33% of 1945.[20]

At the legislative level, the most important postwar law for public administration was the Administrative Procedure Act of 1946.[21] The act prescribed the steps that agencies had to take in rule making and adjudication. It divided these functions into "formal" and "informal" categories, telling agencies when they had to notify affected parties of new rules, allowing them to give comments on them, and determining how much time was required before the new rules took effect. Although the act did not entirely separate the roles of prosecution and adjudication, it did strengthen the office of "trial examiners," increasing their salaries and making them more independent. Section 10 of the act provided for what appeared to be extensive judicial review of agency decisions. Courts could overrule any act that they found "arbitrary" or "otherwise not in accordance with the law." The court should "review the whole record or such portions thereof as may be cited by any party, and due account shall be taken of the rule of prejudicial error."

This was the first attempt to regulate administration through the application of constitutional principles to the organization and operations of federal bureaucracy. With the help of the courts, the nation's legislators accepted the constitutional legitimacy of broad delegations of legislative and judicial authority to administrative agencies, but they sought to infuse the use of that authority with a set of values that privileged legislative over executive or managerial values. Beginning with the Administrative Procedure Act and the Legislative Reorganization Act, both enacted in 1946, Congress accepted the reality of a substantial and administratively centered American state.[22] In response, it reorganized itself internally and positioned itself to exert both broad and finely tailored control over the exercise of administrative power as a counterweight to the continued development of executive management in the presidency.

The Act determined the standards for judging evidence in processes of adjudication, the procedures for hearings of the interested parties, and the mechanisms of participation of interest groups in the decisions of administrative agencies. Moreover, along with the procedural values of open participation and transparency, legislators also sought to bend and sculpt the administrative state to suit the particular interests of individual members, turning agencies into modern patronage machines through casework demands, earmarks, and other levers. The ensuing emendations of the law, the decisions of the Supreme Court, and the new administrative culture that would burst forth in the 1960s together would greatly increase the weight of the representation of interests, citizens' rights, and the political accountability of American bureaucracy's conduct.

Indeed, during the first postwar decade, American politics seemed to have definitively settled into a mixed system that political scientists called "interest-group pluralism."[23] Politics was simply the constant competition among various interest groups, with no overall "public interest" standing above it all. The government's job was to provide the arena in which this contest took place and to ensure that no single group acquired overwhelming power. The new bureaucratic agencies established by the New Deal embedded this new, level playing field.[24] For 20 years after World War II, the New Deal system of "interest group liberalism" would persist, before it met serious challenges from both the left and the right in the 1960s and 1970s.

The Hoover Commission of 1949

After having won the congressional majority in the 1946 midterm elections, the Republicans were especially motivated to undertake administrative reforms, notably reducing and rationalizing bureaucracy, because they expected to win the presidential election of 1948. In 1947, Republican Representative Clarence Brown (R-OH) introduced a bill in the House to establish a mixed commission consisting of Members of Congress, appointees from the executive branch, and representatives from the private sector, to study the organization of the executive branch and to submit recommendations to both the president and Congress. Senator Henry Cabot Lodge Jr. (R-MA) introduced an identical bill in the Senate. On June 26, 1947, the House considered the bill briefly and passed it by a voice vote without dissent. The following day, the Senate acted on the House bill and voted its approval unanimously. The president signed the bill into law on July 7, 1947, and the bipartisan commission was established.[25]

Initially, the commission proposed "to find the places where economics can be effected and the places where there is overlapping and duplication."[26] The commission intended to "promote economy, efficiency, and improved service in the transaction of public business,"[27] through spending limitations, re-ordering administrative jurisdictions, and abolishing services, activities, and functions deemed unnecessary for the efficient conduct of government. In essence, its scope included also the president's general managerial role, as well as personnel management in the executive branch.

Therefore, to understand the pressing circumstances that had engendered such a commission, one must consider several impressive statistics related to the growth of government that resulted from the combination of the 1930s economic depression and World War II. In fact, from the end of the 1920s to 1948, the total number of public employees had passed from 570,000 to over two million; the amount of federal offices had quadrupled, reaching 1,800 units; federal government spending passed from 3.6 to 42 billion dollars; and the annual public debt shouldered by families had grown from 500 to 7,500 dollars.[28]

Therefore, in order to confront and re-order the enormous expansion and complication of the federal government, there was born the Commission on the Organization of the Executive Branch, then named "the Hoover Commission," because of its chairman, the former President Herbert Hoover.

After the Brownlow Committee, the Hoover Commission constituted the largest effort of administrative reorganization of the postwar period. To pursue this objective, thematically specialized task forces were created, while for other matters recourse was made to the suggestions of private counselors. Moreover, the commission worked in close cooperation with the Bureau of the Budget.

In establishing the law of 1947, the following objectives were set forth:

> (1) limiting expenditures to the lowest amount consistent with the efficient performance of essential services, activities, and functions; (2) eliminating duplication and overlapping of services, activities, and functions; (3) consolidating services, activities, and functions of a similar nature; (4) abolishing services, activities, and functions not necessary to the efficient conduct of government; and (5) defining and limiting executive functions, services, and activities.[29]

To those who interpreted these words broadly, the commission's aim was to review, restructure, and reduce the scope of government activities. Commissioners critical of the Truman and Roosevelt administrations tended to see the mandate of the commission as the retrenchment of the federal government, an opportunity to dismantle the New Deal order. In contrast, for the defenders of the administration, the law had to be interpreted narrowly. They argued that the law did not authorize the abolition of substantive functions, and they were concerned that the commission might establish cuts in the fields of social security and veterans' benefits. They wanted the government to continue what it was doing, but they were looking for a reorganization and rationalization, in order to achieve better performance of the governmental functions.

Established by a Republican majority that sought to restore "small government," the first Hoover Commission became the concrete example of how, even among the ranks of the Republican party, in the postwar period there was the affirmation of a culture already permeated by the necessity not of dismantling, but rather of maintaining and better managing the administrative state.

Indeed, the most radical proposals of "fiscal restoration" and "small government" were soon abandoned, in favor of the search for an improved organization of the federal machinery. Even according to the Republicans, the presidency needed the powers to manage the federal administration, to be better organized itself, and to have a wider staff. In continuity with the principles of the Brownlow Committee, the American congressional majority took into account the need to reinforce the presidency and to make the White House the definitive hinge as well as summit of the executive branch.[30]

Numerous factors favored the change of direction with respect to the initial objectives of the commission, as intended by the Republicans. In the end, Hoover showed himself to be more interested in the organizational issues facing the administration than in decreasing the costs of federal government.[31] One of these factors was undoubtedly the close relationship between the Commission and the Bureau of the Budget, which protected the interests of the administration in elaborating the policies related to reorganization. Another factor was that in 1948, contrary to the hopes of the Republicans, Harry Truman won the election, and the Democrats regained their congressional majority. This development brought moderation to the proposals of the commission, imposed by Hoover himself, who understood that if he wished to attain even a limited number of his objectives in economizing and achieving organizational efficiency, he had to cooperate with the White House and Congress. This re-dimensioning of objectives especially held true for the final and most substantial report, that of 1949.

The report considered it to be impossible for the president, at the present time, to perform effective management of the federal administration, and for this reason, it suggested a review of existing legislation, considered by the Hoover Commission to be too restrictive on the power of the White House to reorganize agencies and departments.[32] In fact, the commission noted that

> the executive branch is not organized into a workable number of major departments and agencies which the president can effectively direct, but is cut up into a large number of agencies, which divide responsibility and which are too great in number for effective direction from the top.[33]

To put this program into action, the commission further recommended the rationalization of functions, decentralization into the operating agencies of such functions as accounting, budgeting, recruiting and managing the personnel, and re-grouping them in departments and agencies according to the aimed-for objective, with the goal of reducing waste and multiplications of responsibilities. Other reforms sought to render the executive branch of the government easier to supervise for the president. Instead, at the level of the presidential staff, "the President should not be required to handle a policy problem through any set procedure, or to consult any fixed group of individuals, or to take up problems except at the time he chooses."[34] In order to make this happen, several points were determined:

> This staff would (1) supplement for the President the views and the advice of the operating departments in the formulation of policy, and (2) help the President execute policy by (a) coordinating programs, (b) developing administrative machinery, (c) coordinating the gathering of information, and (d) helping to establish policies to improve the personnel of the government.[35]

These recommendations pursued the transformation that had begun with the Brownlow project, which put the president and the White House staff at the center of the policy-making process. The Hoover Commission sought out the involvement of external experts, to be temporarily enlisted as advisors and strategists for the president's political reforms. Now, the most urgent agenda item was not to develop a competent, neutral, and professional bureaucracy but to supply the president with knowledge and technical means to promote the reforms that he aimed to pursue. Consequently, the role of the expert also changed from that of a skilled and responsible member of the federal government to a counselor and "brainpower" of the presidency. For these reasons, the Hoover Commission strongly advocated the reinforcement of the White House staff, which needed new experts and advisors, in order to fulfill its role in planning and coordinating policies. An unequivocal sign of this shift was the creation by President Truman in 1949 of his own Advisory Committee on Management[36] to study management problems in the federal government from a presidential perspective. This committee was also to advise him with respect to recommendations submitted by the Hoover Commission. The final report of this committee to the president underlined the need for a continuing, rather than occasional, program of public management improvement for all executive agencies, under the guidance of the Bureau of the Budget's Office of Management and Organization.[37]

Implementing the Hoover Commission's Recommendations

The report of the Hoover Commission was transmitted to Congress in 1949. Many of the 277 recommendations elaborated by the commission were adopted and implemented by the legislative branch.

Notwithstanding the rejection of the idea of instituting a Department of Social Service and Education, the plan remained the greatest success in the reorganization of the American executive branch during the entire twentieth century. In addition, Congress renewed presidential powers of reorganization with the Reorganization Act of 1949.[38] The head of the White House now could create and suppress agencies, but he had to specify possible savings and positive impacts, and the law gave Congress veto power, with the majority of only one of the two Houses, to reject plans of reorganization. This narrow path did not hinder President Truman, who sent Congress no less than 35 reorganization plans, in response to the recommendations expressed by the Hoover Commission.[39] Although Congress rejected several modifications, in particular with respect to the creation of new departments, Truman was able to reform the Ministries of the Interior, of Commerce, and of Labor, as well as numerous administrative agencies. A number of recommendations provided a crucial impetus for the passage of new legislation such as the Federal Property and Administrative Services Act, creating the General Services Administration. Following the Brownlow Committee and the prescriptions of the same Hoover Commission, Truman also succeeded in bolstering the support staff of the president, enlarging still further the personnel resources of the White House.

At personnel management level, in mid-1949, Truman submitted Reorganization Plan No. 5 to Congress to change the internal administrative structure of the Civil Service Commission.[40] In his message to Congress, he said this plan "carries into effect one of the major recommendations" of the Hoover Commission in the area of personnel management. The plan tried to distinguish between the commission's ordinary HR work vs. its formal quasi-judicial and regulatory roles. For the former, Truman designated the chair of the commission as (what would now be called) the CEO of the agency. To make clearer the lines of responsibility, the plan abolished the positions of commission secretary and chief examiner. In their place, Truman created an office of executive director who would be the commission's Chief Operating Office, accountable only to the commission chair. For the regulatory and judicial roles of the commission, including recommending executive orders and regulations to the president, Truman assigned a personal assistant to each of the three commissioners to help them carry out those duties.

In analyzing Truman's and Hoover's political actions, Herbert Emmerich later pointed out that "the public relations of Hoover I was a serious professional job, a job which the Brownlow Committee had neglected, and which supporters of Hoover II pushed beyond the limit of credibility."[41] The burden of the past, the Brownlow's vision on scientific and progressive management and the strengthening of the presidency, was still strong. A concentration on the reorganization of departments, agencies, and functions, while important, was inclined to mask what to many was the main achievement of the first Hoover Commission, namely, the enhancement of the presidential office as manager of the government. On this point, Peri Arnold observed that

> it was the supreme accomplishment of the first Hoover Commission, that it masked the managerial presidency with the older values of administrative orthodoxy and, to a significant degree, undercut the conservative and congressional opposition to the expensive executive (...) In the end, Mr. Hoover and his Commission provided the bridge over which the congressional opponents of the Brownlow Committee recommendations and the old political enemies of Franklin Roosevelt could embrace the managerial presidency.[42]

The Second Hoover Commission and the Eisenhower Presidency

The president elected in 1952, the Republican Dwight Eisenhower, did not share Truman's enthusiasm for a comprehensive executive reorganization. Particularly, he was concerned for the results that a congressional initiative, such as a new commission outside of the presidential orbit, could produce. For this reason, at the dawn of his mandate, Eisenhower maintained his distance from Congress and its projects, and sought other ways to manage federal administration. He in fact preferred to keep his focus on his own staff, creating the President's Advisory Committee on Government Organization (PACGO), a committee of consultants divided into task forces autonomous from the political debate and the control of Congress.[43] Eisenhower created a precedent that notably influenced future presidents and the method for elaborating administrative reforms. Compared to the first Hoover Commission and the Brownlow Committee, this initiative had much more modest objectives. The PACGO, however, did maintain continuity with the epoch of Franklin Delano Roosevelt, elaborating solutions and instruments for the enforcement of managerial presidency, especially in the area of national security. This approach on the part of President Eisenhower was dictated both by his military past and by his economic ideas, which made him very little inclined toward drastic reductions of public spending and much more focused on national security, with the aim of confronting the new international scenario of the Cold War.

As previously stated, Eisenhower did not cultivate interest for a wide-range administrative reorganization. For this reason he limited himself to installing the PACGO, which was comprised of three members chosen as expert consultants, one of whom was his brother Milton.[44] This group of trusted individuals, organized by the president himself, had the task of advising Eisenhower on policy and organizational questions, but without interaction with either Congress or administrative agencies. It became operative during the transition from the prior administration, with the goal of designing new plans of executive branch reorganization, and it was given official status as soon as the new president entered the Oval Office.

With the help of PACGO, Eisenhower successfully proposed diverse plans of reorganization in 1953. He managed to override the vetoes against the institution of the Department of Health, Education, and Welfare that Roosevelt and Truman had encountered, and in the same year the two departments came into full legal being with the dismembering of the Federal Security Administration, an agency created by the New Deal. The president directly sponsored the creation of two departments, and he succeeded in convincing a Republican majority that was anxious to free itself from the inheritance of a Rooseveltian agency dedicated to welfare and social politics. Moreover, on May 1, 1953, Eisenhower signed Executive Order 10452 abolishing Liaison Office for Personnel Management (LOPM) by revoking Roosevelt's 1939 executive order that had created it. He transferred to the commission chairman the centralizing presidential role that LOPM had performed. This included advising the president regarding personnel management, assisting the president in planning executive branch-wide personnel policies and executive orders, and promoting improvement in personnel management throughout the federal government. Under this arrangement, the commission chair maintained a separate office in the Executive Office Building next to the White House, with a small staff to handle his presidential role.[45] The formal title of the new position was the President's Adviser on Personnel Management. The commission gained more centrality in human resources, and the idea, advanced by the Brownlow Committee in 1936, to create an independent agency, unbundled by the commission, for personnel management was discarded for the moment by Eisenhower administration.[46]

Later in the year 1953, the renewed Republican Congress intended to concentrate its strongest effort on reducing the public spending of the federal government and on limiting costs through administrative reorganization. Toward this end, the Organization of the Executive Branch, later known as the second Hoover Commission, was re-constituted, since the ex-president was called to preside over it for the second time. The aim was that of returning to the original mission, which was also that of the preceding commission: making more economical the costs of the federal executive branch.[47]

The new commission was established by the Brown-Ferguson Bill, which reaffirmed such objectives as "to promote economy, efficiency, and improved service," and "eliminating nonessential services, functions, and activities which are competitive with private enterprise."[48]

The second Hoover Commission was more politically slanted toward the Republican front, even if it remained bipartisan in its composition. It was more strongly conditioned by the vision of the conservative right, and it counted less on scholars and experts of administration than did the first commission.

In addition, it had fewer ties with the Eisenhower administration than had its earlier counterpart with the Truman one, the Bureau of the Budget was less involved in its proceedings, and the president did not have a particularly good relationship with Hoover. In fact, despite the efforts of Hoover to revive the citizens' committee to bring public opinions to the table of the commission, the Eisenhower administration chose to ignore it on this point.

The reports of the second Hoover Commission reaffirmed that it was opportune for the congressional initiative to re-position and control the organization of the executive branch. These assertions also more strictly cohered with the ideological objectives of Hoover himself, who sought to eliminate or at the very least to scale back the many governmental programs undertaken by the New Deal. However, while this second Hoover Commission contributed to some worthwhile changes in government operations, for example, civil service improvements, it appeared to be adrift, without precise managerial principles for guidance. The second commission did not solve the clash and the contradiction between the canons of administrative orthodoxy inherited by the 1930s and the dominant political values of the moment, namely, Republican anti-statism. The final result was a watered-down compromise which did not provide a new administrative model, as Brownlow and Hoover I did, and did not realize a politics of retrenchment, as Republicans would have wanted.

Some of the solutions proposed by the second commission were implemented through legislative action, but these reforms did not turn out to be particularly problematic, also because they had lost the thoroughgoing quality of those produced by the first Hoover Commission. The main focus now was on the administrative practices of specific agencies, especially those that Hoover considered to be in competition with private enterprise. The commission proposed greater flexibility for the highest rungs of the federal civil service that were meant to move more fluidly between agencies and departments. In other words, a more rapid and flexible turnover rate was prescribed for high-ranking civil servants, but this proposal was never interpreted in this way, nor were proposed changes for the management of policies regarding agriculture and construction, as well as ones for the management of water resources.

While the commission worked on the reports, the congressional majority changed once more and became Democratic in 1956. Thus, the administration implemented only the recommendations expressly supported by Eisenhower. The president quickly understood that if he wished to bring home a tangible result, he now needed to work primarily with the Democrats, and for this reason, he rejected most of the heavily ideological proposals directed against "big government." The true loser to the Democrats was Herbert Hoover, who had to stand by and watch while most of his own ideas for reform were ignored or rebuked.

Indeed, the Truman and Eisenhower reforms had created a personnel structure with the Civil Service Commission at its center. And the commission

was an independent executive branch agency with the primary mission of implementing and protecting the merit system. That was exactly the opposite of
Roosevelt (and Hoover) and his advisors' goal of having the personnel system
within the presidential orbit and with the primary mission of personnel management. Their aim was a presidential personnel director similar to the president's budget director, giving the president central managerial oversight of the
executive branch through the levers of personnel and budgeting. Instead, the
Truman and Eisenhower reforms centralized personnel management into the
Civil Service Commission, and they preferred the maintenance of the merit
system rather than a full-fledged president-centric personnel management.[49]

The Postwar Federal Civil Service

World War II had transformed the body of federal bureaucracy following a sort
of Weberian criteria: a hierarchy, with personnel selected according to meritocratic standards, and with the president at the top, above high-ranking functionaries who took political decisions, and middle- to low-level bureaucrats
employed to implement policies. In 1945 the civil service employed 3.8 million
individuals, more than 92% of whom were chosen through public exams and
interviews.[50] This bloated bureaucracy, which aimed at a clear separation between politics and administration and to promote political neutrality among
civil servants by means of a meritocratic selection process, functioned well for
the war years. A decade and more later, it needed to be reformed, in order to
confront the new period of peace and economic development.

This time, contrary to what had happened after World War I, the growth
of federal administration seemed irreversible, both for the consolidation of the
New Deal reforms, and because the American government was called to a new
role in the world. Undoubtedly, a phase of normalization, steered by the Civil
Service Commission, had to be undertaken because the administration also had
to return to managing diverse, multiple activities and could no longer concentrate only on defense, as it had done in wartime.

Harry Truman reinforced the Internal Revenue Service (IRS) through a
public competition for new, high-ranking bureaucratic positions, which would
be inserted into the system of classification of civil service. Political patronage,
however, would be utilized sparingly. At the end of the 1940s, there were only
70,000 positions available for presidential appointment, which decreased still
further during the following years, reaching 15,000 in 1952.[51] In this sphere,
President Truman demonstrated a continuity with pre-wartime political practice, intent on constructing a neutral and meritocratic bureaucracy.

Meanwhile, however, the problem of political loyalty steadily intensified,
under the pressure that McCarthyism and the "red scare" put on American democracy and its constitutional values. As the Cold War began, radical ideas and
sympathy with communism were called to the bench of the accused. During

World War II, the Civil Service Commission had already conducted 356,000 investigations into employees' political loyalty. In 1946, President Truman issued Executive Order 9835, which imposed reviewing all public workers, in order to prevent eventual threats to national security. Membership in the Communist Party and 90 other radical associations caused exclusion from roles and service in the public sector. When this regulation was revoked in 1953, nearly 4.8 million people had been subjugated to investigations into their political loyalty to the American State.[52] These activities accompanied those of Senator Joseph McCarthy, and of the Commissions for Anti-American Activities, which in those years pursued "anti-subversive" politics through the use of *agents provocateurs* and public hearings of government officials, regarding their activities and political opinions. These commissions, hearings, and related actions were gradually limited by the sentences of the Supreme Court at the end of the 1950s, and they were terminated during the 1960s.

All the same, de-militarization, the controlling of political fidelity, and the growth of the federal civil service weighed heavily on the daily life of bureaucrats. Indeed, alongside this witch hunt was the fact that salaries were much lower than those in the private sector, thus greatly decreasing the morale and motivation of public employees. To compensate for this unpleasant situation, Congress adjusted the pay of federal employees on several occasions. The Federal Employees Pay Act of 1945 and 1946 provided raises averaging, respectively, 15.9% and 14.2%. The Postal Rate Revision and Federal Employees Salary Act of 1948 increased the Classification Act salary rates by $330 annually, for an average pay rise of 11%. A further increase was made by the Classification Act of 1949 itself.[53] Moreover, in October 1948, the commission established a seven-member Fair Employment Board, under the Authority of Executive Order 9980, to consider appeals of agencies on complaints of discrimination.

Then, the first Hoover Commission had made an impact not only on the organization of the administration but also on the conditions of federal government employees. In 1949, numerous federal administration positions were re-classified, a measure which sought to modernize as well as complete the process of normalization of postwar bureaucracy. The same year saw the passing of the Executive Pay Act, which stabilized uniform salaries for similar positions and aimed to bring them to the level of private sector ones. In 1950, the Performance Rating Act was added, which simplified the system of evaluation of public employees enacted in 1930 and which solidified the process of its implementation.[54]

Personnel Management and Eisenhower's Federal Civil Service Reforms

In 1950, moreover, the Korean War began, which caused the Truman presidency's recourse to the capacities of the federal bureaucracy, as had been the case in the two World Wars. When the Korean emergency started, the civil service was again faced with urgent recruitment needs. To meet this need, the commission instructed its operating office to establish boards of examiners to the maximum practical extent. The Board of Examiners demonstrated, during the emergency, that they could do a huge competitive recruitment job with speed and effectiveness. A substantial proportion of recruitment during the Korean War was conducted through open competitive examinations. This was done during a time of high demand for fast recruitment, as well as a restriction on the type of appointment available. Unlike during World War II, most appointments during this period were indefinite and did not confer competitive civil service status. The agencies were invited in 1951 to participate in the process for selecting their own personnel, in order to get a faster recruiting process. Many agencies accepted the invitation and the board program moved forward with steady progress. Indeed, in 1950 there were 1,943,400 civil servants, a figure that rose, in July 1952, to 2,604,300. The conclusion of the conflict brought a new operation of de-militarization, procedures of reduction and re-qualification of federal staff, and the reduction of public expenditures for the administration.[55]

In 1953 Dwight Eisenhower entered the White House, finding there the federal bureaucracy, comprising both career civil servants and appointed political executives, forged by the Democratic presidencies of Roosevelt and Truman. The new president, however, was not interested in expanding positions subject to political patronage, even if only 6.6% of the civil servants had previously worked with a Republican administration. Politically appointed posts amounted to only 15,000, and 95% of the public functionaries inherited by Eisenhower had been selected on a competitive basis.[56]

Eisenhower's new appointments sought to reverse the trend, deploying new hirings and early retirements, as well as relying on massive internal transfers within the administration that led many functionaries to resign and emigrate toward the private sector, a process also favored by the country's economic growth, and by the McCarthyite investigations that undermined the morale of civil servants.

Moreover, a general reorganization of the Civil Service Commission was made in August 1953 in order to tighten its management control and to emphasize its government-wide planning and responsibilities. Further rationalizations and centralization of the administrative structures were undertaken. The reorganization stabilized changes in the commission's functions which had been gradually taking place for years. The commission, looking toward improvement in the Federal personnel program, had been developing steadily in the direction of research, planning, and leadership. It had moved toward delegating certain responsibilities to agencies and guiding them by the establishment of standards, issuance of regulations, and inspection of agency personnel actions; taking corrective action when necessary; and generally giving advice and assistance. As a result of the reorganization, a simplified structure reduced the executive director's span of control from nearly 20 divisions and offices to five bureaus and three staff offices. The Independent Offices Appropriation Act of 1953 required the abolition of the Federal Personnel Council and the transfer of its functions to the office of the commission's executive director.

Eisenhower undertook a major reduction in force. Federal civilian employment was reduced by 212,700 between January and December 1953. About half of the reduction was accomplished by not filling vacancies caused by resignation, retirement, or death. The rest was achieved through reduction in force and termination of temporary appointments. The reduction in force required the separation of many career civil servants with long government service records. A program was established to re-employ these separated careerists. The separated careerist then became eligible to displace indefinites in other agencies in the commuting area, at and below the highest grade he or she had held on or before September 1, 1950. By January 1954, over 3,100 separated career workers had been rehired in the Washington area alone. Moreover, reductions in force procedures were revised and simplified in 1953. The old system recognized six tenured groups, each divided into veterans and non-veterans. In reduction in force, employees in higher groups had retention preference over those in the lower groups. They also had the right of reassignment to a position in the same or lower grade if held by an employee in a lower group. The new reduction in force procedure reduced the tenure groups to three, divided as before into veterans and non-veterans. However, veterans in the lower group were no longer given the privilege of replacing non-veterans in that group. And the right to replace an employee in a lower tenure group was sharply limited.

A form of performance management was introduced in 1954. An act of 1 September, 1954, set up a government-wide incentive awards program for federal civil servants, with the purpose to stimulate them to improve the efficiency and the economy of government operations. Superior performance was to be recognized and rewarded. The program became effective in November 1954 and superseded several awards programs of limited scope which had been in effect for a number of years. It established three types of awards: cash for suggestions, cash for superior performance, and a variety of honorary awards. An agency could make a cash award up to 5,000 dollars. With the approval of the Civil Service Commission, it could make an award of up to 25,000 dollars. Honorary awards, granted independently or in addition to cash awards, could be given for long and faithful service or for acts of personal heroism. In the first three years, the government awarded more than 312 million dollars, and over 200,000 civil servants' suggestions were adopted, and 68,000 superior achievements recognized. Cash awards amounted to over 16 million dollars.[57]

Even during the reduction in force of 1953, the commission did not renounce the promise of recruiting young men and women from the college campuses, deeming them essential to provide a future leadership for federal bureaucracy. Evidence of the validity of this principle was the stature achieved in government by a number of outstanding career executives who were the product of pioneering efforts made during the New Deal and World War II, when brilliant graduates and academics were engaged by the federal machine to face the economic and war emergency. In 1954, the commission's college recruiting program was given new emphasis. The additional fringe benefits authorized in 1954 put the government in a better recruiting position, but something needed to be done to streamline examining procedures. More than 100 individual examinations were consolidated into one, known as the Federal Service Entrance Examination, and definite arrangements were made with federal agencies to fill thousands of jobs with college graduates. The new examination covered substantially every type of professional entrance in government except for engineering and physics, whose program was launched in 1955. More than 900 campus visits were made by government recruiters representing mainly the various hiring agencies themselves, and between 7,000 and 8,000 federal posts were filled through the Federal Service Entrance Examination during the first years. Moreover, to attract qualified personnel, the commission made extensive use of the authority Congress had granted it in 1954, to set starting pay rates above the minimum for the grade in shortage occupations.[58]

As the Cold War confrontation increased and the Space Race began in the late 1950s, the government experienced difficulty in attracting college graduates, particularly in science and engineering, because the starting salary of the General Schedule pay system was significantly below the salaries paid by the private sector. The Federal Employees Salary Act of 1958 enabled the commission to start a plan for recruiting college graduates in science and engineering, with the offer of higher starting salaries. In later years, this program of offering entry to the federal executive at grades GS-7 and GS-9 in recognition of superior academic achievement embraced college graduates in virtually all fields, not just science and engineering, and became an important tool in equal opportunity employment programs seeking to attract high-quality minority graduates.

In the same year of 1958, Congress enacted and the president signed the first Government Employees Training act. The act established fundamental principles for civil servants training in all departments and agencies; authorized many kinds of expenditures for training; provided for centralized training programs under the sponsorship of the Civil Service Commission; and authorized the federal government to purchase training from the existing educational and professional institutions.

In the end, Congress even provided for more benefits for civil servants. In 1959, the Federal Employees Health Benefits Act was approved and signed. Thanks to it, federal civil servants could secure health insurance for themselves and their families at group rates, and the government shared the cost of premiums. The Federal Employees Health Benefits Program offered a variety of plans with different features and coverages, so every civil servant could choose the plan that best fit his/her needs. This new arrangement placed new responsibilities on the Civil Service Commission in managing the health benefits program, contracting with insurance carriers who offered health care coverage under the program, monitoring their activities, and conducting open seasons for employees to sign up for or change insurance coverage.

At the personnel management level, in the Eisenhower years civil servants suffered a great reduction in force, but at the same time their work became more central and more consistently evaluated by the executive branch. The centralization of functions into the hands of the commission simplified recruitment, according to the merit principle, and it strengthened training on the job. Prerequisites and competencies, particularly the ones certified by the university system, became fundamental for hiring and career development. The recruitment of qualified personnel was systematized and incentivized. Moreover, the federal government established a new system to encourage new organizational initiatives and best management practices. A preliminary form of performance management was implemented to award the best efforts. Rights and benefits for civil servants had been expanded by Congress and the presidency, in order to give them stronger welfare protection and job stability.

Eisenhower also sought to achieve a more coherent framework in the machinery of government, in particular between political appointees and professional career bureaucrats. Eisenhower's management of the bureaucracy strengthened the presidency. He carried on the project started by Roosevelt to better control the Civil Service Commission. Philip Young, former dean of the Graduate School of Business at Columbia University, was appointed by Eisenhower as Chairman of the Civil Service Commission, and he also received the new title of Presidential Advisor on Personnel Management. Young was invited to attend Cabinet meetings and to operate as Eisenhower's right hand on personnel matters. Young shared this responsibility with Charles Willis, who supervised the distribution of patronage. But the dual position Young performed was a sign of the increasingly blurred line between political and permanent services. The restructuring of the relationship between the Civil Service Commission and the presidency assumed greater relevance when Eisenhower, with Young's blessing, issued an executive order of March 31, 1953, creating the so-called Schedule C, a list of "confidential or policy-making" positions for those professional bureaucrats most loyal to the president's politics as well as for White House advisors themselves.[59]

The president moved in this direction because the second Hoover Commission had suggested the creation of a Senior Civil Service, a civil servant's super-class devoted to strengthening the link between presidential politics and the executive branch. The political climate was not yet mature enough for such a radical change of organization, and therefore, the creation of "Schedule C" was the preferred choice, adding a new sector but without completely reorganizing the highest spheres of the federal bureaucracy. Eisenhower's aim was to enable the White House and its top political executives to bring them a few people of their own choosing, without going through the strict and more time-consuming merit system procedure. The purpose of the president was not to enlarge the spoils system—indeed at the end of 1954 only 1,127 positions had been placed within the Schedule C category—but to improve his political grip on the federal bureaucracy.[60] His intention was to achieve a better control on policy-making, centralizing it in the White House, following a path traced by his Democratic predecessors.

Nonetheless, the Hoover Commission's proposal would become a long-lasting idea, finding its historic realization with the Civil Service Reform Act of 1978.

Notes

1 1944 State of the Union Message to Congress, 11 January 1994.
2 Dwight Waldo, *The Administrative State* (New York: Ronald Press, 1948), 66–80.
3 Leonard D. White, *Introduction to the Study of Public Administration* (New York: Macmillan, 1926), 2.
4 White, *Introduction to the Study*, 8–9.
5 Luther H. Gulick, *Notes on the Theory of Organizations. With Special References to Government in the United States. Papers on the Science of Administration* (New York: Columbia University Institute of Public Administration, 1937), 6–7.
6 Gulick, *Notes on the Theory*, 7.
7 Luther H. Gulick, *Administrative Reflections from World War II* (Tuscaloosa: University of Alabama Press, 1948).
8 Gulick, *Administrative Reflections*, 40–41.
9 Herbert Simon, *Administrative Behavior* (New York: Macmillan, 1976), 240.
10 Simon, *Administrative Behavior*, 200
11 Simon, *Administrative Behavior*, 52.
12 Simon, *Administrative Behavior*, 253.
13 Simon, *Administrative Behavior*, 53.
14 Simon, *Administrative Behavior*, 186–187.
15 Simon, *Administrative Behavior*, 102.
16 Sheldon Wolin, *Politics and Vision. Continuity and Innovation in Western Political Thought* (Princeton, NJ: Princeton University Press, 1960), 380.
17 Reorganization Act 1949, HR 2361—Public Law No. 109.
18 Brian Balogh, Joanna Grisinger, and Philip Zelikow, *Making Democracy Work: A Brief History of Twentieth Century Federal Executive Reorganization* (Charlottesville: University of Virginia Center of Public Affairs, 2002). See Reorganization Plan No. 2 of 1946 (Washington DC: GPO, July 16th 1946).
19 National Security Act, Public Law 235 of July 26, 1947; 61 STAT. 4.
20 US Personnel Management Office, *Biography of an Ideal: A History of the Federal Civil Service* (Washington, DC: U.S. Civil Service Commission, 2012), 235–236.
21 Administrative Procedure Act, Public Law 404, 60 Stat. 237–244, 1946.
22 Michael W. Spicer, *Public Administration and the State: A Postmodern Perspective* (Tucaloosa: University of Alabama Press), 2016.
23 See Theodore Lowi, *The End of Liberalism. Ideology, Policy and the Decline of the Public Authority* (New York: WW Norton), 1969.

24 A process that was in nuce still in the 1920s as pointed out by Daniel Carpenter, *The Forging of Bureaucratic Autonomy: Reputations, Networks, and Policy Innovation in Executive Agencies, 1862–1928* (Princeton, NJ: Princeton University Press), 2001.

25 The law that instituted the Hoover Commission was Public Law 162, 80th Congress, July 7, 1947 (62 Stat. 246). The commission was to consist of 12 members: four appointed by the President—two from the executive branch (James A. Forrestal and Arthur Fleming) and two from private life (George Mead and Dean Acheson); four appointed by the President of the Senate—two from the Senate (George Aiken and John L. McClellan) and two from private life (Professor James K. Pollack and Joseph P. Kennedy); and four appointed by the Speaker of the House of Representatives—two from the House (Clarence Brown and Carter Manasco) and two from private life (Herbert Hoover and James Rowe). Former President Herbert Hoover was elected as Chairman by the commissioners.

26 Introduction by Lodge to the law, cited in Peri A. Arnold, *Making the Managerial Presidency* (Lawrence: University Press of Kansas, 1986).

27 U.S. Commission on the Organization of the Executive Branch of the Government (Hoover Commission), *General Management of the Executive Branch: A report to the Congress by the Commission on Organization of the Executive Branch of the Government*, February (Washington, DC: Government Printing Office, 1949), vii–viii.

28 Commission on the Organization of the Executive Branch of the Government, *Report on General Management of the Executive Branch* (New York: McGraw Hill, 1949), viii.

29 Public Law 162, 80th Congress, July 7, 1947, Section I.

30 As noted by Peri Arnold, "The First Hoover Commission and the Managerial Presidency," *The Journal of Politics* 38, no. 1 (1976): 46–70.

Every phase of Herbert Hoover's political life showed his interest for administrative reorganization. When he worked at the Department of Commerce between 1921 and 1927, he completely reorganized its structures and agencies. In 1923, he was also one of the prime supporters of the Joint Committee on Reorganization and of the implementation of its recommendations. Moreover, he was the President who asked Congress to cede to the White House the powers of administrative reorganization, if under legislative veto.

31 The reorganization authority was in fact a power that Congress, by majority, had to concede to the President, so that he could reform federal administration.

32 Commission on Organization of the Executive Branch of the Government, *The Hoover Commission Report on General Management of the Executive Branch* (New York. McGraw-Hill, 1949), 3.

33 Memo, Don K. Price to Herbert Hoover, November 1, 1947, in *First Hoover Commission, General Management of the Executive Branch*, Correspondence-Price, Herbert Hoover Presidential Library.

34 Memo, Don K. Price to Hoover, *First Hoover Commission*.

35 Executive Order 10072, 1949.

36 Advisory Committee on Management, "Improvement of Management in the Federal Government," *Public Administration Review* 13 (1953): 38–49.

37 For further details, see "Reorganization Act of 1949," in *CQ Almanac 1949*, 5th ed., *Congressional Quarterly*, 1950.

38 As reported by Balogh, Grisinger, and Zelikow, *Making Democracy Work*, 40.

39 Reorganization Plan No. 5 of 1949, 14 F.R. 5227, 63 Stat. 1067.

40 Herbert Emmerich, *Federal Organization and Administrative Management* (Tuscaloosa: The University of Alabama Press, 1971), 97.

41 Arnold, "The First Hoover Commission," 49–50.

42 The first executive order President Eisenhower signed (10432) created an Advisory Committee on Government Organization (PACGO). See Executive Order 10432,

Establishing the President's Advisory Committee on Government Organization (Washington DC: National Archives and Records Administration, January 24, 1953).

43 Balogh, Grisinger, and Zelikow, *Making Democracy Work,* 43.

44 Bradley H. Patterson, "Teams and Staff: Dwight Eisenhower's Innovations in the Structure and Operations of the Modern White House," *Presidential Studies Quarterly* 24 no. 2 (1994): 227–298.

45 In 1957, the president decided to implement a recommendation of the Hoover II and re-divide the two roles. In Executive Order 10729, he repealed his 1953 executive order and superseded it with the position of Special Assistant to the President for Personnel Management. The duties of the new White House advisor were nearly identical to those that had been delegated to the Civil Service Commission chair in 1953.

46 The commission (1953–1955) had been created by Congress at the beginning of the Eisenhower presidency. The former commissioner Arthur Flemming was, again, a member. In turn, the commission created a Task Force on Personnel and Civil Service. It was chaired by political scientist Harold Dodds, with members including Leonard White, Chester Barnard, and former congressman Robert Ramspeck.

47 Brown-Ferguson Bill, P.L. 108, Ch. 184, 83rd Congress, 1st Sess (S. 106) approved on 10 July 1953; cited in Neil MacNeil and Harold W. Metz, *The Hoover Report 1953–1955: What it Means to You as Citizen and Taxpayer* (New York: Macmillan, 1956), 11.

48 As noted by Mordecai Lee, *A Presidential Civil Service. FDR's Liaison Office and Personnel Management* (Tuscaloosa: Alabama, University of Alabama Press, 2016).

49 Paul Van Riper, *A History of the United States Civil Service* (New York: Row, Peterson, and Co., 1958), 441.

50 Robert Maranto and David Schultz, *A Short History of the United States Civil Service* (Lanham, MD: University Press of America, 1991), 107.

51 Dumas Malone and Basil Rauch, *Empire for Liberty: The Genesis and Growth of the United States of America* (New York: Appleton Century, 1960), 762–763.

52 Office for Personnel Management 2012, 237.

53 Performance Rating Act of 1950, Sept. 30, 1950, chap. 1123, 64 Stat. 1098.

54 Office for Personnel Management 2012, 240.

55 Van Riper, *A History*, 490–492.

56 Office for Personnel Management 2012, 248.

57 David Rosenbloom, *Federal Service and The Constitution* (Washington, DC: Georgetown University Press, 2014), 58–73.

58 Executive Order 10440, Amendment of Civil Service Rule VI, March 31, 1953, National Archives, Federal Register.

59 See Van Riper, *A History*, 495.

Bibliography

Advisory Committee on Management. "Improvement of Management in the Federal Government." *Public Administration Review* 13 (1953): 38–49.

Arnold, Peri. "The First Hoover Commission and the Managerial Presidency." *The Journal of Politics* 38, no. 1 (1976): 46–70.

———. *Making the Managerial Presidency.* Lawrence: University Press of Kansas, 1986.

Balogh, Brian, Joanna Grisinger, and Philip Zelikow. *Making Democracy Work: A Brief History of Twentieth Century Federal Executive Reorganization.* Charlottesville, VA: University of Virginia Center of Public Affairs, 2002.

Carpenter, Daniel. *The Forging of Bureaucratic Autonomy: Reputations, Networks, and Policy Innovation in Executive Agencies, 1862–1928,* Princeton, NJ: Princeton University Press, 2001.

Commission on the Organization of the Executive Branch of the Government. *The Hoover Commission Report on General Management of the Executive Branch*. New York: McGraw Hill, 1949.

Crenson, Matthew, and Francis Rourke. "By Way of Conclusion: American Bureaucracy since World War II." In *The New American State*, edited by Louis Galambos, 137–177. Baltimore, MD: Johns Hopkins University Press, 1987.

Emmerich, Herbert. *Federal Organization and Administrative Management*. Tuscaloosa: The University of Alabama Press, 1971.

Executive Order 10072. National Archives, Federal Register, 1949.

Executive Order 10440, Amendment of Civil Service Rule VI, March 31 1953, National Archives, Federal Register, 1953.

Graham, Otis. *Toward a Planned Society: From Roosevelt to Nixon*. Oxford: Oxford University Press, 1977.

Gulick, Luther H. *Notes on the Theory of Organizations. With Special References to Government in the United States. Papers on the Science of Administration*. New York: Columbia University Institute of Public Administration, 1937.

———. *Administrative Reflections from World War II*. Tuscaloosa: University of Alabama Press, 1948.

Hodgson, Godfrey. *America in Our Time: From World War II to Nixon, What Happened and Why*. New York: Vintage Books, 1978.

Hogan, Michael J. *A Cross of Iron*. Cambridge: Cambridge University Press, 1998.

Hurd, Richard, and Jill Kriesky. "The Rise and Demise of PATCO Reconstructed." *Industrial and Labor Relations Review* 40, no. 1 (1986): 115–122.

Karl, Barry. *The Uneasy State: The United States from 1915 to 1945*. Chicago: The University of Chicago Press, 1983.

Lowi, Theodore. *The End of Liberalism. Ideology, Policy and the Decline of the Public Authority*. New York: WW Norton, 1969.

MacNeil, Neil, and Harold W. Metz. *The Hoover Report 1953–1955: What it Means to You as Citizen and Taxpayer*. New York: Macmillan, 1956.

Malone, Dumas, and Basil Rauch. *Empire for Liberty: The Genesis and Growth of the United States of America*. New York: Appleton Century, 1960.

Maranto, Robert, and David Schultz. *A Short History of the United States Civil Service*. Lanham, MD: University Press of America, 1991.

Memo, Don K. Price to Herbert Hoover, November 1, 1947. In *First Hoover Commission, General Management of the Executive Branch*. Correspondence-Price, Herbert Hoover Presidential Library, 1947.

Milkis, Sidney M. *The President and the Parties*. Oxford: Oxford University Press, 1993.

Moreno, Paul D. *The Bureaucrat Kings: The Origins and Underpinnings of America's Bureaucratic State*. Santa Barbara, CA: Praeger, 2017.

National Security Act, Public Law 235 of July 26, 1947; 61 STAT. 4.

Niskanen, William. *Bureaucracy and Representative Government*. Chicago, IL: Aldine-Atherton, 1971.

Northrup, Herbert Roof, and Amie D. Thornton. *The Federal Government as Employer: The Federal Labor Relations Authority and the PATCO Challenge*. Philadelphia: The Wharton School, University of Pennsylvania, 1985.

Office for Personnel Management, *Biography of an Ideal. The History of the US Civil Service*, 2012.

Patterson, Bradley H. "Teams and Staff: Dwight Eisenhower's Innovations in the Structure and Operations of the Modern White House." *Presidential Studies Quarterly* 24 no. 2 (1994): 227–298.

Performance Rating Act of 1950, Sept. 30, 1950, chap. 1123, 64 Stat. 1098.

Public Law 162, 80th Congress, July 7, 1947, Section I.

"Reorganization Act of 1949." In *CQ Almanac 1949*, 5th ed., *Congressional Quarterly*, 1950.

Rosenbloom, David H. *Federal Service and the Constitution*. Washington, DC: Georgetown University Press, 2014.

Simon, Herbert. *Administrative Behavior*. New York: Macmillan, 1976.

Spicer, Michael W. Public *Administration and the State: A Postmodern Perspective*. Tucaloosa: University of Alabama Press, 2016.

Stigler, George J. "The Theory of Economic Regulation." *Bell Journal of Economics and Management Science* 2 (1971): 3–21.

Thompson, Vincent A. *Without Sympathy or Enthusiasm: The Problem of Administrative Compassion*. Tuscaloosa: University of Alabama Press, 1979.

U.S. Commission on the Organization of the Executive Branch of the Government (Hoover Commission). *General Management of the Executive Branch: A Report to the Congress by the Commission on Organization of the Executive Branch of the Government*. Washington, DC: Government Printing Office, 1949.

Van Riper, Paul. *History of the United States Civil Service*, New York: Row, Peterson, and Co., 1958.

Waldo, Dwight. *The Administrative State*. New York: Ronald Press, 1948.

White, Leonard D. *Introduction to the Study of Public Administration*. New York: Macmillan, 1926.

Wolin, Sheldon. *Politics and Vision. Continuity and Innovation in Western Political Thought*. Princeton: Princeton University Press, 1960.

4

THE 1960S AND 1970S

Administrative Growth, Pluralization, and Management

A Turning Point: The Administrative Growth of the 1960s

As the 1960s began, the country seemed to be gaining speed in a one-way slide toward bureaucratic centralization. Federal expenditures, slightly over 42 billion dollars in 1950, had more than doubled to 92 billion dollars in 1960, and by 1970 they would double once more to 195 billion dollars. Even when these outlays are adjusted for inflation, they reflect a near tripling of national expenditures from 1950 to 1970. The trajectory of central government growth could not be traced only at the absolute level of expenditures, but in the steadily expanding share of the nation's substance that was channeled through federal bureaucracy. In 1950 it was 16.1% of the gross national product, in 1960 18.5%, and by 1970 20.2%.[1] Moreover, through the 1950s and 1960s in particular, the pages devoted to new administrative rules multiplied at a gradually accelerating pace, a prelude to the regulatory explosion of the 1970s. The federal government's growing appetite for revenue seemed to be explained by an ever-increasing extension of bureaucratic control across the country. The "welfare shift," with the approval and implementation of Great Society policies, was the main movement that reshaped the design of federal bureaucracy during the 1960s.

President Kennedy, the Landis Report, and the Failed Reorganization

A turning point, in political terms, for the welfare shift and bureaucratic development was the election of the Democrat John Fitzgerald Kennedy to the White House in 1960. Kennedy took for granted progressive and modern liberal assumptions about the nature of government. He believed that the United

States had outgrown its founding political principles, and that the country now had to deal with technical and managerial problems. He assumed that the ends of government were those of the New Deal welfare state. Kennedy pointed to postwar Western Europe as a model for America. Americans need only consider the means or methods of achieving it. These, he said, were practical, technical matters, and subtle and complicated problems for experts to solve "basically an administrative or executive" project.[2] In cultural terms, bureaucracy needed to become more central in managing welfare programs, and it needed to pluralize itself, by favoring citizens' participation and becoming more diverse.

In his nearly three years as president, however, Kennedy did not bring major innovations to the structures of the federal executive branch. He could count on the federal executives recruited in the Roosevelt and Truman epoch, who still represented the majority of active civil servants, along with the political appointments that he as president could make. Moreover, the new president did not seem at all interested, at least in the first period of his term, in administrative reorganization. By instinct Kennedy was not in favor of the rigid hierarchical organization he had inherited from Eisenhower, since his personal formation, as part of an entrepreneurial and politically progressive East Coast family, inclined him toward more flexible organizations, similar to those of the private sector. In fact, he wished to bypass the problem, rather than directly confront it, concentrating himself primarily on foreign policy and making more use of the White House staff than of the civil service.[3]

The most remarkable initiative of Kennedy's presidency at the reorganizational level was the report on the federal agencies of his expert advisor James M. Landis, who had been president of the Security Exchange Commission during the 1930s and of the Civil Aeronautics Board in the 1940s. At the new president's own request, Landis had compiled a report on the regulatory commissions and federal agencies. In his report, Landis reiterated the progressive shibboleth that bureaucracy was an inevitable product of modernity. "The complexities of our modern society are increasing rather than decreasing," he told the president-elect. "The advent of atomic energy, of telecommunications, of natural gas, of jet aircraft, to cite only a few examples, all call for greater surveillance by the government."

Landis argued that the administrative state needed more independence, though he also occasionally sounded as if he had moved closer to the position of a unitary executive advocated by the Brownlow Committee, which he had objected to in 1938. The old concerns of the New Deal era—especially of the combination of powers in agencies—were shown to be exaggerated. The Administrative Procedure Act had only made the bureaucrats less effective. Excessive judicial review had produced "stagnation." The agencies suffered from inadequate funding and unqualified staff, and they were vulnerable to legislative and executive as well as industry manipulation. Under the Eisenhower presidency, the Bureau of the Budget was "quietly and unassumingly becoming in essence a Bureau of Administrative Management."[4] Landis called for another round of executive reorganization, concentrating power within the White House's Executive Office of the President, which had been established after the Brownlow Committee's report was released.

Landis had been able to confirm what several experts had denounced, namely, the collusion between the regulator and the regulated entity, between commissioners and companies subject to the regulatory action of agencies and commissions. These institutions, most of them created between the 1930s and 1940s, had submitted to the pressure of the private enterprises subject to their regulation and gradually accommodated these business interests, thus losing vigor in their action of maintaining and protecting the interests of the state. The most striking feature of the Landis Report was its avoidance of matters of the ends and purposes of the administrative state. Like Kennedy, he assumed that the political question of the ends and purposes of government had been settled, and that only questions of expert administrative management needed to be considered.

In this vein, Landis had proposed to the president a centralization of the surveillance of the regulatory agencies and the institution of an office within the executive office, compensating for the deficient vigilance of Congress over these phenomena of collusion.[5] At first, Kennedy declared himself in agreement with Landis's proposals, but he did not have enough interest in such problems and procedures to implement reforms in any profound way. Moreover, his prudence was politically well founded. Landis' reforms would not have produced political *clients* capable of reinforcing the president's party, and besides, the politically appointed heads of administrative agencies might well have publicly rebelled against the White House and its reform efforts. They probably would have accused the president of trying to undermine the independence and impartiality of the agencies, by imposing increased executive control over them.[6] Consequently, Kennedy limited himself to introducing five plans of reorganization of the independent commissions, to bolster their staffs and speed up their working rhythm. He abandoned, instead, a more incisive reform action directed toward increasing the executive branch's coordinative power over policies vis-à-vis the independent authorities.[7]

Kennedy did not have time and favorable conditions to implement fully his reforms. In the end, he ignored the most remarkable recommendations of the Landis' report. And even though he was able to design some opening-up policies for the federal civil service, in two years his presidency appeared particularly inconclusive at the executive reorganization level.

In political terms, Kennedy steered toward anti-communism in his foreign policy, a move which enabled him to gain the full collaboration of civil servants who entered the federal government during the Eisenhower administration. The bureaucracy supported the president's foreign policy without any notable resistance.

In addition, the administrative order did not cause problems for John Fitzgerald Kennedy, who responded mainly with immobility regarding organization. The single important action was undertaken in 1962, with the promulgation of Executive Order 10988, which recognized the right of public employees to become members of unions.[8] Although several union organizations were formally accepted, the regulation only furnished an informal mechanism of collective contract negotiation between the unions and the government. Consequently, rights of individual federal employees remained subordinate to the public interest of the agency or of the department for which they worked. The unions could not emancipate themselves from Congress, since the regulation did not allot to collective contracts the power of determining the salary of public workers, and thus, the decision for public wage increases remained a prerogative of legislative power. Salaries thus became the true object of union pressure. Despite these limitations, union memberships made a huge quantum leap, from 180,000 in 1963 to 84,300 in 1969.[9]

Moreover, Kennedy made an effort to pluralize the federal civil service and to raise the pay of civil servants. In 1961, Kennedy established the President's Commission on the Status of Women. In an executive order two years later, the president declared that the federal service would showcase the feasibility of combining genuine equality of opportunity based on merit. The commission greatly restricted the power of department heads to specify one sex as a requirement of qualification for federal jobs. In the next two decades, the commission would draft a more comprehensive Federal Women's Program, designed not merely to remove barriers to employment of qualified women but to open for women employment and advancement opportunities throughout the government. The mission to be accomplished was for women not only to enter the system, but for them to advance to positions of prominence and authority in all areas of the federal bureaucracy. In 1962 Congress, at the urging of the Kennedy administration, took action to address the perpetual questions of how much to pay federal civil servants and on what basis this decision should be made. These questions were answered through the Federal Salary Reform Act of 1962. The new law established a principle for determining future adjustments to the General Schedule pay rates: federal pay should be reasonably comparable to pay in the private sector for work at the same levels of competence and responsibilities. The Act also changed the way individual civil servants would advance within the pay range for the grade level, designing a more managerial, business-like mechanism. For the first time, advancement to the next step in the pay range required demonstration of an "acceptable level of competence," and managers could accelerate advancement though the range by rewarding high quality performance with an additional step increase, which was called "quality step increase." The same act provided a solution to a long-standing problem in the Civil Service Retirement System, related to the increase of annuity rates in line with the rising cost of living. Congress decided that annuity rates should be adjusted in the future by an amount equal to the change in the cost of living index (and indexed to inflation) and set up a procedure to make these adjustments automatically, without having to enact special legislation on the matter.

In conclusion, at the federal civil service level Kennedy's presidency was short but important, because it envisaged the future development of bureaucratic management. There was an expansion of social rights and benefits for civil servants, a growth in terms of pay and guarantees, and a more managerial approach in rewarding excellent performance on the job. Moreover, in the Kennedy years pluralization and diversification in favor of minorities was started, a process which aimed to make federal civil service more representative of a rapidly changing society and equal opportunities in general.

Reorganizing the Executive Branch: Johnson's Presidency

After the tragedy of Kennedy's assassination in November 1963, Vice-President Lyndon Baines Johnson took his place in the Oval Office and obtained a landslide victory in the following election of 1964. In administrative terms, the ambitious objective of the new president was that of realizing the political changes envisioned by the reforms of the Great Society, in other words a program of public initiatives designed to strengthen welfare and to guarantee an increasing pluralism of civil rights in American society.

Johnson decided to act immediately in reforming the executive branch that needed to be ready to serve as best as possible the Great Society's policies implementation. The president wished to stay a step ahead of Congress, before the possible returning in vogue of an idea similar to that of the first Hoover Commission, which would have given the legislative branch powers to initiate administrative reforms.

For this reason, once he had entered the Oval Office, Johnson preferred the use of presidential task forces, with experts and special advisors employed to develop reform plans and political strategies. He created the first one in the summer of 1964 and entrusted its presidency to Don K. Price, an important political scientist who had founded the School of Public Administration at Harvard University, and had already been an advisor to President Kennedy. Initially the group consisted of nine members, to which ten were added during the succeeding month. Among them were members of the president's cabinet, high-ranking functionaries and academics like the historian Richard Neustadt, and the political scientist Stephen Bailey. The group did not have a public identity, nor did it interact formally with the Congress, and it limited itself to referring to the president himself—and even with him it did not engage in regular confrontation. Johnson did not seem particularly interested in supervising administrative reorganization from the White House, but he sought congressional involvement to stimulate the creation of a specific commission modeled on the first Hoover Commission.[10]

In November 1964 the Price task force presented its first report, based on information drawn from the Bureau of Budget and on the theoretical elaboration of its constituent experts. The fundamental philosophy was that of reinforcing presidential power, rendering the executive branch more responsible and reactive to the White House. The official document was extremely wide-ranging and included classic themes of administrative reorganization, such as the organization of powers, the reform of high-level bureaucracy, and the "departmentalization" of reform projects relative to health, education, and welfare. It recommended re-grouping the numerous administrative entities already operative in these areas into new and better-organized agencies. In addition, it proposed guaranteeing increased autonomy to departments, in the management of personnel, and as with preceding cases this task force also declared the necessity of assigning permanent power to the presidency for administrative reorganization.

The task force's recommendations were sent to Johnson through the filter of the Bureau of Budget.[11] All the same, the Bureau ignored the section of the group's requests concerning the relationship between Congress and the executive branch, as well as the suggestion to strengthen the evaluation of public policies on the part of the administration. In short, Johnson received a partially watered-down version of the original, and the president did not give it serious consideration. The task force's work concluded with an empty result, and with hindsight this failure can be understood as being essentially tied to two factors: (1) the group of advisors was too distant from the daily operations of the president—thus deprived of the possibility of cultivating a strong relationship with him—and (2) the White House itself had never specified its own priorities to the group of consultants.

Johnson thus decided to act autonomously and with reoriented ambitions of reform. In the first year of his mandate he obtained the extension of reorganizational powers to 1968, on the basis of the Reorganization Act of 1949. Many of his plans were accepted by Congress with only slight modifications. The agency dedicated to fighting illegal drug trafficking was moved from the Treasury to the Justice Department; the Department of Commerce would now include functions related to environmental protection, and the Public Health Service ended up as part of the Department of Health, Education, and Welfare.

As noted above, the president renounced the creation of super-departments but introduced several innovations. Within the Executive Office of the President, the Office of Economic Opportunity was installed, and two new departments were created between 1965 and 1966—one appointed for city management and public construction, and the other for transport. The birth of these new structures was fundamental to the political objectives of the president. These were not a response to situations of crisis, as was often the case in the history of American government when new departments were created, but instead they formed part of the project of improved confronting of the long-term problems, such as urban development and the politics of mobility.[12]

The presidential interest in reorganization increased, with the effort to contain, coordinate, and streamline the enormous public costs for the Vietnam War, which were added on to those for the Great Society programs. Seeking to attain his own objectives and to obviate the problem of another congressional commission on reorganization, Johnson instituted in 1966 a second task force called *Task Force on Government Reorganization*, chaired by Ben Heineman. In his speech of January 24, 1966, the president himself underlined the need for a more efficacious process of implementation at the administrative level:

> In moving forward the goals of the Great Society, the enactment of substantive legislation is only the first step... If these laws are to produce the desired results—effectively and at minimum cost to the taxpayer—we cannot afford to cling to organizational and administrative arrangements which have not kept pace with changing needs.[13]

This time, therefore, the fundamental change was that this second task force responded directly to the president and acted according to precise instructions provided by the White House.

The final report of the Heineman group was presented in 1967 and proposed a centralization of government departments, amalgamating them into super-departments which had as their heads the members of the Presidential Cabinet, thus simplifying management by the top level of executive power.[14] In particular, there was the proposal to create a Department of Economic Development, which would combine the departments of Labor and of Commerce, and a Department of Natural Resources, comprising various other departments. Beyond these proposed changes, there was the suggestion to augment the staff of the Executive Office and to institute new offices that would be focused on the coordination and the development of the president's program. Nevertheless, none of the proposed reforms saw the light of day. This outcome was due both to the political climate of the time, concentrated almost exclusively on Vietnam and the internal disorders linked to movements for civil rights, and in part to the insufficient commitment that President Johnson gave to reforming the executive branch, which remained a marginal theme for the entirety of his occupancy of the White House.[15]

Lyndon B. Johnson and the Federal Bureaucracy

The succession of Lyndon Johnson after Kennedy's assassination did not alter the lines of administrative politics. Indeed, the social reforms mapped out by his predecessor were put into practice by President Johnson. These reforms took the name of the Great Society and they were articulated in three dimensions.[16]

The first was the elimination of poverty in the United States, the so-called war on poverty. In his State of the Union address of 1964, the president declared unconditional war on poverty and indicated the necessity of urgently approving a package of new laws, including the Equal Opportunity Act—approved later that year—designed to ensure income-bearing integration for the indigent, and labor training and other social services for the poor.

The second dimension was that of civil rights, to which Johnson dedicated himself all the way, in order to recognize equal rights and opportunities for blacks and other minorities. The American government would commit itself to guaranteeing not only equal opportunity for all but also equal results.

The third dimension of the Great Society consisted in believing in the capacity of government to adjust the economy in a way that would maintain perennial growth. The economic theory in support of this policy was based on the reduction of taxes, approved in 1964, that had increased investments and work positions. The intervention was the typical example of a Keynesian economic politics, based on a combination of fiscal reform, lowering of fees and tax payments, and the succeeding redistribution of surplus to the needy through an accentuated government activism. In this exceptional historical phase, public and political trust in technocrats and the capacity of the federal government to work for economic growth reached its highest level in the history of the United States.

The result of these three objectives was the most sizable increase in spending for social programs since the New Deal. In 1965, public spending, on a par with military spending, amounted to 37.7 billion dollars. Nine years later, in 1974, the government spent almost 140 billion dollars.[17] The interventions of the Great Society were concentrated in seven areas: income support, health, public construction works, education, centers for employment and jobs training, civil rights, and programs for assisting low-income communities.

The legislation of this period was prolific, and among others the Economic Opportunity Act, Medicaid and Medicare, the Jobs Corp, the Elementary and Secondary Education Act, the Higher Education Act, the Civil Rights Act, and the Voting Rights Act were passed. Of key importance for the implementation of these programs through executive power was the work of administrative reorganization that Johnson had succeeded in accomplishing early in his mandate, with agencies and offices already in place to manage the new social programs.

The American way toward the welfare state began with the New Deal neared its fulfillment in this period.[18] Government activism in social and economic contexts attained its apex, as did the expansion of social rights favoring underprivileged and minority groups. These changes reflected on the federal civil service. In 1965, at the height of the national debate on civil rights and in continuity with his predecessor, President Johnson, by Executive Order 10925, assigned responsibility for equal employment opportunity to the Civil Service Commission and declared that

> it is the policy of the United States to provide equal opportunity in federal employment for all qualified persons, to prohibit discrimination in employment because of race, creed, color or national origin and to promote the full realization of equal employment opportunity through a positive, continuing program in each executive department and agency.[19]

The commission stated that agencies were responsible for equal employment opportunity in their personnel practices and required them to formulate and file with the commission equal employment opportunity plans. To support agencies' efforts, the commission set up a training program for federal managers and supervisors, and an educational program to provide information to minority communities about opportunities in the federal service. The commission sent its personnel program evaluation staff to agencies both to provide advice and to assess the level of equal employment opportunity in agency manpower. Furthermore, the commission overhauled the entire collection of its qualification standards and its civil service examinations to identify and remove any unintended obstacles to hiring minorities and women, without compromising the principle of merit in examining and selection. Beyond recruitment there was the issue of career organization, then the commission set up "Operation MUST—Maximum Utilization of Skills and Training." The plan was that many of the government's minority and female employees were trapped in clerical occupations at lower grade levels, and these posts did not offer the possibility of a significant leap into the higher levels of the civil service General Schedule. The aim of the program was to identify these employees and to offer them training and reassignment opportunities to qualify for entry and advancement to work that offered better salaries and increased promotion opportunities.[20]

Moreover, Johnson's administration aimed to make federal bureaucracy more technocratic and professionalized. The commission's classification standards program established new posts for technicians in most of the administrative fields—personnel, budgeting and financial management, procurement, management analysis, logistics, transportation, and other areas in which these positions did not exist previously. The commission urged departments and agencies to review specialists' jobs in those fields that did not require the full qualifications of the specialist, but which could be placed into new technician posts that would be accessible to people who were previously working in the lower, clerical, grades. The model for this reform was the one used for engineers and scientists, in which federal employees with technical experience in specialized fields assisted engineers and scientists by running experiments, recording data, making measurements, and realizing infrastructural projects. These tasks tapped into skills that could be learned or improved on the job, and that did not need the attendance of college and university. Moreover, between 1963 and 1971, the Civil Service Commission established three Executive Seminar Centers in different locations. These centers offered a two-week seminar for middle-level managers of the government. The seminars were used to share information and experiences with other federal managers, to discuss new initiatives and best practices, to improve skills, and to get a better knowledge of management principles. In 1968, the commission set up the Federal Executive Institute, and it added its premier program for top-rank civil servants (GS 16–17–18). The core program, in this case, lasted two months. The executives were hosted at the Institute and they attended seminars, forums, classes, field trips, and other educational activities that were designed to expand the understanding of their role in the wider context of the government, the nation, and the world.[21]

Moreover, in the wake of Eisenhower's Schedule C, President Johnson issued in November 1966 the Executive Order 11315.[22] The Civil Service Commission, with the cooperation of the executive agencies and the departments, created a new Executive Assignment System, embracing federal executives in jobs at super-grades of the General Schedule, GS-16, GS-17, and GS-18. The corps of top-level civil servants included people of great experience and managerial skills who could fill executive-level positions anywhere in government. The system established that the commission, departments, and agencies made an inventory of executive talent throughout the government, and, when departments and agencies had executive positions to fill, the commission would signal executives from other departments and agencies for them to consider along with their own executives. A new category of positions was created, and they were called Noncareer Executive Assignments (NEAs), whose members, in recognition of their direct involvement in policy-making and advocacy, were exempted from the usual civil service requirements. Johnson, like Eisenhower, established non-career positions to enhance the responsiveness of the bureaucracy to his directives. Contrary to Eisenhower, however, Johnson's reform focused only on top-level positions, and not on such lower-level jobs as Schedule C, and it was more ambitious in its scope. The concern was to transform the ranks of the highest civil service by creating a new grade of top civil servants who could be promoted and transferred at the discretion of the president, thus breaking down the rigid rules of the merit system, which traditionally protected career civil servants from executive control.[23] Creating a new category of positions meant a constriction of the competitive civil service, exposing the bureaucracy to stronger political control. NEAs gave to the president a stronger political control on the agencies. But the criteria the administration used to fill these positions emphasized loyalty to the president's program, rather than a narrower personal commitment to Johnson. Moreover, the principle to which this program was dedicated, envisioning an expansive and novel role for federal government, tended to boost the status of the federal civil service.[24]

In conclusion, the Great Society spending programs obviously had an impact on federal administration in terms of organization, personnel policies and practices, and the size of the federal bureaucracy. The number of federal government employees grew from 2.5 million in 1965 to over 3 million in 1969, at the end of Johnson's presidency.[25] In addition, the Great Society extended the merging of politics and administration that characterized the reform of the executive branch during the 1930s. As Sidney Milkis observed, "in program development and staffing the Johnson administration attempted to transcend party politics in order to strengthen and enlarge the focus of presidential politics."[26]

A Movement of Criticism of the Status Quo: The New Public Administration

The scarce interest for administrative reorganization shown by the presidencies, the gridlock of the vested interests in the institutional process, the Great Society's flood of new programs of social spending, the intellectual crisis of public administration, and the managerial pretext of governing the economy from government offices provoked criticism and discontent in the community of public administration experts over the course of the 1960s. Not only conservative academics but also those on the radical left attacked the administrative system imposed by the political programs of the Democratic presidency. This movement took the name of New Public Administration, and it attacked the weaknesses of conventional bureaucracy and the theoretical approach based on the dichotomy between politics and administration. This critique of the capacities and integrity of public officials became both a theoretical bias and a rhetorical campaign destined to influence the presidencies of Nixon, Carter, and Reagan.

In a certain sense, the federal administration had raised expectations too high during the 1960s. The promise that technocrats could manage and direct the economy, drastically reduce poverty, remedy social pathologies, and at the same time accomplish planning with unprecedented efficiency had exposed the bureaucracy to the judgment of experts and citizens alike. The practical problems of implementing the politics of the Great Society, the explosion of the deficit, and the difficulties of the Vietnam War had put into question the role of government as well as that of federal civil servants. The pedagogical style of 1960s progressive technocracy gradually lost its own ideological and political impetus, because the economy slowed down, the conflict in Vietnam eroded faith in the politico-administrative class, and bureaucratic mismanagement showed the first cracks in the architecture of the welfare state.

Theorists of administration agreed that the growing complexity of government, its expanding size, rapid changes, and the rise of new technologies together imposed the need to overcome the old hierarchical organization on which federal bureaucracy had been based. It was opportune to render administration less hierarchical, more representative, and socially legitimate, as well as faster in adapting to organizational changes.[27]

The promoters of this new administrative approach held a meeting in September 1968 at Syracuse University, which would pass into history as the Minnowbrook Conference. Participants included the most important scholars of the era, such as Dwight Waldo, George Frederickson, and Frank Marani. The end of the meeting saw the affirmation of common conclusions that provided the new conceptual framework for public administration and for the public organization of the government. The salient arguments were the following: social equity needed to cohere with the search for efficiency and economy, as the objective of public functionaries; ethics and honesty had to guide the actions of administrators; agencies needed to grow, change, and reflect the needs of their clients, and the social problems that they were supposed to resolve; the hierarchical organizations had to be superseded, to make way for more flexible structures that would better satisfy the needs of their users; and an efficacious public administration could be achieved only in a context of active, participatory citizenship.[28]

George Frederickson, one of the founders of the "new public administration," for example, argued that public administrators should seek "to change those policies and structures that systematically inhibit social equity."[29] In his argument, he urges upon public administrators a set of purposes that, whatever may be their intrinsic merits, are clearly substantive in character. Frederickson wants public administrators "to work for changes which try to redress the deprivation of minorities" and "to enhance the political power and economic well-being of these minorities."[30] From the point of view of new public administration, what public administrators should strive for ideally, therefore, is some sort of a redistributive state, directed at promoting greater substantive equality in income and wealth among its citizens. He looks forward to "quantitatively inclined public-organization theorists ... executing a model or paradigm" in which social equity will "be elevated to the supreme objective"; with the help of such a model, in Frederickson's view, we might be able then to "assess rather precisely the likely outcomes of alternative policies in terms of whether the alternative does or does not enhance equity."[31]

The central point remained the overhaul of the old bureaucratic order, an order that suffocated the very authority of the state represented by civil servants. In addition, new public organizations needed to be flexible and capable of interacting with the populace. The clear-cut separation between politics and administration, in other words the paradigm that since the 1880s had prevailed in American political theory, was no longer an acceptable distinction.

In the new academic vision, public administration was to be politicized, so that it would acquire a socially extroverted mission. For these experts, the political neutrality of the civil service was the excuse for public functionaries to reinforce their own power, whereas now the administration needed to adjust its approach, and assume responsibility for promoting equity and social change without regard for the political opinions of the presidency. Civil servants had to be more intently representative of the interests of the American people whom they were called to serve. They also could become protagonists of modernization. Federal bureaucracy had to be capable of effectively reaching its own objectives and responsible with respect to the values of American democracy. This approach clearly aspired for an increased centrality of civil servants, called to fill in the gaps linked with elected politicians in the context of social policies. In this sense, the theorists encouraged a process of politicization of the bureaucracy and of its becoming more interventionist in formulating policies. In this theorization, a fundamental role was played by the political climate of the late 1960s, when public demonstrations often blamed academics and politicians of being excessively conservative, hierarchical, and corporate. In this context, the experts of public administration chose to denounce the failures of government in applying social policies, and they envisioned a new kind of function for the nonelected executive branch, capable of satisfying the demand for emancipation that was emerging from American society.

At the practical level, the influence of the New Public Administration showed itself in multiple initiatives. For example, at the beginning of the 1970s, the American government strove to make bureaucracy more representative in its composition. This trend was favored both by the contribution of the Civil Service Commission, which outlined more inclusive policies toward ethnic minorities, and by the sentences of the Supreme Court during the late 1960s, which adhered to the same course, reaffirming the principle of increased representative practices by the civil service and the necessity for it to uphold the principle of merit.[32]

Moreover, the trade unions were to be more actively involved through the formalization of collective bargaining, the increased participation of non-managerial employees, and the strengthening of procedures for the care and maintenance of the workplace.[33]

Again, through spontaneous initiatives and the intervention of judiciary courts, the federal agencies, particularly independent regulatory agencies,[34] opened their decision-making process to the participation of citizens and their associations. This resulted from the diffusion among jurists of the doctrine of *standing*, that is, the right to bring cases to court involving a decision of the agency. This trend also reflected the introduction of formal rules and procedures that permitted the interested parties, or ones damaged by an administrative measure, to contest the decisions of the administrative agencies.[35]

Furthermore, the Minnowbrook Conference and the recommendations of the liberal area of New Public Administration had a significant impact on the organization of federal bureaucracy, with the aim of making it more representative of ethnic minorities and women, and closer to actual social conditions. These policies became institutionalized in the following years, reaching their apogee in the late 1970s.[36]

A different path was followed by the right wing/conservative branch of the New Public Administration, which contested the excessive managerial powers of public administration and exorbitant state intervention in the economy. Theodore Lowi, for example, argued that the crisis of the interventionist and Welfare State—"big government"—was inevitable.[37] His thesis argued that government had passed from simply constructing infrastructures and defending citizens to desiring to direct economic and technological development, and to resolve social problems, making it prey to special interest groups, lobbies, and professional advocates who proliferated alongside the political parties, making it impossible to govern the nation in all its complexity.

Thus, citizens' distrust in the government and its institutions was on the rise. These problems were emphasized by theorists like William Niskanen, Edward Savas, Steven Ginsburg, and Vincent Ostrom.[38] These commentators held that the structure of government institutions and the ways in which public services were provided had to take account, in a liberal society, of individual incentives for operations both within and outside of the government. In other words, bureaucracies had become excessively focused on their own interests, on the construction of large-scale structures, and on their own planning procedures, neglecting to consider the diverse choices and preferences of individual citizens.

In such a context, an over-inflated bureaucracy undermined the responsibility of governments, becoming dispersed through the multiple structures of the executive branch, and it also blocked the provision of quality services, hindering incentives for improved performance. In a different guise, then, there returned the idea already developed in the United States during the 1920s of an administration based on the improvement of civil servants' efficiency and productivity through economic incentives.

Others, like Victor Thompson, openly criticized the new ideas of the New Public Administration, accusing the movement of being illogical with respect to premises and conclusions, as well as immature for its excessive idealizations about administration. For Thompson, in fact, it was pure utopia to think that one could render bureaucracy more socially responsible and more representative of American demography. This kind of policy, he claimed, in the long run would disable the system of merit and of equality, by introducing preferred spaces reserved for minorities. In essence, for Thompson the project of making the federal administration more compassionate meant sacrificing the pursuit of efficiency, and furthermore it would complicate the decision-making process of the government.[39] The result would not be that of humanizing, politicizing, and decentralizing bureaucracy, as the progressive theorists thought, but to render government services more costly and complicated. The comments of Thompson, Lowi, and others showed how there was disagreement about the direction of the New Public Administration, just as there had been about the development of Great Society programs. In fact, according to these theorists, both one and the other needed to be changed. Their ideas remained minority ones until the late 1970s, but they were emerging in the Nixon era, and above all they constituted the basis for the administrative reforms of the Reagan years.

The Paradox of the Federal Government Expansion and the New Social Regulation

Paradoxically, the greatest ever expansion of the federal bureaucracy took place at a time of cresting intellectual criticism of the federal government. In the late 1960s and early 1970s both left- and right-wing scholars lambasted the system of interest-group liberalism. From the left, Cornell political scientist Theodore Lowi's 1969 book, *The End of Liberalism*, was probably the best-known of these analyses. Lowi described the New Deal state as "the second republic of the United States," succeeding the first, classically liberal or laissez-faire republic. Now both political parties had come to accept positive government, but they had no sense of the ends or purposes of positive government, and no substantive deliberation about justice. The rule of law had been replaced by unrestrained logrolling. "Interest-group liberalism possesses the mentality of a world [of] universalized ticket-fixing," Lowi argued. The ethos of the new order was to "destroy privilege by universalizing it. Reduce conflict by yielding to it."[40] For many left-wing critics, the cynical political theory of interest-group liberalism prevented full-blown statism. They rejected it, together with any system of limited government. Its policies were "basically conservative, co-optive, de-moralizing, and contrary to the very best sentiments and goals expressed by the liberals themselves."[41]

On the libertarian right, scholars of the "public choice" or "law and economics" movements—associated with the economists of the Universities of Chicago and Virginia—applied economic theory to political behavior to explain the rise of twentieth-century big government. They ridiculed the progressive idea that an independent, apolitical bureaucratic class would pursue the "public good." Rather, public individuals and groups behaved just like private individuals and groups. Legislators would promote policies that would maximize their chances of reelection, trading favors for votes. Bureaucrats would seek to maximize their powers and budgets.[42] For different reasons, then, the libertarians agreed with the liberals that private groups had turned public power to their own benefit.

Moreover, the new liberalism of the 1960s produced a new kind of regulation, the "new social regulation," seen most prominently in the fields of environmental protection, workplace safety, public health, and consumer rights.[43] Rather than the broad delegations of the New Deal–era statutes, the new regulatory legislation included specific mandates that agencies had no choice but to meet—what has been called "command and control" legislation. The old agencies had largely eschewed general rulemaking in favor of ad hoc, case-by-case adjudication. Congress now sought to encourage rulemaking. The new agencies would protect the large, diffuse, unorganized, and relatively powerless parties against the organized and concentrated interests that exploited and duped them.

The new wave of administrative reform grew out of the "New Left" culture of the 1960s. The new reformers regarded the old, pluralist New Deal system as corrupt and hoped to make government responsive to the public interest through the participation of ordinary citizens. The old pluralism rejected the idea of a public interest apart from a collection of private interests, and the libertarian critics of regulation also tended to reject the idea of a "public interest."

In part, the new social regulation constituted a change in the political economy that required unprecedented centralization of the national government's administrative power. Business found the new social regulation particularly problematic, since it allowed executive agencies to intrude into broad problem areas with detailed prescriptions for the manufacture and sale of products. As Bernard Falk of the National Electrical Manufacturers' Association pointed out about the expansion of the government's regulatory role: "In the past, going back ten or fifteen years, you didn't have a consumer movement. The manufacturer controlled the make-up of his own product, and Washington could be ignored. Now we all have a new partner, the federal government."[44]

The New Social Regulation was the work of a "new class" of administrators that desired to reshape not just the American economy but American society and culture. Progressivism and New Deal liberalism had largely limited themselves to economic stability; 1960s liberalism encompassed a wider range of "lifestyle" issues.[45] The new regulatory class came out of the greatly expanded middle class of postwar America, and especially out of its burgeoning universities. Many had rebelled against the bureaucratization of the mega- or multiversity, where students were treated as numbers. They similarly protested the Vietnam War, which had been a product of the national-security bureaucracy. Many of them would end up leading such bureaucracies after graduating. This new class looked like a technically trained cadre of experts, who could see the public good above the selfish and crony interest-group politics. From this class, new ideas and movements from both the left and the right were spawned, but above all there began a process of delegitimization of the postwar administrative order.[46]

Indeed, the explosion of regulation and the recasting of administrative institutions coincided with, and to a degree contributed to, increasing public doubt about the expansion of government.

An Administrative Time of Transition: The 1970s, Nixon's Presidency, and the Crisis of Government Legitimation

Reorganizing the Executive Branch: Centralizing Policy-Making for Decentralizing Administration

In 1968 the Republicans returned to the White House with the election of Richard Nixon, who was an ardent creator of new administrative institutions. As the scholar Richard Nathan has noted, Nixon adopted the strategy of the "administrative presidency," which implied the exertion of greater discretionary powers in the implementation of pre-existing laws, rather than promoting new laws and their approval by Congress.[47] Furthermore, if in the programming and propagandistic contexts the new president claimed that he wished to combat an excessively centralized and bureaucratic government and to promote a new federalism that would decentralize administration, in practice he showed his readiness to expand his powers of managing and controlling the executive branch and to pull all the levers of command the presidency offered him.

Underlying the continuity with his Democratic predecessor Johnson in administrative matters, historian Barry Karl has written: "Expansion of government programs in all areas ... moved with surprising ease from the Johnson administration to the Nixon administration."[48] A sign of continuity in this sense was the creation of new administrative agencies both through legislation, such as the Occupational Safety and Health Administration and the Consumer Product Safety Commission, and through administrative reorganization, such as the Environmental Protection Agency.[49]

Nixon partly achieved his program of New Federalism that took seriously, for the first time since the New Deal, a plan eventually to devolve management of this program to the local and state governments. As a result, Karl concluded,

> the equation–familiar since the New Deal days—of expanded federal programs and a strong presidency with liberalism, the opposite with conservatism, no longer applied, for Nixon as much as Johnson wanted to centralize control of the bureaucracy in the White House.[50]

To accomplish his program, Nixon intended to acquire greater control over the policies promoted by the federal government, to centralize operations and decisions in his office, and to enlarge the White House personnel. Nixon's priority was to increase the presidency's control over executive branch operations and organization. The White House had to play a stronger role in the coordination of the administrative structures both for making political decisions and for putting them into action.

To begin with, Nixon enlarged the White House staff. In 1939, there were 37 staff members, who numbered 53 by 1945, 283 in 1953, dropped to 250 by

1968, and rose again to reach 510 in 1973.[51] Nixon aimed to expand the reach of presidential power and, by doing so, to achieve political and policy objective autonomously. For this reason, the first phase of Nixon's administrative program was to create a White House counter-bureaucracy that could take on the liberal opposition that Nixon considered rooted within the career civil service.

In addition, the president wanted to have greater control over his Presidential Cabinet, and at the same time, a higher number of experts engaged with the execution of his political program. First, he created a series of Cabinet subcommittees to assess matters such as the economy and the environment, and then he sought to replicate for domestic politics the model of the National Security Council, a technocratic organ founded in 1947 that assisted the president with strategic decisions related to foreign policy and coordinated various agencies responsible for activities abroad.

He therefore entrusted his advisor, the lawyer John Ehrlichman, with the task of installing an analogous domestic affairs department before the end of 1969. In March 1970, with Reorganization Plan No. 2, there was born the Domestic Council, which would be dedicated to the coordination of public policy.[52] Furthermore, the Bureau of Budget (BOB) was renamed the Office of Management and Budget (OMB), and it was recalibrated on the development of managerial practices and costs control within the executive branch. Its tasks were to evaluate the performance of agencies, to improve managerial techniques, and to develop information systems as well as training programs for civil servants. In 1971, the OMB, moreover, replaced the system of the Planning Programming Management System in budget matters, with the Management by Objectives (MBO), a procedure that allowed greater focusing of the budget on the achievement of the presidency's high-priority objectives.

The new Domestic Council was instead composed of the president, the vice-president, the Cabinet secretaries, and several agency chiefs, who operated at the level of domestic affairs. It was also organized into task forces, composed of experts and professional bureaucrats, who carried out much of the actual work. The plenary meetings in fact were rare, and these sub-groups of experts played a fundamental role. The Council had five principal functions: definition of objectives, development of alternatives, formulation, coordination, and control of policies. The aim was to provide the presidency with a comprehensive vision of all things concerning the government on the domestic front. The hired experts gradually increased in number, and the Domestic Council eventually had 70 components, among them political analysts, economists, statisticians, and management experts.[53]

In 1968, during the transition between presidencies, the newly elected Richard Nixon had created a task force for the reorganization of the Executive Office, headed by Roy Ash, formerly chief executive of Litton Industries.[54] Ash was then named by Nixon to head the Advisory Council on Government

Organization, created by the president after his full installation in the Oval Office in 1969.[55] Three of the four members of the Council, including Ash himself, hailed from private industry. The fourth was John Connally, former governor of Texas and a Nixon supporter. As with Eisenhower's PACGO and Johnson's Heineman Task Force, the Ash Council was tightly linked to the president, and being his trusted associates, its members succeeded in meeting with him on a frequent basis.[56] The 1969 budget of a million dollars enabled the Council members to recruit 35 new staff members, who grew to 47 in number in 1970.[57] The president meant to centralize power in the executive branch, and in particular he wanted to reinforce the numbers and the functions of Presidential Cabinet members, in order to be much more free to concentrate his attention on foreign policy.

Richard Nixon who had come into office convinced that many of the problems facing government could be solved by reorganizing the federal establishment along sound political management principles. He did not see the purpose of reorganization as being the implementation of neutral principles of economy and efficiency. On the contrary, the principal aim of reorganization, for him, was to alter the terms of political power. In Nixon's mind, the objective was to reorganize in order to enhance the power and capacity of the president. Paradoxically, his goals were not to make the president powerful for the institution's sake but to create leverage for definitively decentralizing government. The political power had to be centralized, for then being properly decentralized. Nixon's purpose was to move much of the power away from Washington and toward the states and localities (New Federalism). In this vein, the mission of the Ash Council was to suggest ways and means to the president on how policy-making could be centralized while administration decentralized.[58]

The Ash Council sent Nixon 13 memoranda between 1969 and 1971, on various themes such as the reorganization of the Executive Office, changes in the regulation of the environment, and the reorganization of independent administrative authorities. All of these recommendations were incorporated into legislative proposals by the president in 1971.[59] The reorganizational power of the executive branch was extended through the end of 1971, and Nixon succeeded in getting his reorganizational plan passed by the Bureau of Budget, which was re-named the Office of Management and Budget, and in creating an Office for Policy Development, which would concern itself with economic politics.[60] These were probably the two most important among Nixon's various successes in reorganizing the executive branch.

With this phase concluded, the Ash Council sought to increase the centralization and to re-define the contours of presidential power within the executive branch. The Council also proposed creating super-departments linked to the Presidential Cabinet. Nixon aimed to re-politicize numerous functions, on the one hand abolishing a series of departments, and on the other hand removing functions from independent administrative agencies, making everything converge in new departments such as Human Resources, Community Development, Natural Resources, and Economic Affairs.

Nonetheless, there remained a problem for the creation of super-departments. In fact, following a modification to the Reorganization Act of 1949 made in 1964, the president could not autonomously implement this reform by using an executive order or a simple reorganization plan, but had to accept the necessary legislation of Congress. The reform of the departments never left the congressional committees, and in definitive terms, it never was put into practice.

Despite this failure, the president and his staff planned new institutions to centralize the direction of social policies within the federal government. For example, they founded the National Goals Research Staff, which worked on objectives of social reforms, as well as on the monitoring of policy; they created the first Population Commission for urban planning and the supervision of population dynamics; and they sought to make federal government-owned lands more productive.[61]

While the Ash Council's most detailed recommendations met with success, its general proposals encountered failure. In a political climate of growing doubt and mistrust, caused by the Watergate scandal, the idea of creating super-agencies and super-departments frightened members of Congress and the specific interests that they represented. History has demonstrated how the task forces and the councils, composed of the president's loyal associates, were effective in reforming the institutions closest to the presidency, but proved to be too remote from public opinion and from the legislative to construct vast support for more complex and ambitious administrative reforms. Finally, both the evidently irresolvable Vietnam War and the Watergate scandal had weakened credibility and the legitimacy of nearly all American constitutional institutions and their members. The experience began in the 1930s with the Brownlow Report, then formed of attempts in the following decades to increase the centralization of the White House's powers, was about to end.

Nixon's Civil Service Reform

Like his Republican predecessor Eisenhower, Richard Nixon seemed to be more opposed to government interventionism and the development of the welfare state in his intentions than in his actions. He inherited an enormously expanded federal civil service, focused by Lyndon Johnson on the struggle against poverty and on social programs, but this notwithstanding he did not seem to have, at least initially, very clear ideas about administrative reforms. Besides, the president was primarily concerned with the Vietnam War which, despite his optimistic electoral declarations, appeared to be more complex and difficult to resolve than it seemed from outside the White House.

Also like Eisenhower, he won his first-term elections in 1968 with an extremely narrow majority, and he could not count on a Republican administrative establishment, neither among career bureaucrats nor among his new appointees. Partially constrained by the Democratic majority Congress and partially by the pressures of conservative public opinion, he continued to implement the Great Society programs, enlarging federal interventionism, albeit through a new funding method which relied on local and state governments.

In this context, Nixon understood that he could not engage in ideological battles to make government policies align with his own positions. He advised his cabinet with urgency:

> if they did not act quickly, they would become captives of the bureaucracy they were trying to change... We can't depend on people who believe in another philosophy of government to give us their undivided loyalty or their best work... If we don't get rid of these people, they will either sabotage us from within, or they will just sit back on their well-paid asses and wait for the next election to bring back their old bosses.[62]

In his 1971 State of the Union message, he expressed his distrust toward professional bureaucracy:

> The idea that a bureaucratic elite in Washington knows best what is best for people everywhere and that you cannot trust local governments is really a contention that you cannot trust people to govern themselves. The notion is completely foreign to American experience.[63]

Nixon had no serious objections to the ends and purposes of the liberal state consolidated by his predecessor Lyndon Johnson, but he was determined to get the bureaucracy under presidential control. He believed that the career civil servants in the agencies opposed him. He complained about the network of interest groups, congressional committees, and bureaucrats who regulated the society "regardless of changes in administrations." Nixon revived the effort—undertaken at different levels by every president since Franklin Delano Roosevelt—to centralize the administration under presidential control.

The president elaborated plans to re-orient management of White House personnel. He intended to use the organs with which presidential personnel was managed to install people favorable to Republican Party ideas in the governmental subcabinets and other subordinate positions. This entailed thorough usage of internal administrative transfers, and the rotation of commissions, to inhibit the careers of those professional bureaucrats who created political problems for policy choices.

These practices left their mark on the administration, even though a good part of the administrative reforms foreseen by Nixon failed, because of the Democratic majority in Congress, the difficulties of managing the Vietnam War, and then the Watergate scandal. With this strategy he managed to place at key points of the top-level bureaucracy both career bureaucrats and politically nominated ones who shared his conservative ideas, launching a true change from those with Democratic views, inherited in 1968 from previous administrations. He was able to close the ranks of leadership positions, through the use of interviews and promotions geared toward testing the ideological preferences of the bureaucracy. He also gave politically appointed executives greater power, especially in the management of social policies and programs. In this way he could accomplish dilatory tactics on the implementation of some Great Society policies or re-direct financial resources to shut down or limit certain programs.

Another of the Nixon administration's concerns was to achieve better control of the federal executive administrative personnel. Seeking out and placing in key leadership positions individuals philosophically compatible with and loyal to Nixon became the stated objectives of the White House personnel organization. A management study prepared by the White House stated that

> management control could be achieved by attracting the best qualified individuals who are philosophically compatible and loyal to the President, placing them in leadership positions, motivating them by recognizing and promoting outstanding performance, and removing any whose performance is poor. At the same time, personnel decisions should be made and announced to maximize political benefit and minimize political loss.[64]

The question arises as to how was it that the White House hoped to successfully influence the selection of top officials, a process supposedly protected from such incursions by a host of civil service rules and regulations. Obviously, the president was expected to name his own appointees to important political positions. However, the essence of the administrative presidency argument is that White House influence was to extend to the career civil service as well.

Shortly after Nixon's first term began, the White House Personnel Operation (WHPO), headed by Harry Flemming, was established to identify and place individuals in presidential appointment positions.[65] Following initial White House disappointment with Flemming's direction of the personnel operation, Frederick Malek (then Health, Education and Welfare Deputy Undersecretary) was asked to study the Flemming operation and to project a comprehensive plan. Ultimately the White House Personnel Manual was issued and distributed in November 1972 as a guide to executives in the hiring and placement of personnel.[66]

The first step, according to the manual, was to identify vacancies. When no vacancies existed, some would have to be created and the manual provided specific guidelines for this activity:

> There are several techniques which can be designed, carefully, to skirt around the difficult problem of firing established career executives. You simply call an individual in and tell him he is no longer wanted ... you expect him to immediately relinquish his duties. There should be no witnesses in the room at the time.[67]

If this "frontal assault" (the manual's own terminology) was not successful, the manual went on to suggest transferring unwanted personnel to regional offices, described by the manual as "dumping grounds." If the transfer technique failed, the manual recommended other "special assignments" as well as other techniques. But the strategy was clear: where no positions at the senior career levels were open, political executives were instructed in the art of creating such openings by encouraging the firing or transferring of personnel.[68]

In addition, once an open position was identified, the White House wanted to ensure that "its" personnel were appointed to that position. Malek described this process in Senate testimony as follows:

> What we are doing in the case of a career position is we would be submitting the name of a person to a department and asking them to determine where this person would be qualified and competitive, to serve in that position, to try to get them into it. So, what we were really doing is facilitating the personnel process in getting somebody in that door, where, without the political push, they may not have been getting into the door.[69]

Thus, through the process of first identifying vacancies and second by ensuring that candidates supportive of the administration's position were referred to appropriate political personnel contacts in the departments and agencies, the White House expected to maximize the placement of "its fellows" in senior career positions. In this manner, the Nixon administration hoped to circumvent the "normal" civil service process and to achieve a high degree of managerial control over the federal bureaucracy.

Moreover, Nixon's administration developed an increasing political attention to the civil service personnel management, which also led to an attempt to re-classify positions within the administration. In fact, for over 20 years, the federal government had not updated the classification of civil servants' duties, and consequently, it did not possess a system of evaluation that accounted for the technical specifications of every single position. The 1949 Classification Act had been perceived as too rigid, cumbersome, and bureaucratic by agencies and departments since the 1950s. There had been accumulating complaints about position classification, the form, and the style of classification. The approval of the Job Evaluation Policy Act of 1970 offered the opportunity to address the question, since with it Congress expressly delegated the Civil Service Commission to study a homogeneous system of classification and evaluation for the entire workforce of the federal government.[70]

Indeed, in 1968, a subcommittee of the House Committee on Post Office and Civil Service, chaired by James M. Hanley, studied the job evaluation system of government and issued a highly critical report.[71] In 1970, Congressman Hanley pushed through both Houses of Congress a Bill calling for the Civil Service Commission to make a study of the government's job evaluation system that would embrace all separate systems then existing in the civil service.[72]

The commission convened experts to study an appropriate evaluation system.[73] Thus was born the Job Evaluation and Pay Review Task Force, directed by Phillip M. Oliver, who worked on a final report, presented in January 1972, after which the study group was dissolved. The Task Force proposed an evaluation system based not only on the rung of the organizational ladder at which the civil servant was placed but also on the type of tasks assigned to her or him, and it proposed a thorough re-structuring of the classification system. In particular, it recommended a "Coordinated Job Evaluation Plan," a new classification system with six different job evaluation systems: executive positions, supervisor and manager positions below the executive level, administrative and technological occupations, clerical and technician occupations, employment trades and jobs paid on an hourly basis, and special occupations (e.g. police, doctors) that did not fit in any other system. For the bulk of the federal jobs subjected to the General Schedule, the Task Force suggested the creation of two systems for evaluating job performance, both of them using the tabulation of points: one was valid for those who engaged in intellectual labor, research, and policy, while the other applied to those who were employed to carry out clerical and technical work.[74] In fact, the report was only partially put into effect, since in 1972 the commission decided not to alter the tasks and duties classification system that had been installed by the Classification Act of 1949. A points-based evaluation system for federal executives was inserted, but within the parameters of the old structure.[75]

Also in 1970, Congress approved the Federal Pay Comparability Act, which aimed to equalize the salaries of federal government employees with those found in the private sector.[76] The legislation had already confronted this point in 1962, but economic politics had given priority to other sectors, and in 1967, public sector salaries were 23% lower than those offered by private companies.[77] The law established that the president had the power to analyze private sector salaries and to adjust on an annual basis the level of growth of compensation for civil servants. This adjustment would be confirmed with a simple executive order, having automatic and immediate effect. At the same time, the law allowed for the possibility of freezing or only slightly increasing salaries, in case of national emergency or if higher wages could compromise the general welfare of the nation. Nixon immediately had to confront the economic crisis which exploded in 1971, and he never succeeded in raising the wages of federal employees to make them match private sector levels.

Recruiting practices were also the object of several revisions, which can be shown to have a continuity with the preceding period, in which the presidency was occupied by progressive Democrats. The Civil Rights Act of 1964 determined that the competition for obtaining a specific post in the administration needed to have a verified correlation with the tasks that the position effectively required: this measure was designed to prevent hiring procedures from penalizing some ethnic minority groups who would be applying for publicly advertised jobs. In 1972, thanks to momentum from a Democratic majority Congress, this law was amended to strengthen anti-discriminatory policies.[78] This amendment ensured that for access to both first-time hiring and promotions, as well as to transfers within the administration, one could take tests and examinations, as long as these were written in a way that did not discriminate against any participants, on the basis of ethnicity, gender, or other social differences. This meant, for example, that the same exams could vary according to one's ethnic background, in order to balance out or neutralize possible discriminations.

In conjunction with the 1972 amendments, the Equal Employment Opportunity Coordinating Council (EEOC) was created, which was formed by members of the Civil Service Commission, by those of the Equal Employment Opportunity Commission itself, and by several bureaucrats and policy-makers of the Departments of Labor and Justice. This Council issued guidelines for avoiding racial discrimination in public exams and job applications and interviews, which had to be observed by all federal agencies and departments. Furthermore, in cases where possible discrimination would occur, even when the guidelines were observed, the civil servants charged with supervising job applications or exams were obliged to devise acceptable nonstandard tests in order not to perpetrate abuses.

In many respects, the Nixon era did not excessively stray from the policies of preceding years, in the area of public administration. On the one hand, Nixon sought to centralize control over the Presidential Cabinet's political decisions, as well as those made in his own office, attempting to create super-departments, to increase political supervision of bureaucracy, and to expand the federal government by installing new agencies; on the other, he sought to make the operations of the federal civil service even more technical as well as politically controlled, through programs of formation and job performance evaluation, returning bureaucracy to positions within more rigorous but also more egalitarian rules and boundaries of selection and personnel management.

All the same, several of the president's intended reforms failed or were only partially carried out. Meanwhile, federal bureaucracy had to confront new turmoil, linked to the economic crisis, to the financial squeeze that this imposed, to a political invasiveness that grew ever stronger—dragging civil servants into various scandals—and finally to public opinion that was increasingly mistrustful and diffident toward the permanent federal government.

In general, the Nixon presidency can be interpreted as the expression of a time of public and administrative transition, destined to veer toward crisis, which finally did explode with the oil crisis of 1973 and the Watergate scandal. Nixon tried to centralize still further the White House's political decisions, to politicize public office appointments based on personal loyalty criteria, and, at the same time, to roll back the social policies he had inherited, without reversing the trend toward the multiplication of administrative agencies. The Nixon presidency was a controversial period, distinguished by only a few personal victories for the president and by a variety of failures in the administrative field. The old order had gone into full crisis, in terms of both management efficiency and political legitimation, but the emergence of a new order was slow to arrive.

Notes

1 Matthew Crenson and Francis Rourke, "By way of Conclusion: American Bureaucracy since World War II," in *The New American State*, ed. Louis Galambos (Baltimore, MD: Johns Hopkins University Press, 1987), 159.
2 Papers of John F. Kennedy. Presidential Papers. President's Office Files. Speech Files. Address at Yale University, 11 June 1962.
3 As noted by G. Calvin MacKenzie, *The Politics of Presidential Appointments* (New York: Free Press, 1981), 24–28.
4 These quotations are taken from James M. Landis, *Report on Regulatory Agencies to the President-Elect* (Washington, DC: US Government Printing Office, December 21, 1960).
5 Landis, *Report on Regulatory Agencies*.
6 Carl McFarland, "Landis' Report: The Voice of One Crying in the Wilderness," *Virginia Law Review* 47 (1961): 392–416.
7 See William L. Cary, *Politics and the Regulatory Agencies* (New York: McGraw Hill, 1967).
8 Executive Order 10988, *Employee-Management Cooperation in the Federal Service*, 17 January 1962.
9 See OMB (2012), 246.
10 See Herbert Emmerich, *Federal Organization and Administration Management* (Tuscaloosa: University of Alabama Press, 1971).
11 Price Task Force, *Memorandum, Task Force on Government Organization to L. B. Johnson*, White House Central Files, Box 43, Austin, TX: Johnson Library, 15 December, 1966.
12 See Emmette S. Redford and Marlan Blissett, *Organizing the Executive Branch: The Johnson Presidency* (Chicago, IL: University of Chicago Press, 1981).
13 Lyndon B. Johnson, *Public Papers of the President*, 1966, Annual Budget Message Congress, 24 January, 1966, 65.
14 Price Task Force, *A Final Report by the President's Task Force on Government Organization*, Outside Task Forces, Austin, TX: Johnson Library, 15 June, 1967.

15 Arnold, *Making the Managerial Presidency*, 276.
16 Robert Maranto, and David Schultz. *A Short History of the US Civil Service* (Washington, DC: University Press of America, 1991), 115.
17 Sar A. Levitan and Robert Taggart, *The Promise of Greatness* (Cambridge, MA: Harvard University Press, 1976), 21.
18 According to the reconstruction made by the historian Daniel T. Rodgers (*Atlantic Crossings*, 2009), the American establishment's cultural absorption of ideas relative to European-style social policies can be read from the long-term standpoint, with reference to the period starting at the end of the nineteenth century and ending in the 1960s.
19 See Executive Order 10925, *Establishing the President's Committee on Equal Employment Opportunity*, 6 March, 1961.
20 On equal opportunity employment, see David H. Rosenbloom, "The Civil Service Commission's Decision to Authorize the Use of Goals and Timetables in the Federal Equal Employment Opportunity Program," *Western Political Quarterly* 26, no. 2 (1973): 236–251; G. B. Lewis, "Progress Toward Racial and Sexual Equality in the Federal Civil Service?" *Public Administration Review* 48 (1988): 700–707.
21 See Office for Personnel Management 2012, 248–249.
22 Executive Order 11315, *Amending the Civil Service Rules to authorize an Executive Assignment System for positions in grades 16, 17, and 18 of the General Schedule*, November 18, 1966.
23 The executive order implemented a recommendation of the Report on the President's Task Force on Government Reorganization, November 6, 1964, Johnson Library.
24 See Sidney M. Milkis, *The President and the Parties* (Oxford: Oxford University Press, 1993), 192.
25 Godfrey Hodgson, *America in Our Time: From World War II to Nixon, What Happened and Why* (New York: Vintage Books, 1978), 245.
26 Milkis, *The President and the Parties*, 191.
27 On this point see Allen Schick, "The Trauma of Politics: Public Administration in the Sixties," in *American Public Administration: Past, Present and Future*, ed. (Tuscaloosa: University of Alabama Press, 1975).
28 H. George Frederickson, "Minnowbrook II: Changing Epochs of Public Administration," *Public Administration Review* 49, no. 2 (1989): 97; Dwight Waldo, "Public Administration in a Time of Revolution," in *Classics of Public Administration* (Oak Park, IL: Moore Publishing, 1968), 310–317.
29 H. George Frederickson, *New Public Administration* (Tuscaloosa: University of Alabama Press, 1971), 312.
30 Frederickson, *New Public Administration*, 311.
31 Frederickson, *New Public Administration*, 330.
32 See the cases Elrod v. Burn, 427 U.S. 347 (1976), and Branti v. Finkel 445 U.S. 507 (1980)
33 Patricia Ingraham and David H. Rosenbloom, "The New Public Personnel and the New Public Service," *Public Administration Review* 49, no. 2 (1989): 118–119.
34 These agencies are similar to the independent administrative authorities in European organizational frameworks.
35 On this point, see John A. Ferejohn and Larry D. Kramer, "Independent Judges, Dependent Judiciary: Institutionalizing Judicial Restraint," *NYU Law Review* 77 (2002): 962–1009.
36 M. E. Guy, "Minnowbrook II: Conclusions," *Public Administration Review* 49, no. 2 (1989): 219–220.
37 Theodore Lowi, *The End of Liberalism*, 2nd ed. (New York: Norton, 1979).
38 E.S. Savas and Sigmund G. Ginsburg, "The Civil Service: A Meritless System?" *The Public Interest* 32 (1973): 70–85; William Niskanen, *Bureaucracy and Representative*

Government (Chicago, IL: Aldine-Atherton, 1971); and Vincent Ostrom, *The Intellectual Crisis in American Public Administration* (Tuscaloosa: University of Alabama Press, 1974).

39 Vincent A. Thompson, *Without Sympathy or Enthusiasm: The Problem of Administrative Compassion* (Tuscaloosa: University of Alabama Press, 1979).

40 Theodore J. Lowi, *The End of Liberalism: The Second Republic of the United States*, 40th anniversary edition (New York: Norton, 1969), 297.

41 Lowi, *The End,* 225.

42 George J. Stigler, "The Theory of Regulation," *Bell Journal of Economics and Management Science* 2 (1971): 3–21.

43 David Vogel, "The New Social Regulation," in *Regulation in Perspective: Historical Essays*, ed. Thomas K. McCraw (Cambridge, MA: Harvard University Press, 1981), 155–185; William Lilley III and James C. Miller, "The New Social Regulation," *Public Interest* 47 (1977): 49.

44 Falk, cited in Jeffrey M. Berry, *The Interest Group Society* (Boston, MA: Little Brown, 1984), 36.

45 See Sidney M. Milkis, "Remaking Government Institutions in the 1970s: Participatory Democracy and the Triumph of Administrative Politics," *Journal of Policy History* 10 (1998): 51–74.

46 See Paul H. Weaver, "Regulation, Social Policy and Class Conflict," *Public Interest* 50 (1978): 45–63; David Vogel, "The Public Interest Movement and the American Reform Tradition," *Political Science Quarterly* 95 (1981): 607–627; Philip Hamburger, *Is Administrative Law Unlawful?* (Chicago, IL: University of Chicago Press, 2014).

47 See Richard P. Nathan, *The Administrative Presidency* (New York: MacMillan, 1983), where the author has denominated this strategy as "administrative presidency strategy."

48 Barry Karl, *The Uneasy State: The United States from 1915 to 1945* (Chicago, IL: The University of Chicago Press, 1983), 226.

49 Reorganization Plan No. 3 of 1970 (July 9, 1970) - message from President Nixon to Congress about reorganization plans to establish EPA and the National Oceanic and Atmospheric Administration (NOAA).

50 Karl, *Uneasy State,* 226.

51 Data reported by Graham, *Toward a Planned Society,* 230.

52 U.S. Congress, House of Committee on Government Operations, *Hearings on Reorganization Plan no.2 of 1970*, 91st Congress, 2nd Session, April–May 1970.

53 E. L. Harper, "Domestic Policy Making in the Nixon Administration: An Evolving Process," *Presidential Studies Quarterly* 26 (1996): 41–56.

54 Arnold, *The History,* 276.

55 The Council was born on 5 April, 1969. See *U.S. Weekly Compilation of Presidential Documents*, Vol. 5, 14 April, 1969, 530–531.

56 The other members of the task force were George Baker, Harvard Business School Dean; Frederick Kappell, President of the AT&T; and Richard Paget, founder of a top-level consultancy firm.

57 See U.S. Congress House, Committee on Government Operations, *Reorganization of Executive Departments*, Hearings, 92nd Congress, 1st session, Government Printing Office, Washington, 1971,184.

58 See Ronald C. Moe, *Administrative Renewal* (Lanham, MD: University Press of America, 2003), 86–95.

59 Ash Council, *President's Advisory Council on Executive Organization (Ash Council)*, White House Central Files, 1969–1971.

60 US Public Papers of the President Richard M. Nixon, 1969, "Special Message to the Congress Requesting New Authority to Reorganize the Executive Branch," January 20, 1969, 32–33.

61 See, for example, the report by U.S. National Goals Research Staff, *Toward Balanced Growth: Quantity with Quality* (Washington, DC: US Government Printing Office, 1970).
62 Cited in Carl M. Brauer, *Presidential Transition: Eisenhower Through Reagan* (Oxford and New York: Oxford University Press, 1986), 150.
63 *Public Papers of the Presidents*, Richard Nixon, 1971, 55.
64 Subcommittee on Manpower and Civil Service of the Committee on Post Office and Civil Service, *Final Report on Violations and Abuses of Merit Principles in Federal Employment* (Washington, DC: Government Printing Office, 1976), 411.
65 Richard L. Cole, and David A. Caputo. "Presidential Control of the Senior Civil Service: Assessing the Strategies of the Nixon Years," *The American Political Science Review* 73, no. 2 (1979): 399–413.
66 Subcommittee on Manpower and Civil Service, 1976, 573–686.
67 Subcommittee on Manpower, 1976, 163.
68 Cole and Caputo, "Presidential Control of the Senior Civil Service," 399–413.
69 Subcommittee on Manpower, 1976, 166.
70 Public Law 91-216, 1970.
71 Committee on Post Office and Civil Service and Subcommittee on Position Classification, *Report on Job Evaluation and Ranking in the Federal Government* (Washington, DC: GPO, February 27, 1969).
72 These were: the General Schedule, the Postal Service, the Foreign Service, the Medical Service, the Coordinated Federal Wage System.
73 Committee on Post Office and Civil Service (House of Representative), *Interim Progress Report of the Job Evaluation and Pay Review Task Force* (Washington, DC: GPO, March 31, 1971).
74 See Jack Rabin, *Handbook of Public Personnel Administration* (New York: Marcel Dekker, 1995), 98.
75 *Job Evaluation and Pay Review Task Force Report* (Washington, DC: GPO, September 1972).
76 Federal Pay Comparability Act of 1970, Pub. L. 91-656, 84 Stat. 1946 (Washington, DC: GPO, January 8, 1971).
77 U.S. Office of Personnel Management, *Biography of an Ideal. A History of the Federal Civil Service* (Washington, DC: Government Printing Office, 2002), 262–275.
78 Public Law No. 92-318, 86 Stat. 235 (June 23, 1972), codified at 20 U.S.C. §§ 1681–1688.

Bibliography

Arnold, Peri. *Making the Managerial Presidency*. Lawrence: University Press of Kansas, 1986.
Ash Council. *President's Advisory Council on Executive Organization (Ash Council)*. Washington, DC: White House Central Files, 1969–1971.
Balogh, Brian, Joanna Grisinger, and Philip Zelikow. *Making Democracy Work: A Brief History of Twentieth Century Federal Executive Reorganization*. Charlottesville: University of Virginia Center of Public Affairs, 2002.
Berry, Jeffrey M. *The Interest Group Society*. Boston, MA: Little Brown, 1984.
Bon, Cristina, and Glauco Vecchiato. "Un grande amministratore per una Great Society: la riorganizzazione dell'esecutivo federale di Lyndon B. Johnson." *Giornale di Storia Costituzionale* 36, no. 2 (2018): 331–350.
Brauer, Carl M. *Presidential Transitions: Eisenhower through Reagan*. Oxford and New York: Oxford University Press, 1986.

Cary, William L. *Politics and the Regulatory Agencies.* New York: McGraw Hill, 1967.

Cole, R. L., and D. A. Caputo. "Presidential Control of the Senior Civil Service: Assessing the Strategies of the Nixon Years." *The American Political Science Review* 73 (1979): 399–413.

Committee on Post Office and Civil Service and Subcommittee on Position Classification. *Report on Job Evaluation and Ranking in the Federal Government.* Washington, DC: GPO, 27 February, 1969.

Committee on Post Office and Civil Service (House of Representatives). *Interim Progress Report of the Job Evaluation and Pay Review Task Force.* Washington, DC: GPO, 31 March, 1971.

Crenson, Matthew, and Francis Rourke. "By Way of Conclusion: American Bureaucracy since World War II." In *The New American State*, edited by Louis Galambos, 137–177. Baltimore, MD: Johns Hopkins University Press, 1987.

Emmerich, Herbert. *Federal Organization and Administrative Management.* Tuscaloosa: The University of Alabama Press, 1971.

Executive Order 10925. National Archives, Federal Register, 1961.

Executive Order 11315. *Amending the Civil Service Rules to authorize an Executive Assignment System for Positions in Grades 16, 17, and 18 of the General Schedule*, Federal Register, 1966.

Federal Pay Comparability Act of 1970, Pub. L. 91–656, 84 Stat. 1946. Washington DC: GPO, January 8, 1971.

Ferejohn John A., and Larry D. Kramer. "Independent Judges, Dependent Judiciary: Institutionalizing Judicial Restraint." *NYU Law Review* 77 (2002): 962–1009.

Frederickson, H. George. *New Public Administration.* Tuscaloosa: University of Alabama Press, 1971.

———. "Minnowbrook II: Changing Epochs of Public Administration." *Public Administration Review* 49, no. 2 (1989): 95–100.

Graham, Otis. *Toward a Planned Society: From Roosevelt to Nixon.* Oxford: Oxford University Press, 1977.

Guy, M. E. "Minnowbrook II: Conclusions." *Public Administration Review* 49, no. 2 (1989): 219–220.

Hamburger, Philip. *Is Administrative Law Unlawful?* Chicago: University of Chicago Press, 2014.

Harper, E. L. "Domestic Policy Making in the Nixon Administration: An Evolving Process." *Presidential Studies Quarterly* 26 (1996): 41–56.

Heatherly, Charles L. *Mandate for Leadership: Policy Management in a Conservative Administration.* The Heritage Foundation, 1981.

Hodgson, Godfrey. *America in Our Time: From World War II to Nixon, What Happened and Why.* New York: Vintage Books, 1978.

Hogan, Michael J. *A Cross of Iron.* Cambridge: Cambridge University Press, 1998.

Hood, Christopher. *The Art of the State.* Oxford: Oxford University Press, 2000.

United States Civil Service Commission, *Job Evaluation and Pay Review Task Force Report.* Washington, DC: GPO, September 1972.

Johnson, Lyndon B. *Public Papers of the President.* Washington DC: GPO, 1966.

Karl, Barry. *The Uneasy State: The United States from 1915 to 1945.* Chicago: The University of Chicago Press, 1983.

Kennedy, John F. *Presidential Papers.* President's Office Files. Speech Files. Address at Yale University, 11 June 1962.

Landis, James M. *Report on Regulatory Agencies to the President-Elect.* Washington, DC: US Government Printing Office, 1960.

Levitan, Sar A., and Alexandra Noden. *Working for the Sovereign: Employee Relations in the Federal Government*. Baltimore, MD: Johns Hopkins University Press, 1983.

Lewis, G. B. "Progress Toward Racial and Sexual Equality in the Federal Civil Service?" *Public Administration Review* 48 (1988): 700–707.

Light, Paul C. *The True Size of Government*. New York: Volcker Alliance, 2017.

Lilley III, William, and James C. Miller. "The New Social Regulation." *Public Interest* 47 (1977): 49–61.

Lowi, Theodore J. *The End of Liberalism: The Second Republic of the United States*, 40th anniversary edition. New York: Norton, 2009.

Lynn Jr., Laurence E. *Public Management New and Old*. London: Routledge, 2006.

MacKenzie, G. Calvin. *The Politics of Presidential Appointments*. New York: Free Press, 1981.

———. *The In and Outers*. Baltimore, MD: John Hopkins University Press, 1987.

Mackenzie, G. Calvin, and Robert Shogan. *Obstacle Course*. New York: Twentieth-Century Fund, 1996.

Maranto, Robert, and David Schultz. *A Short History of the United States Civil Service*. Lanham, MD: University Press of America, 1991.

McFarland, Carl. "Landis' Report: The Voice of One Crying in the Wilderness." *Virginia Law Review* 47 (1961): 392–416.

Milkis, Sidney M. *The President and the Parties*. Oxford: Oxford University Press, 1993.

———. "Remaking Government Institutions in the 1970s: Participatory Democracy and the Triumph of Administrative Politics." *Journal of Policy History* 10 (1998): 51–74.

Moe, Ronald C. *Administrative Renewal*. Lanham, MD: University Press of America, 2003.

Moreno, Paul D. *The Bureaucrat Kings: The Origins and Underpinnings of America's Bureaucratic State*. Santa Barbara, CA: Praeger, 2017.

Nathan, Richard. *The Plot that Failed: Nixon and the Administrative Presidency*. New York: John Wiley and Sons, 1975.

———. *The Administrative Presidency*. New York: MacMillan, 1983.

Niskanen, William. *Bureaucracy and Representative Government*. Chicago, IL: Aldine-Atherton, 1971.

Office for Personnel Management, 2012.

Ostrom, Vincent. *The Intellectual Crisis in American Public Administration*. Tuscaloosa: University of Alabama Press, 1974.

Price Task Force. *Memorandum, Task Force on Government Organization to L. B. Johnson*.

Price Task Force, *A Final Report by the President's Task Force on Government Organization*, Outside Task Forces, Johnson Library, 15 June, 1967.

Rabin, Jack. *Handbook of Public Personnel Administration*. New York: Marcel Dekker, 1995.

Redford, Emmette S., and Marlan Blissett. *Organizing the Executive Branch: The Johnson Presidency*. Chicago, IL: University of Chicago Press, 1981.

Rosenbloom, David H. "The Civil Service Commission's Decision to Authorize the Use of Goals and Timetables in the Federal Equal Employment Opportunity Program." *Western Political Quarterly* 26, no. 2 (1973): 236–251.

———. *Federal Service and the Constitution*. Washington, DC: Georgetown University Press, 2014.

Savas, Emmanuel. *Privatization and Public Private Partnership*. New York: Seven Bridges, 2000.

Savas, E. S., and Sigmund G. Ginsburg. "The Civil Service: A Meritless System?" *The Public Interest* 32 (1973): 70–85.

Schick, Allen. "The Trauma of Politics: Public Administration in the Sixties." In *American Public Administration: Past, Present and Future*, edited by Frederick C. Mosher, 142–180. Tuscaloosa: University of Alabama Press, 1975.

Schultz, David A., and Robert Maranto. *The Politics of Civil Service Reform*. New York: Peter Lang, 1998.

Simon, Herbert. *Administrative Behavior*. New York: Macmillan, 1976.

Stigler, George J. "The Theory of Economic Regulation." *Bell Journal of Economics and Management Science* 2 (1971): 3–21.

Subcommittee on Manpower and Civil Service of the Committee on Post Office and Civil Service. *Final Report on Violations and Abuses of Merit Principles in Federal Employment*. Washington, DC: Government Printing Office, 1976.

Thompson, Vincent A. *Without Sympathy or Enthusiasm: The Problem of Administrative Compassion*. Tuscaloosa: University of Alabama Press, 1979.

U.S. Congress, House Committee on Government Operations, *Reorganization of Executive Departments*. Hearings, 92nd Congress, 1st session. Washington, DC: Government Printing Office, 1971.

U.S. National Goals Research Staff. *Toward Balanced Growth: Quantity with Quality*. Washington, DC: US Government Printing Office, 1970.

U.S. Personnel Management Office. *Biography of an Ideal: A History of the Federal Civil Service*. Washington, DC: U.S. Civil Service Commission, 2012.

US Public Papers of President Richard M. Nixon. "Special Message to the Congress Requesting New Authority to Reorganize the Executive Branch." January 20, 1969.

U.S. Weekly Compilation of Presidential Documents, Vol. 5. April 14, 1969: 530–531.

Van Riper, Paul. *History of the United States Civil Service*, New York: Row, Peterson, and Co., 1958.

Vogel, David. "The New Social Regulation." In *Regulation in Perspective: Historical Essays*, edited by Thomas K. McCraw, 155–185. Cambridge, MA: Harvard University Press, 1981.

———. "The Public Interest Movement and the American Reform Tradition." *Political Science Quarterly* 95, no. 4 (1981): 607–627.

Waldo, Dwight. *The Administrative State*. New York: Ronald Press, 1948.

———. "Public Administration in a Time of Revolution." In *Classics of Public Administration*, edited by Jay M. Shafritz, 310–317. Oak Park, IL: Moore Publishing, 1978.

Weaver, Paul H. "Regulation, Social Policy and Class Conflict." *Public Interest* 50 (1978): 45–63.

White House Central Files, Box 43, Johnson Library, 15 December, 1966.

Wilson, James Q. *The Politics of Regulation*. New York: Basic Books, 1980.

Wolin, Sheldon. *Politics and Vision. Continuity and Innovation in Western Political Thought*. Princeton: Princeton University Press, 1960.

5

TOWARD THE NEO-MANAGERIAL AGE

Entering a New Era

In the aftermath of Nixon's effort to centralize control of the bureaucracy in the White House, Congress reasserted its influence over the executive branch. As the economic woes of the 1970s caused many people to focus on the price of regulation, Congress cooperated in an unprecedented campaign to deregulate many of the nation's major industries. The election of a markedly conservative president in 1980 suggested that the 1970s deregulation movement might turn into a wholesale dismantling of the twentieth-century welfare state. Congress reasserted its powers in a variety of ways. Its 1973 War Powers Act attempted to impose a "legislative veto" on the power to declare war that it had effectively delegated to the president. The Independent Counsel Act tried to provide for an outside prosecutor to deal with cases where the Constitution's executive branch law enforcers were themselves suspected of violating the law. Another important innovation was the Budget Control Act of 1974. The act prohibited the "impoundment" of appropriations that Nixon had imposed, and it established a Congressional Budget Office as a legislative counterpart to the White House's Office of Management and Budget. Above all, it adopted "baseline" budgeting, with automatic increases in spending based on inflation and population growth, which helped to lock in earlier bureaucratic expansions.[1]

In terms of public policy, the most remarkable development of the late 1970s was the dismantling of major parts of the New Deal economic regulation of large industries, such as railroads, trucking, airlines, and telecommunications. The social science literature of the period emphasized the entrenched power of the "iron triangles," composed of congressional committees, industry lobbyists, and captured bureaucrats, that guarded these cartels. With benefits concentrated among a small number of interests and costs diffused among the general population, these private interests were supposed to be all but immune to majoritarian politics. By the end of the decade, however, these industries were opened to competition at the expense of organized and concentrated insider-beneficiaries and to the benefit of diffuse consumer-outsiders. The economic malaise of the 1970s fed the deregulation movement. This was the only decade other than the 1930s that left Americans poorer than when the decade began. This situation contributed to ending the dominant postwar paradigm of Keynesianism. Indeed, after World War II, Americans came to accept that Keynesian economists had figured out the business cycle and could provide full employment and stable prices by fiscal and monetary "fine tuning." This view was put in crisis by rising "stagflation"—the combination of high unemployment levels, stagnant consumer demand, and inflation. Economists challenging Keynesianism demonstrated that regulation contributed to stagflation. The "monetarists", led by Nobel Prize winner Milton Friedman, explained that inept regulation of the money supply by the Federal Reserve was the main explanation of the economic chaos. Regulations acted like taxes and business could only pay these taxes by raising prices or reducing employment, the latter especially when productivity growth was low or negative. Regulation had long been promoted as a corrective to "market failure." Inflation was so clearly a "government failure," however, that deregulatory ideas gained credibility.[2]

In conclusion, many factors concurred to a changed perception in the 1970s. Watergate and its aftermath caused many Americans to reconsider the role of government, as well as its size. The enormous growth and concomitant cost of many programs developed in the 1960s disappointed elected officials and citizens alike. Declining economic conditions forced reconsideration of citizens' ability to tolerate slack in the system and the inefficiencies it implied. Frustration was widespread, but both solutions and problems were somewhat uncleared. Many looked for a scapegoat and they found it in the bureaucracy. The National Journal began an article about administrative reform this way:

> Bureaucrats. If you are not one of them, you probably can't stand them. You figure that they are lazy and overpaid, that they arrive at work late and leave early and take long lunch hours. But you can't do anything about it, because it's impossibile to fire a bureaucrat.[3]

In this political and cultural context, Jimmy Carter had won the presidency in 1976 running as an "outsider" and had overseen the first significant revision of the administrative state. The election of Ronald Reagan in 1980 was even more of a challenge to administrative government, because he capitalized on the theme that government was the problem, not the solution. A new era was beginning, and the federal civil service would be consistently affected by this ideological and political shift.

Reorganizing the Executive Branch: Jimmy Carter's Project

In contrast to his predecessors, Jimmy Carter, elected president in 1976, quickly showed his strong interest in reorganizing the executive branch. He aimed to obtain Congressional renewal of his power of reorganization, with the purpose—already stated in his electoral campaign—of putting in order the "horrible bureaucratic mess" into which the federal administration had been transformed: this would be accomplished through the president's being delegated more extended capacities of reorganization. As a candidate, he had affirmed that were he to win the election, the new Carter administration would "give top priority to a drastic and thorough revision of the federal bureaucracy."[4]

The new chief of the White House had included administrative reform among the points of his platform, and a group had been formed within his transition staff for the planning and reorganization of the executive branch. Their directives would be implemented by Carter, once his term of office actually started. President Carter personally considered reorganization as part of an exercise to cleanse Washington of its corruptions. Structural reform was viewed by the new president not as one of the many possible tools for addressing the idiosyncratic problems of departments and agencies. Rather, reform was considered as the lynchpin of the new administration's reorganization package: already during the transition period, the Office for Management and Budget (OMB) and the White House cast about for "problems" that structural change could address.[5]

As we have seen, the evolution of theories of the private enterprise economy and social organization had brought 1960s and 1970s experts of administration to seek an alternative to the managerial presidency that was forged in the Roosevelt years.[6]

The old paradigm of the scientific management therefore seemed incapable of assuring impartiality and efficiency, since lobbying practices allowed a few regulated parties to heavily influence the regulators (interests capturing); and, at the same time, the federal government had grown too much in its interference in national economy, burdening the private sector with excessively high taxation. Trust in professional bureaucracy and its designated rules was eroding, and this trend left space for accusations of corruption and favoritism.[7]

To address these problems of political legitimacy, a new sense of morality in public administration was needed. The president wrote in 1977, "Nowhere in the Constitution.... or the Declaration of Independence.... or the Emancipation Proclamation, or the Old Testament or the New Testament do you find the words 'economy' or 'efficiency.' Not that these two words are unimportant. But you do discover other words like honesty, integrity, fairness, liberty, justice, courage, patriotism, compassion, love—and many others which describe what a human being ought to be. These are also the same words which describe what a government of human beings ought to be."[8]

In 1977 Carter set up a group within the OMB for the reorganization of the executive branch. The choice of the OMB was not a random one, since it put reform plans under the supervision of the president. Carter claimed that he wished to maintain a gradual approach to reorganization, and that his mission was not, as had been the case in the past, the strengthening of executive authority, so much as the ways with which the government operated. Despite this rhetoric, however, the recommendations of his Presidential Reorganization Project (PRP) turned out to be very similar to those of the commissions and task forces that had preceded it.

Carter named a new director of the OMB, Bert Lance, whose mission was to pursue a new project called the PRP. The administrative philosophy of this reorganizational project was more pragmatic than its precedents, focused more on the facts rather than the principles expressed by administrative theories. The vice director of the OMB John White declared, "Reorganizations should proceed from problems which had been identified towards solutions rather than from preconceived notions of idealized structure."[9]

This approach connected with the changes that were developing in the private sector. American capitalism was launching itself toward a new phase, based on innovation of industrial processes, and more large-scale competition. The old top-down structures were perceived as no longer satisfactory for an expanding market that demanded increased flexibility and adaptation. Evidence of these changes had already appeared during the Truman presidency, when Charles W. Wilson, President of the General Electric Company and formerly Vice-President of the War Production Board during World War II, had put in doubt, in a Senate hearing on the consolidation of the Armed Forces, the theorem that centralization would produce greater efficiency. Companies like General Electric were successful precisely because they had decentralized decision-making through diverse managerial divisions "that were coordinated, not controlled by the 'top man'."[10] Furthermore, research in the field of corporate organization demonstrated that the hierarchical theory was unsatisfactory for describing the way in which organizations actually functioned, and on this basis experts progressively moved toward the study of human relations, developing new theories.[11]

According to Carter's team, the process of administrative reform should evolve from a top-down to a bottom-up model. Operationally, the reform program was a solid one. Forty new external advisors were hired, and the OMB's own budget grew by over two million dollars, which were spent on employing 32 new civil servants.[12] The PRP, in contrast to almost every other initiative for the reorganization of executive power, did not produce a final comprehensive report on all its recommendations. The two key elements of the project were, on the one hand, the drastic reduction of the number of administrative agencies—to be accomplished, however, in a gradual way—and, on the other hand, the reorganization of the federal departments. In particular, the proposal was made for the creation of a Department of Energy, with the aim of centralizing in a single structure all the policies pertaining to a sector of such vital importance for the geopolitical role of the United States. The project also proposed detaching the purview of instruction from the Department of Health, Education, and Welfare, for the sake of creating a Department of Education, precisely to underline the Carter administration's political commitment to this issue. Ten reorganization plans were sent to Congress, all of which were accepted by the legislative body. Among the most important results were the reorganization of the Executive Office, the reduction of its structural components, the creation of an inspectorate for the extraction of petroleum in Alaska, the creation of the two new departments mentioned above, and the centralization of the management of emergencies in the Federal Emergency Management Agency.[13]

As had been unsuccessfully tried by the Johnson and Nixon presidencies, the project envisioned the creation of super-departments tied to the presidential Cabinet, and Carter sought to implicitly create these new departments under his reorganizational authority, re-naming and eliminating the old offices. At the same time, Congress opposed the attempt to evade the limits imposed on the president's reorganizational powers, which disallowed the possibility of installing new ministries without legislative approval. Therefore, despite the power granted to the president by the Reorganization Act, Congress prohibited him from proceeding with such ample changes, without specific parliamentary authorization.

In fact, notwithstanding Carter's declared intents, the Reorganization Act of 1977 did not arrange for significant expansion of presidential authority: the legislative veto was maintained, and there was the rejection of giving the president the possibility of instituting or abolishing not only departments but also agencies. In addition, he was constrained to specify, in his own plans of reorganization, estimates of eventual increases in public spending. Carter's success was thus only a partial one. Among the positive results for the president was the definitive concession of the possibility to submit to Congress's attention a maximum of three reorganizational plans at the same time.[14]

The president succeeded in making forward progress on other fronts as well. For example, he instituted the Department of Energy in 1977 and that of Education in 1979. Moreover, Congress supported the president's initiatives to reduce the size of the Executive Office, consolidate the separation of functions of federal officials, centralize the management of emergencies in the Federal Emergency Management Agency, and redistribute the functions of the Civil Service Commission across two different organizations.[15]

Carter's successes derived from the realism of his political strategy, since the White House never underestimated Congress's lack of will for radical change in the reorganization of the executive branch, something which legislative power had never fully tolerated. Not by chance did the Reorganization Act of 1977 pass through Congress and confer upon the president powers to emend reorganization plans: it was sent through the House and the Senate only after the polling of the opinions of congressional committees and the same governmental agencies. The president's strategy of consultation about the reforms with other institutional players had worked well.

Carter was probably the first president of the post-Roosevelt era who did not seek to reorganize the executive branch in order to facilitate the presidency's management of administrative agencies or exclusively to reach his own policy objectives. With realism, and by applying "de-politicized" and more technical solutions, he sought to simplify government and to improve performance following.

The Civil Service Reform Act of 1978: A Dividing Line between Past and Future

Whereas the direction of civil service reforms under discussion prior to 1978 had been toward establishing more regulations and rules to insulate the federal civil service from political interference, Alan K. Campbell, the newly appointed Chairman of Civil Service Commission, declared that the real problem was quite the opposite of the apparent one—more rules were not needed to separate politics from administration. Indeed, what was needed was to make the meritocratic civil service more responsive to the president's executive direction and leadership. The general direction on the civil service reform which emerged with Carter's presidency was to free managers from excessive restrictions ("let managers manage"), to make managers more accountable to the political leadership, and to give them incentives to be responsive. At the same time, the reformers hoped to insert the concepts and the machinery of modern performance management throughout all the layers of the civil service.

These lines of reform emerged with particular clarity with the reform of the Civil Service in 1978. In 1977 the president had launched a research commission composed of political appointees, career bureaucrats, experts, and academicians to reform federal bureaucracy. Basing its work primarily on the ideas of the Hoover Commission of the Truman epoch, the commission translated its own proposals of reform into the Civil Service Reform Act of 1978.

The new legislation aimed to reinforce the president's control over policymaking, and it sought to do so by creating a new class of professional bureaucrats who would be dedicated more to the study and formulation of policies than to pure administration. These new civil servants would operate directly under the political control of the president, who would acquire increased agility in his enhanced guidance of the entire federal bureaucratic apparatus. Although this might appear to be a reform giving further strength to presidential power, in reality the 1978 Act seems to have altered the relationship between politics and administration in the other direction. In fact, it increased the influence of high-level administrators in public policy-making, while it favored a decline of presidential power.

There was also, however, an exchange: if on the one hand the political voice of the bureaucracy grew more resonant and influential, on the other hand there was a rise in the number of political appointees and in the power of the presidency to manage bureaucratic careers.

For example, awards incentives based on performance results were systematically introduced into the highest levels of the civil service. An elite section of the Senior Executive Service (SES) was also created. This entity was composed of the three highest levels (GS-16, GS-17, GS-18) of the federal administration, and their functions were more fully personalized according to the capacities and responsibilities of the involved individuals, with respect to the rest of the federal civil service. Furthermore, these high-ranking bureaucrats could more readily take a year's sabbatical, for the purpose of training, and enjoyed increased opportunities for the advancement of their careers.

These top civil servants would be all the more occupied with policy-making, that is, with research and evaluations for presentation to political officials and much less with delivery or the practical implementation of the input provided by political decisions.[16] This process was designed to make the chain of command between the president and the executive branch more fluid, with the creation of intermediaries between the political and administrative levels. Experience had in fact shown that faced with the political resistances of Congress and those of the bureaucracy, especially regarding slight or absent implementation, the presidents' reforms risked getting bogged down in administrative terrain. For this reason, an élite administrative corps was established, which on the one hand had the task of providing the president with calculations of what was possible and on the other hand had that of spurring the civil service to translate political impulses into practice. Thus, the Senior Executive Civil Service was born as an institution of mediation between the White House and governmental machinery.[17]

Reorganizing the Federal Bureaucracy

With the Reorganization Plan No. 1 of 1978 the administration took the entire matter of equal employment opportunity out of the Civil Service Commission and transferred to the Equal Employment Opportunity Commission.[18] The commission and the new Merit System Protection Board (MSPB) would share responsibility for acting on discrimination appeals from federal employees. The operational responsibility for equal employment opportunity in the federal civil service moved to the Equal Employment Opportunity Commission and out of the hands of the central personnel office of the government.

Then, with the Reorganization Plan No. 2 of 1978, the Civil Service Commission was abolished, 96 years after the Pendleton Act and after having created and implemented successfully a merit-based civil service, and it was divided into two organs: the MSPB, which was assigned to the two functions of protecting career bureaucrats from politically nominated ones and adjudicating appeals from federal employees on all matters affecting their employment,[19] and the Office of Personnel Management (OPM), which served as the agency for the government's personnel. In addition, the law codified collective bargaining, created the Federal Labor Relations Authority (FLRA) to supervise programs concerning industrial relations in the public sector, increased research into occupational trends in the public sector and into the implementation of the reform, bolstered protection for government whistleblowers,[20] and directed the OPM to design a system of evaluating performance, in order to determine the awarding of income bonuses.[21]

This final point posed some problems of implementation, and in fact the polls taken during the following years among members of the SES showed how high-level bureaucrats were favorable to performance evaluations for lower-level employees, but denounced their politically appointed superiors, since the latter did not seriously respect the new evaluation system, or they changed their posts too rapidly to understand it in full.

Senior executives, moreover, paid for the flexibility and prestige of their new postings with an increased mobility. Job assignments were made by top-level political appointees, and this meant that a high-ranking bureaucrat could be moved from one function or department to another in the administration whenever a new president took office. The law prescribed a total of 120 days from the installation of the new president before new postings were to be started, but often this waiting period was bypassed through "voluntary" transfers.[22]

In effect, that system of the SES was a mix of a spoils and a merit system: though they might have long careers distinguished by multiple promotions, professional bureaucrats, once they reached the level of the SES, did not remain secure in their administrative positions and instead could be moved from one department or function to another by sheer political *fiat*. This meant that the ideological and political orientations of a senior executive could determine his or her potential rise to high-ranking positions according to the president in charge.

Not all positions within the SES were entrusted to professional bureaucrats, since 10% of the total number of posts and 25% of those inside each administrative unit were reserved for political appointees. This system weakened the merit system. For example, it was not mandatory that all positions reserved for professional bureaucrats would have a current occupant, and this permitted the practice of reserving the chief posts of some structures, like the agencies, exclusively for political appointees.

Performance Management and Merit Pay System

The Civil Service Reform Act 1978 required agencies to develop performance appraisal systems for their SES managers, apart from the systems for other employees. They were to base performance criteria on both the individual performance of the executive and the organizational performance of the program the executive headed. Under the act, senior executives could lose their executive status for less than fully successful performance. To balance these "high-risk" features of the SES, the act authorized some "high-rewards" features: a set of impressive compensation incentives in the form of high base pay and a series of performance awards. The awards included the possibility of substantial annual bonuses, plus selection for the ranks of "Meritorious Executive" (with a one-time award of 10,000 dollars) or "Distinguished Executive" (with a one-time award of 20,000 dollars) granted by the president.

The act established a merit pay system for the lower ranks, and it provided similar performance-based incentives to managers, supervisors, and management officials throughout the General Schedule at the organizational levels next below the SES (grades GS-13, GS-14, and GS-15). The law abolished the ten steps in those grades for managers and supervisors, and it provided them funds from which, in addition to their base pay, they could receive annual merit pay increases based on the level of performance of the individual and the organizational unit in meeting the goals and objectives of the department or agency. Moreover, the act provided for cash awards of up to 25,000 dollars or more with the president's approval to any civil servants who provided suggestions, inventions, superior accomplishments, or improvements for governmental operations, or who performed special acts or services.[23]

For the civil servants of the lower grades, the act repealed the government-wide performance rating system that had become a routine exercise for managers and employees every year, but without impact on career steps. In its place, the law assigned to agencies and departments the task to build a new performance appraisal system for all their employees. The results of the appraisals each year would be used specifically as the basis for personnel actions affecting the employee: to recognize and reward employees whose performance warranted it, to identify and assist employees whose performance fell short of goals, and to reassign, move, or remove civil servants who continued to show unacceptable performance.[24]

By these provisions, the reformers intended to instill throughout government the values of performance appraisal and responsiveness to managerial directions. One of the main characteristics of the neo-managerial wave of the late 1970s was based on the view that individuals and organizations could achieve more efficiency and effectiveness introducing a business-like performance evaluation. The idea of a performance-focused management system remained resilient through the next decades, becoming a lynchpin of the New Public Management (NPM).

Bureaucratic Representativeness

Another element that emerged in the 1970s was the debate on the representative status of bureaucracy. In this case, there also was present a cyclical aspect that had already emerged in the Jacksonian epoch and that returned with the request to make administrators more representative of the people they had been called to serve. During World War II, the federal civil service became much more socially diverse, opening itself to female and African American workers. Still, the Executive Order 11246 on equal opportunity issued by Roosevelt applied only to the private sector in its relations with the public sector—the provider of services—and to the armed forces, where the segregation of African Americans was abolished. The legislation had left out the federal bureaucracy, and in the 1960s there began the academic and political movements, especially on the part of the New Public Administration to make administration more socially representative.

In 1974 an amendment to the law on discrimination made it illegal for the government to discriminate against those citizens between 40 and 65 years of age who were applying for publicly available employment. In 1972, instead, the Equal Employment Opportunity Act had extended to the administration and to government agencies Title VII of the 1964 Civil Rights Act, which prohibited discrimination based on race, color, creed, sex, and national or ethnic origin. The legislation was implemented by the Civil Service Commission, which enjoined agencies and departments to draft plans for guaranteeing equal opportunity to all those who competed to enter the ranks of public service.

These reforms were also based on data relative to competitive selections and the principle of merit. In the 1960s, in fact, most of these selections hinged upon highly standardized tests, such as the PACE test, which was used to recruit over 100 positions at various levels in the federal administration. In 1978 the test was taken by over 135,000 people. The results indicated that 58% of whites succeeded in passing the exam, while among blacks this figure decreased to 12%.[25] The PACE test was put on trial, accused of racial discrimination, and the plaintiffs won their case with full juridical support. On the basis of this evidence, the Carter administration decided to do away with the test, elaborating different screening procedures and hiring African Americans and Hispanics on the basis of proportionality with the overall population. The Reagan administration was not initially enthusiastic about this system of minorities protection, but in the end chose not to change the new regulations.

During the same period, there intensified the pressures to guarantee equal opportunity to men and women in the federal civil service, at the levels of both careers and salaries. In numerical employment terms, this equality was gradually attained through the Carter, Reagan, and Bush presidencies.

This transformation of representative bureaucracy, achieved mainly through judicial measures, brought about a re-conceptualization of the principle of merit. In fact, until the early 1920s, the principle simply meant choosing the most qualified person for a position, without considering sex and ethnic background. From the 1960s and 1970s onward, the courts had challenged this principle, maintaining that equal representation for some groups was more important than the principle per se, and that this criterion needed to be recognized by recruiting and hiring procedures. Thus to meritocratic selection were added other criteria designed to construct social representation through application of the law and to protect minorities through ad hoc norms that guaranteed quotas of representation.[26]

The 1978 Civil Service Reform Act restated commitment to affirmative action principles and to the need for more women and minorities in the career federal civil service.[27] Veterans' preference was reduced and this increased opportunities for these groups, which enjoyed additional provisions for increased recruiting.[28]

Labor Relations and Ethics: A New Approach

Progress was also made on the labor unions front. As noted above, Kennedy was the first president to recognize unions for the federal bureaucracy, while Nixon regularized collective negotiation and created the Federal Labor Relations Council to mediate judicial disputes regarding labor. Unionization grew during the 1960s and 1970s, and by 1980 86% of blue-collar workers, and 54% of white-collar workers were members of unions, which represented 1.2 million workers and more than 61% of federal government employees.[29]

The 1978 reform of the civil service contributed to modifying relations with the unions. The law codified how the executive orders of Kennedy and Nixon legally guaranteed collective negotiations, and it expanded the points which could be the object of agreements between the respective parties. Nonetheless, the level of salaries and the system of classification of the positions continued to exist outside the criteria of so-called collective bargaining, which did indeed include the rights of employees. In addition, the Federal Relations Council was transformed into the FLRA, a genuine agency with the power of judging disputes between the government and its dependents. The unions sought to use FLRA to expand the range of collective negotiation, but their efforts obtained mixed results under the Carter administration, and even fewer successes with Reagan, who appointed agency chiefs less inclined to make compromises with the union representatives.

The public sector unions also proved to be weaker than their private sector counterparts. The FLRA and the government had closed ranks, conceding very little to the unions in terms of rights, especially regarding the right to strike. Such rights remained subordinate to public interest or to the particular needs of government agencies, and Congress never renounced its own power to exert control over compensation and salaries, a fact which transformed the unions into a lobby prepared to pressurize the legislator in order to obtain enhanced juridical protections in the area of federal labor.

In addition to these changes, a separate piece of legislation, approved in 1977, established an Office of Government Ethics and made it responsible for promulgating and enforcing standards of ethical conduct in the federal civil service, particularly in the matter of financial disclosure and conflict of interest. The legislation made the Office of Ethics part of OPM at first, and later it became an independent agency.[30]

An Important Turning Point

In sum, the Civil Service Reform Act of 1978 and the attached legislation worked to resolve both the procedural and organizational problems behind much of the criticism of the civil service. It aimed to make performance of federal civil servants more important and easier to deal with, and it sought to sort out the various conflicting responsibilities of the Civil Service Commission by creating a number of new organizations focused on particular aspects of the civil service: equal employment opportunity, protection of the merit system, labor relations, ethics, and personnel management.

In conclusion, the Carter era can be considered a time of rupture, between the social reforms of the 1960s and the crisis of the early 1970s, and the rise of the new managerialism in the 1980s. Carter showed himself to be pragmatic at the administrative level: on the one hand he based his own reforms on the originally Weberian but then progressive idea of constructing a strong professional bureaucracy, and on the other hand he reinforced the presidency's holdover policies and administrative practices with the Federal Civil Service Act of 1978. Professional bureaucracy was strengthened by this process, with the creation of the élite corps of the SES, but at the same time the presidency succeeded in changing the dichotomy between politics and administration. Carter raised the level of top-level administrative control over policy, but he tempered it with the spoils system and with a system of less rigidity and more guarantees for the highest-ranking civil servants. At personnel management level, with the abolition of the Civil Service Commission, the Carter administration completed the transition from the predominance of the merit system to the one of presidential management. However, the basic elements of a merit system had become such a deeply established institution and the presidential management overlapped with these elements. The concept that the permanent workforce of any governmental unit be merit-based had rooted deeply into the core of American political culture. Nonetheless, in the late 1970s, the American society came definitely to defer to the wisdom of management, whether those senior managers were in the private or public sectors. Management should not have been a fallback choice, or, at least, it should not have provided an easy alibi to blame for failure someone or something else. There could be no blame game on the career civil servants when an elected chief executive failed. Eliminating the Civil Service Commission took away any such easy excuse for any future president.

Carter's approach thus seemed to be a gradual one, even if under the ashes of this transition there smoldered transformations that would explode and then be resolved in the course of the 1980s and 1990s. The federal administration continued to become more representative, through legal and jurisdictional care and protection of minorities, breaking with the orthodox interpretation of the principle of merit and introducing a new concept of public representation; the unions gained political and contractual power, eroding presidential control of bureaucracy; the courts progressively reduced the leverage powers of political patronage and removed the limitations on the political activity of civil servants. Moreover, Carter himself interpreted the electorate's deeply rooted feelings of distrust toward government and its bureaucracy; consequently, he promoted a new ethical approach to cleanse corruption problems and he directed harsh anti-statism toward the programs of the Great Society, which later would be exploited with great political profit by Ronald Reagan. At the beginning of the Reagan epoch, therefore, the tensions undergone by the federal administration had multiplied, and the solutions to these new conflicts would characterize the first term of the new Republican presidency.

"Government Is Not the Solution, but the Problem": The Neo-liberal Reforms of Ronald Reagan

Ronald Reagan ran as an outsider in the Republican presidential primaries, promoting an ideological program oriented toward challenging "big government," reducing fiscal pressure, and favoring the liberalization of the economy. In contrast to Carter, however, who showed a much more moderate vein once he had won the White House, Reagan remained an outsider even from within the Oval Office.

Reagan's campaign was anti-bureaucratic, contrary to government intervention in the economy and society, and profoundly adverse to Washington politico-administrative establishment. His victory can be considered the triumph of a neo-liberal brand of conservatism and the defeat of a certain kind of centrist, directional pragmatism that had permeated the 1960s and 1970s, and that had witnessed the profound involvement of the federal bureaucracy. The "ancient principles" of self-government, of individual liberty, and of free enterprise pervaded reaganite rhetoric and proposals, wrapped in the promise of new, vigorous economic growth and the defeat of socialism on the global scale.

Reagan's plans to reform bureaucracy were based on a simple idea: government had to cost less and become more efficient, by observing the private sector and importing from it managerial techniques for public administration.

This was an idea that, on the intellectual level, had already been ripening for a decade, as a response to the economic and political crisis of the 1970s, and which was now gaining affirmation in the practical world of politics.

The Grace Commission on Cost Control

In 1982 the president instituted the President's Private Sector Survey on Cost Control, directed by J. Peter Grace, formerly president and Chief Executive Officer (CEO) of W. R. Grace and Co. The Grace Commission was composed of 161 volunteer members who had worked in the private sector, that is, mainly as company managers. These individuals were called upon to evaluate administrative organization on the basis of "the techniques and experiences with which they had become familiar in their respective economic realities."[31]

The Grace Commission was entrusted with the power to inspect the operations of agencies and departments of the federal government, with the aim of finding areas where costs could be cut or where practices could be introduced that would render administrative activity more efficient. As the commission's report would state, "We welcomed the chance to bring to bear on the Executive Branch of Government our experience and expertise acquired in managing private sector business enterprises." It also affirmed that "the President charged the members to scrutinize the Government with the same careful attention that they might give to a potential acquisition of another company."[32]

Like the earlier Carter Project, the Grace Commission dismissed the idea that any general principles of organizational management were unique to the public sector or the federal government. Indeed, the commission rejected the peculiarities of the public sector altogether. The opening paragraph of the Grace Commission report stated,

> Most reports of presidential commissions begin with a lengthy introduction detailing the origins, premises, and methodologies of their studies before focusing on the results of the study. We are omitting such matters because we do not want to risk losing even one reader who would be turned away by having to wade through such preliminary material.[33]

The operating premise was that the government was poorly organized, mismanaged, and plagued by waste and abuse. In the early line of the report the commission argued, "it is with private sector management tenets in mind that the Grace Commission findings have been developed."[34] The dominant argument was that public and private sectors were alike in their essentials and should be analyzed with the same set of economic variables and managerial principles. Government should be organized like a large commercial corporation, with a structure permitting a top-down control. As is evident, the rhetoric of management and business pervaded the lexicon of the new administration. In both official rhetoric and policy-making, the commission was the explicit manifestation of the transpiration between the public and private sectors and of a new managerialism, which inherited from the early twentieth century a rationalism centered on efficiency, mixing it with the neo-liberal objective of dismantling the entrepreneurial American State and contracting out public services.

"For decades," the report continued, "the federal government has not managed its programs with the same eye to innovation, productivity, and economy that is dictated by private sector profit and loss statements and balance sheets."[35] According to the Grace Commission, the logic of marketing discipline would bring long-term benefits to the public sector.

> The members of the President's Private Sector Survey on Cost Control (PPSS) believe that the disciplines necessary for survival and success in the private arena must be introduced into Government to a far greater degree than previously has been the case. It is that belief which motivated the PPSS effort. A government which cannot efficiently manage the people's business will ultimately fail its citizenry by failing the same inescapable test which disciplines the private sector: those of the competitive marketplace and of the balance sheet.[36]

The commission recognized, however, that

> the public sector performs roles which have no counterpart in the business community or, indeed, anywhere in the private sector... The Survey, therefore, focused much of its attention on those critical factors which have a comparable impact upon both the management of Government and the management of the private sector[37]

such as the administration of human resources and financial management.

The commission also sought to improve supervision of governmental accounts. Its members wrote 47 reports, containing 2,478 recommendations for eliminating wasteful practices in 784 areas of the federal government. In a letter to Reagan, the Grace Commission claimed to have obtained savings of up to 424 billion dollars in three years, rising to 1.9 trillion dollars per year, by the year 2000.[38] The political line was that of cutting costs, instead of raising taxes, and the report specified that

> the need for a major undertaking to reduce government spending is widely perceived, as witnessed by the public's present concern that budget deficits are out of control and are expected to run at about 200 billion dollars a year indefinitely.[39]

The commission argued that "the federal government has significant deficiencies from managerial and operating perspectives, resulting in hundreds of billions of dollars of needless expenditures that taxpayers have to bear each year." It continued:

> It is, admittedly, a staggering task to manage an organization whose size dwarfs even the largest private sector corporations. Still, the federal government is also an organization with human and financial resources of gigantic dimensions, and it would appear that one administration after another has simply not been as effective as it should have been in productively employing those resources.[40]

In addition, the commission targeted the duplication of functions in the Departments of Agriculture, of Commerce, and of the Defense. It overcame problems of management in some agencies by having recourse to private business practices, and it plumbed even deeper by analyzing the financial management of the units, the use of paper, the costs of communication, and the benefits of federal employees. It determined that there was excessive centralization of financial resources and their control. As a final point, it recommended cost-cutting measures, as well as steps for the improvement of management, through the institution of an Office of Federal Management within the Executive Office, to have a government-wide responsibility for establishing, modernizing, and monitoring management systems.[41]

Reagan accepted many of the recommendations of the commission, but Congress, requested to vote on most of them, did not give its approval.[42] An analyst concluded, "the overwhelming number of the commission's recommendations were ill-founded, and many of the savings estimates were groundless."[43] In substance, the report was used more for political propaganda than for concrete reforms, since the commission's report gave the president numerous examples with which to attack "big government."

Finally, Reagan sought to reorganize the government by using the classic instrument of congressional authorization. He attempted to revise and extend the powers of the Reorganization Act of 1977, first in 1981, when the legislative proposal was not approved by the House of Representatives.[44] The president tried again three years later, but Congress definitively shifted the equilibrium of power in its own favor: instead of giving consent to the automatic enactment of the presidential plan in absence of a legislative veto, the 1984 amendment imposed the obligation of a resolution of common approval on the part of both congressional chambers and extended the Reorganization Authority only until December 31 of the same year.[45] In other words, Reagan had had only a few months to reform the agencies and departments of the executive branch, but he did not succeed in using them to full advantage for getting approval of his plans of reorganization. After the 1984 legislation, little advantage remained in the reorganization plan process because the procedure had become too cumbersome. In short, it was easier to simply follow the regular legislative process. None of the following presidents requested the reintroduction of the reorganization plan authority.[46]

Political Appointments and the Reform of the Federal Bureaucracy: Pushing the 1978 CSRA to the Limit

Also important was the impact of Reagan's administration on the federal civil service. As has been seen, the landslide victory of 1980 was made possible not only by the communicative abilities of the Republican leader but also by a message of a radical contesting of the state's role in the economy, and of its bureaucratic apparatus. The conservative think-tank called the Heritage Foundation played an especially influential role: in the same year, it had mapped out a project for administrative reform, entitled "Mandate for Leadership," centered on the idea of a sweeping change at the top levels of administration, and an expansion of the spoils system, with the aim of realizing the massive package of reforms promised by Reagan.[47] Many of the authors of the report prepared themselves to obtain postings at the head of administrative agencies, making the Heritage Foundation's role especially important both for planning policy and for informing the presidential staff. The transition was the fastest, most efficient, and best planned in American history, since in fact it was prepared six months before the elections. For example, Pendleton James, future personnel director at the White House, travelled for nine months across the entire country, meeting potential candidates for the presidential appointments and reporting the results to Edwin Meese, chief of staff of Ronald Reagan's electoral campaign.[48]

Moreover, the reaganites were well aware of the difficulties encountered, especially by the three previous presidents, when presidential reforms were to be implemented. The fundamental *nuclei* of the most important policies called for being realized immediately, while the opposition was not yet fully organized, and the presidential approval rating high. For this reason, the government focused primarily on economic matters, because reaching rapid results with the budget, in terms of both cuts and the redistribution of resources meant being able to continue working on the administrative implementation of these. The legislation of economic questions, in short, was the main vehicle for the realization of the political program of Ronald Reagan's first term of office.

Together with this strategy, a parallel one was developed for political appointments. In contrast to Carter's approach, the new president's team borrowed a checking technique from Eisenhower's and Nixon's experiences with bureaucratic appointments. First, whoever was nominated to an executive post had to be attentively examined, and then pass an ideological loyalty test, to respect the president's plans. As Henry Salvatori, a long-time member of the

Reagan Cabinet, underlined, "The three principal criteria were: first, was he a Reagan man? Second, was he Republican? And finally, was he a conservative? Probably our principal concern was that conservative ideology would be appropriately represented."[49]

The adhesion to the conservative project and the capacity for teamwork were applied on a vast scale and extended even to low-level appointments, on which little media attention was focused, but which proved to be fundamental for the implementation of policies. In the past, once it had been formed, the Presidential Cabinet was left a certain autonomy, and its members could arrange for the appointing of subcabinet members, and of still lower-ranking functionaries. This time, instead, the president's closest advisers, appointed at the top levels of the administration, continued to control the process of nomination and to exercise veto power over all available nominees. The mantra of the new staff became "policy is people," meaning that Reaganism was not possible without the reaganites themselves. The nominating process was expanded through a multiplicity of interviews, tests, and declarations, becoming so long and intricate that some candidates were discouraged to participate. One federal observer described the selection process that lasted several weeks as a "zoo" with a continual turnover of examiners and little or no certainty about the duration.[50]

It might seem that a stronger form of the old-style spoils system came back with Reagan, in order to achieve a better control over the federal bureaucracy particularly in terms of policy implementation. In reality, the only available statistical study shows an increment of a mere 5% between 1978 and 1987 of political appointees, most of which were made during Carter's term in office.[51] "Responsive competence" was language that came into fashion during the Reagan administration to replace the ideal of "neutral competence." However, this is probably the most remarkable element on Reagan's personnel management strategy; the idea of responsiveness was not intended to mean responsiveness to those in Congress or even in the courts. The intent was for bureaucracy to be more responsive to the White House and its key appointees.

In this context, as had been anticipated, Reagan did not reject the idea of centralizing decisions, and of reinforcing the presidency. This happened through a dispassionate as well as biased use of the 1978 Civil Service Reform Act, and especially of the option to transfer professional bureaucrats from one position to another. The reaganites were convinced that the rotation of assignments for career senior civil servants was fundamental for avoiding the risk that the reforms might be obstructed by employees who had spent years in a particular sector of public administration.[52] Very often the transfers became "voluntary," that is, pressure was exerted on the individual in question, who would be promptly transferred, to speed up the process with respect to the 120 days of transition prescribed by the law. A letter by the *Government Accountability*

Office (GAO) confirmed how, among hundreds of transfers, the overwhelming majority were "voluntary," as a result of this governmental strategy.[53]

It also often happened that when a high-level career bureaucrat was removed from office, the place would be taken by a political appointee, and this enabled Reagan to have politically loyal men in positions considered to be key ones for the administration. The CSRA also permitted "playing" with promotions and compensations, and in fact the Reagan administration, remaining within legal boundaries, pushed for career advancements and prizes for senior executives who aligned themselves with presidential policy and for politically appointed officials, while those who resisted were penalized in their careers or neutralized through transfers.

These strategies of bureaucratic management on Reagan's part raised questions among experts on administration. Huddleston, for example, maintained that

> while the operation of the SES has remained, to date, within the bounds of the law, the provisions of the CSRA have so expanded the managerial prerogative as to raise reasonable doubts about the long-term stability of the balance between the responsiveness and neutrality of the civil.[54]

A 1984 report of the MSPB indicated that more than 50% of the members of the SES felt themselves exposed to the arbitrary action of politics, and more than 40% believed that the system was not free from undue political influence.[55] The general impression was that career bureaucrats felt themselves to be less secure and protected than in previous administrations.

Cutting Federal Administration Manpower: The Reduction in Force and the OMB's Role

To this situation were added the budget cuts of President Reagan's first years in office. As noted above, the conservative rhetoric of the period considered government to be part of the problem, and not the solution, and for this reason, the block of turnovers in the federal administration was the first act of the presidency.

Next, the first substantial reduction (reduction in force) of public employees since the time of Eisenhower was launched between 1981 and 1982. The Reduction in Force (RIF) implied that several high-ranking functionaries would be transferred or demoted to lower administrative levels to compensate for the lack of assumptions of new employees. In other words, even while maintaining the same salaries and benefits, professional bureaucrats were asked to cover gaps opened by retirements, and consequently to occupy different positions than the ones they originally held. During the Reagan years, around 30,000 civil servants were subjected to RIF, mainly in the agencies and in the OPM.[56]

On the purely occupational level, however, in 1982 there were 2,777,000 employees, instead of the 2,821,000 two years before. Only in 1984 did the number of federal employees return to the levels of 1980, and this recovery depended most of all on the increase in the number of workers in the Departments of State and of the Defense, while employees in other agencies and departments remained fewer in number than in previous years. The most sweeping cuts, according to the data released in 1987, were in the fields of education, construction, commerce, and labor.[57]

The president's rhetoric focused especially on the elimination of waste, administrative abuses, and federal government corruption. To reach this objective, various techniques were combined. In the first place, Reagan transformed the OMB into the political arm of the president on administration. Under David Stockman, the first director of the OMB during the Reagan era, the agency was strengthened and given powers of controlling the regulations of other agencies to limit the proliferations of bureaucratic procedures and to ensure a positive rapport between costs and benefits of the undertaken administrative initiatives.

This policy was supported also at the legislative level, with the approval of the Paperwork Reduction Act of 1980, to cut regulation and, with the issuing of an executive order, to make obligatory cost-benefit analyses of laws and regulations.[58] This was probably Reagan's most important step to control the bureaucracy involving executive orders that required agencies to perform "cost-benefit analyses" of new rules and to clear them with the OMB, particularly its Office of Information and Regulatory Affairs (OIRA). The OMB used both mechanisms to monitor the operations of the agencies and to realize the objectives of the White House, namely, the reduction of social expenditures and regulatory power, the promotion of liberalization policies, and the introduction of market mechanisms in the public sector.[59]

The Centralization of Performance Management

At the beginning of the Reagan presidency, budget problems undermined the application of the merit pay system established by Carter in 1978 and severely constrained the funds available for distribution. Meanwhile, many merit pay civil servants who had spent their careers under the one-size-fits-all General Schedule believed the merit pay system's highly decentralized approach introduced the risk of inequalities across different government's agencies and departments. As the disenchantment among merit pay employees grew, a new legislation was enacted to address the perceived problems.

In 1984, Congress passed legislation that created the Performance Management and Recognition System (PMRS) to replace the merit pay system.[60] PMRS established a government-wide pay structure, based on an employee's performance appraisal but more closely in line with the pay progression of the

General Schedule. Using annual merit increases instead of the General Schedule's within-grade step increases, PMRS could deliver higher compensation sooner.[61] Moreover, PMRS retained the lump-sum bonus features of the merit pay system but established government-wide funding and payout requirements. A distinctive feature of the PMRS was a centralized performance appraisal system that standardized the number of performance levels and how appraisals would operate. The pendulum had clearly swung back to a highly centralized approach to pay-for-performance for managers. In addition, OPM extended this re-centralization when it revised the government-wide regulations for appraising all non-senior executive servants and it established a uniform approach based on the statutory PMRS.[62] The creation of PMRS is notable for putting "performance management"—which meant performance planning and assessment for financial recognition—firmly in place. It corrected and, at the same time, consolidated the managerial rhetoric and business-like practices set up at the end of the 1970s.

Minorities and Unions

In addition, President Reagan did not pursue policies of integrating minorities aimed at reserving for them a certain number of positions, in order to raise their proportional percentage in the composition of employed staffs. Nonetheless, the Republicans did not reverse the trend of such policies and did not cancel preceding legislation, but refused to enact further development in this area. At the same time, the number of white male employees in the federal administration decreased from 50.2% to 41.8% between 1976 and 1986, the number of men and women workers became equal, 16% of the workforce was African American, and 9% represented other minorities.[63]

All this notwithstanding, the distribution of posts remained unequal, given that high-level positions continued to be occupied by aging white males, because no incentives were made for the promotion of women and minorities in the top branches of the administration.

The president's approach with the unions also differed from that of his predecessors. Thanks to the spoils system established by the Civil Service Act of 1978, Reagan succeeded in placing his own loyal followers within the agencies concerned with industrial relations between the government and its employees, such as the FLRA and the MSPB. The most dramatic conflict with the unions occurred at the dawn of the Reagan epoch, in 1981, when there exploded the protest of PATCO, the association that united the flight controllers' unions. At the start of negotiations, the Carter administration had promised these unions a reduction in working hours and an improvement of conditions, especially for those who worked in the international and busiest airports.[64] The Reagan administration put a freeze on negotiations to pursue its policy of public spending reductions and the downscaling of union power. In part, the impasse arose from PATCO's demands to obtain bargaining rights similar to those used in the private sector, threatening to go on strike, and in part from the presidency itself, which made three moves to precipitate the situation. First and foremost, in February 1981 the administration hired as a negotiator a law firm that expressed a strongly anti-union orientation. Second, it nominated Lynn Helms as the head of the Federal Aviation Administration (FAA), who also had a reputation as a fierce opponent of the unions. Finally, the FAA revised Carter's plan on flight controls, worsening the conditions imposed on the controllers. In addition, the number of permitted daily flights was increased, a measure taken to lessen eventual inconveniences caused by a strike. Within a few months, negotiations broke down, and the PATCO declared a strike on August 3, 1981.[65]

This strike violated the Taft-Hartley Act, which prohibited federal employees to strike. Four hours after the declaration of the strike, Reagan counter-declared that the controllers who did not return to work within 48 hours would be fired. Five thousand controllers did return to work, while more than 11,000 lost their jobs. Moreover, the FAA requested and obtained from the FLRA the cancellation of PATCO as a union.[66]

This episode probably represented the most hard-line reaction to public sector union action of any presidency in American history, and it was undoubtedly the low point in relations between these institutions. Reagan most likely contributed to provoking this clash, which was resolved with the presidency and its ideology prevailing over the public sector unions, which in the years to come would gain very little at the negotiating table.

A Final Appraisal

We can trace a final general appraisal of Reagan's administrative policies.

The president's strategy was based on an unscrupulous yet legal use of the powers and the organization determined by the 1978 CSRA and of the "reduction in force," which gave the administration greater ideological uniformity, precisely thanks to the tighter control over the appointments process and a numerical reduction as well as a strategic redistributing of professional functionaries. In other words, on the one hand the Reagan administration strove to reduce the size of the civil service and on the other hand to protect its own policies, appointing people of unquestioned ideological loyalty to the key positions in the administration, at both the high and low levels. There were two significant movements, one of depoliticization and the other of politicization: the first sought to reduce the "political power" of government bureaucracy as a social actor, through the reduction of public personnel and increase in transfers of top-ranking career bureaucrats, and the second was designed to augment the control of presidential policy over administrative implementation, through ideologically secure political appointments, in the key junctures of the federal machinery. The eight years of the Reagan presidency, therefore, did not undermine the dichotomy between politics and administration, since there was never any serious revision of the principle of merit nor any politicization of the professional bureaucracy through the abrogation of the Hatch Act. On the contrary, the dichotomy came out strengthened, because politics increased the hold on the high administration to likewise increase control over the implementation of the policies delegated to this entity. The two roles were never confused, and there was not a politicization of career civil servants. Yet political power became predominant over bureaucratic power, thanks to the political and ideological clout of the Reagan presidency. In broader terms, the administration of Ronald Reagan continued the populist wake of the Carter years with the managerialist recommendations of the Grace Commission and the reduction in force. The Carter and Reagan reorganization exercises and civil service reforms rejected the orthodox concept of a strong institutional presidency, the one theorized from the Brownlow Report of 1937 to Nixon's Ash Council, opting instead for the stronger political presidency then in academic vogue.[67] As the 1980s proceeded, an intellectual void emerged, without the design of a comprehensive organizational management counter-theory able to replace the orthodox principles now in disfavor. However, there was a common coherence in the Carter and Reagan reorganization plans and civil service reforms, and it was a general movement toward deconstructing the state.

George Bush and the Return of the "Administrative Aristocracy"

The Republican George Bush, elected president in 1988, had an approach that differed from that of Reagan and his team. Bush came from a career in public service, having been named ambassador to China, then director of the CIA under President Gerald Ford and, finally, having served as Vice-President during Ronald Reagan's eight years in the White House. Thanks to his long career in its institutions, his sympathy for the federal civil service was much more marked, in comparison to his predecessor.[68] Bush's presidency was probably the most favorable toward peaceful cooperation with public employees since the time of Hoover, and the actions undertaken during his term served to reconnect the relationship between political leadership and federal bureaucracy.[69] The new president was a centrist, moderate Republican, much less interested in the ideology of his administrative appointees than had been Ronald Reagan. He focused primarily on competency, ethical propriety, and managerial capacities than on political loyalty. Instead, he believed that a positive relationship between the White House and the federal bureaucracy would itself guarantee reciprocal and fruitful collaboration. Moreover, in contrast to Reagan, who had appointed as functionaries party activists mainly hailing from the country's periphery, Bush chose political appointees who were familiar with

Washington and its political-institutional logic. In fact, 13 of his 16 Cabinet members already lived in the Capital, as did more than 50% of his appointees to the government's subcommittees.[70]

With respect to his predecessor, he was also much more attentive to ensuring the representation of gender, ethnicity, and geographical background. He did not enforce quotas, as Clinton would do later on, but he still arranged for a certain balance among the appointees. With Bush the style of government also changed, becoming more collegial, almost a form of "cabinet government," less centered on the White House itself, as had been the case with Reagan. No longer were there ideological tests for selecting administrative candidates, and ample space was left for presidential cabinet members to suggest names to the president, for their various areas of responsibility. This approach was appreciated by the high-level career bureaucrats, who in a 1994 poll declared by a sizable majority that they considered Bush's political appointees more competent, more moderate, and more reliable than preceding ones.[71]

Regarding the president's moderation, some scholars have maintained that it was facilitated by the Republicans' long-standing hold on power, meaning that career bureaucrats were used to the ideology and policy preferences of that party. This strategy would have been followed by a vast number of civil servants, ready to advance their careers through loyal cooperation with their own political department heads, who decided on promotions. For this reason, according to several analysts, Bush had little or no need to insist on the politicization of his nominees.[72]

This fact, however, did not prevent the appointments from becoming more politically pluralistic, since Bush's candidates were 70% Republicans, 18% Democrats, and 6% independents. In Reagan's case, the Republicans surpassed the level of 90% in number.[73] This meant that an important part of the reaganites were not re-confirmed and, in fact, the data indicates that only 35% of the appointees made by Bush's predecessor were indeed re-confirmed. Thus two-thirds of those who had served during Reagan's presidency were expelled from the Bush administration.[74]

A particularly important figure of Bush's administration was Constance Newman, an African American woman appointed to lead the Office of Performance Management, who identified as main objectives the raising of civil servants' stipends and the reform of the system of performance assessment. In this context, the practice of "locality pay" was immediately installed, which sought to calibrate public employees' paychecks to the cost of living in their cities of residence. This reflected the fact that during the 1980s the cost of living in the major cities had risen notably, and buying power varied considerably from area to area, from metropolitan centers to small cities. "Locality pay" was approved by Congress in 1991 and provided for a pay raise of 8% for civil servants resident in the most expensive cities. This measure also ratified peace with the public employees' unions who supported the reform.[75]

Newman brought to the president's attention another fundamental problem: the difficulty of recruiting competent and prepared personnel. This occurred both at high levels, where many senior executives chose to switch to working for private companies, and at lower ones, where administrative assistants opted for better-paying jobs in the private sector. The result, Newman argued, was that public careers were chosen by less capable, diligent, and well-trained people. The director of the OMP came up with a solution that mixed salary increases with continuous training in cooperation with local schools, facilitated hiring and firing practices, and higher bonuses based on job performance, which came to prevail over the scheduled steps to seniority. Consequently, advertised jobs in the public sector returned to having, among both blue- and white-collar workers, more applicants than there were positions to be filled, meaning that public employment had once again become attractive to the middle class. Moreover, for the SES, salaries increased by 22%, and this fact made for fewer defections toward the private sector on the part of high-ranking bureaucrats.[76]

Along with these moves, there arrived other initiatives, like the report of the National Commission on Public Service, presided over by the ex-Chairman of the FED Paul Volcker and the ex-Cabinet Secretary Elliot Richardson who proposed numerous recommendations for reinforcing federal bureaucracy. They argued for the necessity of reducing the number of political appointees from about 3,000 to only 2,000, seeking to strengthen the role of career civil servants. According to them, this decrease would be useful both for limiting the pressures and avoiding the little scandals that occurred during the Reagan presidency and for increasing the efficiency and skills of public officials. In fact, the authors of the report claimed that a higher number of political appointees did not necessarily ensure enhanced political control of bureaucracy, and for this reason, such appointments ought to be fewer, thus obtaining better coordination and better organization. Another objective was to address the "quiet crisis" in government, namely, an erosion of attractiveness of public service to talented young people, which in turn was undermining government effectiveness. The commission organized its recommendations around the themes of leadership, talent, and performance. The proposals also advocated greater diversification in favor of women and minorities, growth in productivity, investment in technology to support government agencies, and the development of new systems of compensation and performance. Bush gave his support to most of the proposals, except for the reduction of politically appointed positions, but he did not have enough time to thoroughly implement what the report recommended. Rather, the Bush administration continued the effort to increase public sector pay and sent a new proposal to Congress, which was enacted as the Ethics Reform Act of 1989. It included a 25% pay increase for Executive Schedule employment, and the president acted to extend this raise to the SES as well. Still, a renewed attention on performance measurement and management was promoted in the Bush era. In particular, the Total Quality

Management (TQM) movement gained much attention. Promoted by Dr. W. E. Deming and others, the "TQM" approach emphasized the performance of work units and organizations rather than the individual employee.[77] Single civil servant determinations were limited, while more attention was paid to measuring overall organizational improvement. TQM served as a harbinger of the shift in the civil service from focusing on individual employee performance to measuring organizational performance. In the case of the federal sector, the focus was on how effectively and successfully it was delivering goods and services to the American people. Government agencies adopted and adapted many cornerstones of TQM, and they began to develop reliable measures to determine progress and customer satisfaction.[78]

Furthermore, consolidating a trend that had started with Carter and would continue with Bush's successor, there was also an increase in contracting out. This policy provoked aversion from the unions as well as many experts of public administration, but the Bush administration maintained that it would reduce costs and improve efficiency of public services, thanks to competition among private enterprises. Critics of these policies argued that this assumption regarding savings was more ideological than real, that public managers would become de-legitimized, opportunities for corruption would be extended, and the integrity of the federal government would be weakened, getting pulverized in a mishmash of public and private players. Nevertheless, both Bush and Clinton, alike imbued with the neo-liberal and neo-managerial ideology, continued to widen the range of services open to competitive bidding.[79]

Finally, in 1990, there was the congressional attempt to abolish the Hatch Act. Bush, however, put his presidential veto on the maneuver, and the Senate failed to override it, if only by a single vote.[80] Democrats favored the move, since they thought they held a majority among public employees, while blue-collar workers were also in favor of it, because they wanted to free themselves from limitations placed on their political activism. This stance did not apply, however, to the majority of high-level civil servants, who were worried about a potential increase in politicization and an undermining of the impartiality of public administration. The same argument was used by President Bush in his rejection of the legislation modifying the Hatch Act.

The National Performance Review: Bill Clinton's Great Plan for Administrative Reform

The Theoretical Background: Reinventing Government

Until the summer of 1992, almost all Washington analysts predicted the re-election of George Bush, who instead failed in his bid for a series of reasons. First, the American economy had entered a phase of recession, and the Bush administration, which expected an upswing before the election, was unable to provide convincing explanations for the slowdown. Second, Bill Clinton conducted a highly efficacious campaign focused on three themes: economic recovery, renewal of the political class, and the promise of universal access to a health system guaranteed by public intervention. The Republicans did not manage to regain their capacity to dictate the agenda on these points. Third, the billionaire Ross Perot became a candidate with his own party, and drew votes away from President Bush, obtaining almost 19% of the popular vote. Finally, Clinton was a moderate candidate who avoided the "tax and spend" approach, embracing a more free-market economic vision founded on tax cuts for the middle class and on the remodulation and reduction of bureaucracy. He gained 43% of the consensus, a low proportion, but enough in a three-way race to win the White House, even if Congress remained in Republican hands. This result probably demonstrated the sensibility of the American electorate, in favor of the reduction of the public deficit and taxes on businesses, a conservative argument, but also in favor of the improvement of welfare, a progressive argument.

Thus, Clinton brought the Democrats back to the White House, at the same time maintaining continuity with his Republican predecessors on the level of administrative reorganization. In this case as well, the leading objective was therefore to reduce the scale and the inefficiency of the administrative state.

In contrast to Carter, who sought to pursue objectives related to social justice through administrative reform, Bill Clinton and his Vice-President Al Gore accepted the idea that the techniques refined by business management could be transposed into the public sector, and they therefore proceeded along the path traced by the reaganite Grace Commission. In terms of administrative philosophy, the Clinton administration aimed to give an answer to a universal problem: the public's disappointment with government. Numerous studies and polls of the time indicated increasing frustration by the public with the way in which federal bureaucracy performed its duties and delivered services. In the 1980s there was a considerable effort in promoting privatization and contracting-out policies in order to move government toward private sector practices.[81] But privatization was not enough for those, in Al Gore and Clinton's inner circle, who embraced the NPM paradigm. The "old administrative paradigm," based on law and regulations, was the cause, in their view, of the "red tape" that had undermined the introduction of contemporary management practices. Rather, in the entrepreneurial management paradigm, the agency manager was central. The central management agencies, such as the OMB, were imbued by the old administrative management paradigm and therefore ought to be downgraded. And the executive branch was in need of restructuring. Agencies should be given wide power over their personnel, compensation, acquisition, and contract policies, as well as the applicability of regulations.

The reform program came to be called the National Performance Review (NPR), a name that expressed the quest for speed and efficiency in obtaining tangible results in the context of public policies. The NPR incorporated the paradigm of NPM, which aimed to put "consumer satisfaction" at the center of relations between the citizens and public administration.

NPM's intellectual foundations were microeconomics, public choice theory, and transaction cost analysis developed in the 1970s and 1980s. Moreover, in political terms, as Robert Durant noted,

> NPM also was consonant with the perpetually reigning image in America of public organizations as rational machines or brains to be fine-tuned. In addition, its market- and business-based reform agenda was highly consistent with American exceptionalism's emphasis on limited government, economic liberalism, and civic responsibility. Also advantageous was its resonance with the dominant neoliberal economic spirit of the times and the propensity of elected officials to want to control administrative behavior to advance their own agendas and institutional interests.[82]

NPM proponents argued that metrics—market competition, performance measurement, outcomes-based administration, and citizen satisfaction scores—should override bureaucratic procedures as accountability mechanisms. Their prescription for controlling public agency behavior for efficiency and effectiveness was to (1) determine core agency competencies and expertise; (2) hive off non-core tasks to subnational, private, and nonprofit actors; (3) aggressively downsize the remaining agencies and cut the number of bureaucratic layers; (4) alter the decision calculus of public managers away from traditional procedural controls; (5) refocus managers on realizing goals by measuring agency and employee performance "outcomes" or "results" and citizen satisfaction; (6) link these performance metrics to budgets; (7) deskill agencies to minimalize existing expert opinion relative to political goals; and (8) substitute a vocabulary of metrics for the professional jargon boundaries of existing agency professionals, thus diminishing the power of the latter.[83]

In consequence, the administrative philosophy of the NPR set out to "melt the rigid boundaries between organizations. The federal government should organize its work according to customers' needs and anticipated outcomes, not bureaucratic turf."[84] The reformers argued to change the public law basis of an agency's mission and replace it with an "outcomes" mission orientation as defined by the agency's management. The executive branch was to be culturally reorganized, not organizationally reorganized, to reflect the entrepreneurial values of the private sector. The reformers' vision was to break down the barriers between the sectors and create a society of government/private partnerships. The partnerships, in their mind, would be largely autonomous bodies run by civil servant-managers to meet negotiated performance standards. The entrepreneurial position argued that managers should be deregulated, given freedom from congressional micromanagement and less supervision by the president and his central management agencies. The goal was a greater managerial autonomy to achieve more efficiency and effectiveness.

This body of ideas was developed in a much-debated book written by David Osborne and Ted Gaebler, published in 1992 with the title *Reinventing Government*.[85] In this influential work, the authors explained their neo-managerial vision which lied at the basis of the "reinventing government movement."[86] They fervently expressed their desire for a more mission-oriented and less rule-oriented form of governance and administration in their wish that government should more closely emulate the practices of business and in their emphasis on the importance of defining, within the political process, a clear and consistent set of goals and objectives for government policies. John Dilulio, another prominent writer in this field, expressed much the same vision of governance when he argued that public organizations are the "hands and feet" of important public purposes and that public management as a field of enquiry should search for "ways to realize public goals by the most appropriate administrative arrangements possible."[87]

Michael Barzelay and Babak Armajani, in a perhaps more radical vein, called for what they characterized as a "Post-Bureaucratic Paradigm" in public management. They argued that "concepts of mission, services, customers, and outcomes are valuable because they help public servants articulate their purposes and deliberate about how to adapt work to achieve them."[88]

The essential thesis of Osborne and Gaebler's book was that the fall of communism, the globalization of markets, and the spread of information technology had rendered out-of-date and illegitimate the hierarchical and monolithic bureaucracies inherited from the Progressives of the 1920s. Just as private companies were evolving toward new models, so too bureaucracy had to undertake an itinerary of change following the same principles. The book was well written, easy to understand, and replete with case studies, and these qualities enabled it to become the manifesto of a much longer academic elaboration that had informed the neo-managerial paradigm.[89]

This elaboration was based on a series of principles, such as competition in public services and the diffusion of managerial culture, that would allow public administrations to be more efficient, innovative, and conscious of consumers; the liberalization of providers of public services with the involvement of private entities and the third sector; and the reduction of red tape as well as regulation of the public sector. From these principles there derived a series of policies, like the obligation of compulsory competitive tenders open to both public and private providers; voucher systems for citizens who chose the most efficient service; rewards for executive agencies that had best integrated market mechanisms; multidisciplinary approaches and teamwork for public managers; the introduction of multi-annual budgets to leave more discretionary options to public managers in their expenses management; the introduction of penalties and rewards with regard to the results of administrative units; and the use of new technologies as a means for measuring results.

In other words, the aim was to transfuse into governmental structures those methods that characterized the management of American private corporations.

Into the Practice of New Managerial Paradigms

The ideological and lexical influence of this intellectual paradigm was transposed into Clinton's plans of administrative reform, particularly in the first report of the NPR. In this text, the awareness and usage of history in designing policies of administrative reform seems worthy of special note:

> From the 1930s through the 1960s, we built large, top-down, centralized bureaucracies to do the public's business. They were patterned after the corporate structures of the age: hierarchical bureaucracies in which tasks were broken into simple parts, each the responsibility of a different layer of employees, each defined by specific rules and regulations. With their rigid preoccupation with standard operating procedure, their vertical chains of command, and their standardized services, these bureaucracies were steady—but slow and cumbersome. And in today's world of rapid change, lightning-quick information technologies, tough global competition, and demanding customers, large, top-down bureaucracies—public or private—don't work very well. Saturn isn't run the way General Motors was. Intel isn't run the way IBM was.[90]

"Through the ages," the NPR continued,

> public management has tended to follow the prevailing paradigm of private management. The 1930s were no exception. Roosevelt's committee—and the two Hoover commissions that followed—recommended a structure patterned largely after those of corporate America in the 1930s. In a sense, they brought to government the GM model of organization. By the 1980s, even GM recognized that this model no longer worked.[91]

The neo-liberal rhetoric had not faded away: on the contrary, the Democrats themselves had now thoroughly adopted it. For example, the NPR website's homepage proclaimed that the administration had "put an end to the era of big government." Beneath, the presidency's successes were listed: reduction of the numbers of federal employees, cuts in the various levels of government, simplification of agency rules, and closing of unnecessary offices. In addition, the administration cited its success in strengthening the partnership between the public and private sectors, and the change in the relationship between private business and the government.[92] The report affirmed that the reforms made government more focused on actual results and on the satisfaction of the citizen-customer. The proposals had a certain success, for, as we will see, they were small and incremental reforms, and many of them came from the agencies themselves.

To a certain extent, Clinton's reorganization of the executive branch was part of a long cycle of initiatives, undertaken by the end of the 1970s, that shared a common goal: reduce the public sector's space of intervention in the economy, transpose private sector managerial techniques to bureaucratic organization, and eliminate wastes and duplication of services and functions.

Political Appointments: Making It More Difficult

Nonetheless, the start of Clinton's presidency was complicated and above all behind schedule in naming political appointees. First, the Democrats had been absent from the White House for 12 years, and during the transition they were inundated by requests from party members to occupy civil service posts in Washington. Moreover, in order to centralize the process of appointments, Clinton concentrated the relevant team at the White House, instead of leaving choices to single Cabinet members: they thus would have greater influence and control over the naming of appointees. Furthermore, since 1978 the appointee-making process had become all the more unwieldy, due to the passage of the Ethics in Government Act, which entailed political appointee candidates to provide data on their own financial status and to separate themselves from their own financial and entrepreneurial activities, forming trusts or blind trusts, to avoid conflicts of interest. Clinton added to these rules a five years' ban on engaging in lobbying activities on behalf of private interests or for the governments of other countries, applied to any politically appointed functionary after the termination of his or her time in office.[93] The country had entered into a process of stronger political polarization than had existed in the past, and consequently the interest groups and the minority currents both in one's own party and in the adversary's rendered much more complex the hearings for candidates and their confirmation as appointees. Then there were the pressures exerted by the media that scrutinized the lives and curricula even of potential political executives, increasing the possibilities of scandals, embarrassments, and investigations. This made the politics of public appointments all the more cautious and apprehensive, significantly slowing down procedures. To give an idea of the declining pace, during the Kennedy presidency it took an average of two and a half months to name and confirm an appointee, during the Bush presidency eight months, and by the Clinton years nine and a half months.[94]

Finally, the president and his staff wished for a diversification of appointees, who would represent the variety of genders, ethnicities, and geographical regions of the United States. The nominations were made not on an individual basis but in groups, and this new method contributed to the cumbersome nature of the process. Fifteen percent of the nominees were African–American, 6% Hispanic, and 46% women to demonstrate the pluralism inherent in the new liberal ideology incarnated by Clinton.[95]

Even though the Clinton administration was slower than preceding ones, it was possible to make a parallel between it and the Wilson presidency, and that of Eisenhower, where the appointment processes were much slower than in prior administrations. All three administrations returned their respective parties to government after many years of absence from the White House, and if we combine this factor with sociopolitical changes, we can conclude that this brought greater difficulty to making the administrative machine quickly ready and efficient.

Regarding political bureaucracy, the Clinton presidency disrupted the relationship with career civil servants. For example, the first "reduction in force" since the Reagan years was applied, and the cutting of positions caused the number of civil servants to fall to the lowest level since the Kennedy era. The unions were revitalized by the new administration, especially in the agencies, where the links between public managers and union support were reinforced. All the same, there were cases of isolation of top-level officials, who did not meet with union approval. In addition, the gender and ethnicity question began to weigh more heavily even on promotions for career bureaucrats, a policy that dismayed several white males who perceived that the road to promotion was blocked by the new premium on the care and support for minorities.[96] Finally, Clinton signed the modification of the Hatch Act, relaxing the relationship between career functionaries and political activism, which for decades the former had prohibited. While political propaganda remained forbidden in federal workplaces, as did potential coercions based on political opinions, from this moment on government functionaries were free to participate in democratic life.[97]

Administrative Reform: Traditions and Changes

The electorate's new expectations, especially that of keeping public accounts in order, without renouncing improved services and reduced fiscal pressure, produced a more aggressive administrative neo-managerialism during the Clinton era: career bureaucrats had to turn themselves into public managers, endowed with increased autonomy at the level of budget management, and, above all, they had to gear their own actions toward efficiency, without jeopardizing the successful delivery of public services. For this reason, management needed to be less hierarchical and more results-oriented, and to follow the model of private business organization.

From the business sector arrived successful studies like Charles Peters's *How Washington Really Works*[98] and Thomas Peters and Robert Waterman's *In Search of Excellence*, which argued that greater efficiency and innovation could be attained by liberating employees of any given organization, making it less rigid, encouraging change, rewarding successes, and cutting the levels of management and of bureaucracy which slowed down and burdened the functioning of a given structure.[99]

Government agencies needed to take customers' opinions into greater consideration, to encourage continual training, to be less conditioned by internal rules, and to be more dedicated to the achievement of objectives. Once more, ideas from the world of private business swept over public bureaucracy. In 1993, the best-seller *Reengineering the Corporation* suggested re-structuring the entire productive process, mapping out procedures which would allow for the continual training of employees. Through these techniques of reorganization, innovation would be encouraged, providing more flexibility and autonomy to individuals and reducing costs of transaction in the various production phases.[100] All of this also happened through the use of information technology, which increased the number of activities that a single employee could accomplish. In fact, the re-engineering was none other than the re-visitation of Taylor's "scientific management," which envisioned less hierarchical structures and less routine work for the lower levels of organizations.

In comparison to the Reagan era—when bureaucrats were considered to be *rentiers*, lazy, privileged, and disorganized—during this phase the attention shifted on to structures. According to the reformers of the Clinton administration, the civil servants were top-notch individuals, who only appeared to be less than efficient, because of excessively complex and bureaucratic organizations: the latter needed to be reformed in order for better results to be obtained.[101]

These principles and this multiplicity of policies formed the basis of the NPR, which in fact was only launched in 1993 by Vice-President Al Gore. On March 3, 1993, President Clinton announced his plan to improve the efficiency and quality of government illustrating the objectives: "Our goal is to make the entire federal government both less expensive and more efficient, and to change the culture of our national bureaucracy away from complacency and entitlement toward initiative and empowerment."[102] The president's language clarified how the NPR would need to transform the government into a provider of services, whose performances could be enhanced through the use of techniques and concepts borrowed from the business management experience of corporate re-engineering. On this issue, the administrative theorist Steven Cohen published a book targeted at practitioners, asserting that "effective public managers try to make things happen; they pursue programmatic goals and objectives by thinking and acting strategically." According to Cohen, "One of the primary motivators of public employees is their desire to be involved in critical missions," and he suggested that "it is important to build on that predisposition and explicitly connect the work of your organization to important objectives."[103]

Interpreting the new Democratic centrism, Clinton maintained that Americans wanted "better schools and health care and better roads... but they want...a government that works better on less money and that is more responsive."[104] The president had fully embraced the new managerialist doctrine: "we intend to redesign, to reinvent, to reinvigorate the entire national government."[105] The NPR, therefore, took up the provocations of the billionaire independent candidate Ross Perot, who had claimed that the government was a broken-down machine, and similar ones made before him by the Republican President Ronald Reagan.

The reform proceeded under the strict observation of the presidency, since the task force's staff, composed of 250 people, did not have autonomous powers, nor a budget, nor its own personnel. Its members were mainly high-level career bureaucrats who came from a variety of agencies. The choice was a strategic one: bureaucracy did not need external interventions, presidential advisers, academic experts, and business world managers, as in the 1970s and 1980s, but could reform itself based on political input.[106] This strategy would impel federal civil servants to take up the battle of ideas to give the government greater efficiency and would create fewer problems of implementation, once the NPR was approved. The task force worked busily, also due to the high-profile media pressures imposed by President Clinton, and in September 1993 presented its first report with its principal recommendations.

The members of the task force formulated four principles which would guide administrative reorganization: (1) put the consumer at the center of attention, (2) empower federal agencies to better satisfy consumers, (3) remove bureaucracies and rules that impeded these actions, and (4) reduce wasteful practices. All of this was integrated with reform plans for individual agencies that, based on the schema designed by the center, could develop their own practices autonomously in order to reach objectives.[107]

In its substance, the reform joined the ranks of the "new managerialism" that had been experimented with in more sophisticated forms, in countries like New Zealand, the United Kingdom, and Australia, which sought to combine reduction of public spending with a dose of efficiency based on managerial techniques imported from the private sector.[108] The NPR aimed to have a swift and visible impact. Vice-President Gore was convinced that in order to have success, the reform needed to gain credibility and popularity, not only among federal functionaries but also in Congress, and more generally with the electorate. The expected benefits, along with the obtained ones, would need to be publicized as well as possible to convince the country that the administration was capable of making viable reforms.

Al Gore committed himself to accomplishing a series of meetings with federal civil servants of all levels to promote the new managerialism, seeking out those personalities who could adapt to innovations within public administration. On

June 25, 1993, Gore organized a major conference on *Reinventing Government* in Philadelphia, bringing together groups of federal bureaucrats and private sector directors, in which the latter would explain to the former how to reorganize an institutional structure in more efficient ways.[109]

As scheduled, on September 7, 1993, the first NPR report was published, entitled *From Red Tape to Results: Creating a Government that Works Better and Costs Less.* This publication was a compendium of what had already been announced by the White House, with regard to efficiency and the struggle to reduce waste.[110] Each chapter was dedicated to a different theme: simplification of the administrative process, further decentralization of policy-making and personnel management into agencies, contracting-out for public services, elimination of waste, and increase of productivity. The report was simple and legible, and each section was seasoned with anecdotes illustrating the governmental dysfunctions that the new system would repair. The strategies of reform, therefore, could no longer neglect the needs for communication and popular legitimization of the initiative. In addition, the chapters were interconnected by a comprehensive design: for example, if one wished to decentralize personnel management, it was fundamental to deregulate the sector and bypass the 10,000 pages of the Federal Personnel Manual. In other words, simplification, efficiency, autonomy, and economy were interdependent, and that which emerged most definitively was that any single part of the reform could not do without the other concomitant parts. Thus, the text conveyed the idea that on the whole, the Clinton administration was focused on transforming government into a provider of services and citizens into consumers of these services. The system would be less fiscally burdensome, and the practical realization, or delivery, of public services would be enhanced.[111]

After September 1993, implementation of the report began, and this transpired in two ways. First, there were several recommendations that could be carried out from the top level such as the reduction of civil servants. This policy was particularly important, because it could be accomplished in the short term, and the Clinton administration could affirm that it had reduced waste and public spending, as had been promised during the electoral campaign. The report promised a cut of 108 billion dollars in five years. At the level of personnel management, this meant reducing by 252,000 units the federal civil service, an objective that was in fact raised to 272,000 by Congress. The reduction of the workforce indeed exceeded expectations, with a reduction of 316,000 in the number of employees registered by March 1996.[112]

The second type of implementation, by contrast, arrived from the lower ranks, for example, the training of personnel for improving the standard of services and the simplification of procedures. Roles linked with public relations grew in importance, and especially those involving communication—for sharing the results of the NPR—and technology for digitizing practices and information.

During its first year, the reform achieved good results, thanks to the work of the task force and to the delegated responsibilities that it was able to instill, favoring cooperation and coordination among the various administrative entities. The task force never imposed a hierarchical leadership, nor did it seek to solidify relations with Congress, but instead concentrated on the promotion and communication of the reforms. It was the White House, with the support of legislative power, that gave a real boost to the reform, in order to prepare itself for the 1994 midterm elections. In fact, for Al Gore, success in "reinventing" government meant not only reaching the objectives of a reform to which he himself had significantly contributed but also reinforcing his own political position. In Congress, even the most skeptical lawmakers agreed to implement most of the recommendations, because these promised to reduce bureaucratic costs and simplify administration for citizens. Not by chance did the Government Performance and Results Act (GPRA) of 1991 make its proposals match those of the NPR, and to them were added new requirements established by the 1993 GPRA for strategic planning by government agencies.[113]

The GPRA received broad support from both parties in Congress and by the Clinton administration itself. The law aimed to tackle the classic questions of government: accountability and performance. However, the GPRA was different from earlier attempts at similar reform, because it required that agency results were integrated into the budgetary decision-making process. Moreover, the law was not an executive branch initiative, but it was statutory: its performance measurement requirements were law, and almost all agencies and departments were subject to GPRA requirements. Under the Act, agencies developed multiyear strategic plans, annual performance plans, and annual performance reports. Agencies now had to align individual employee performance with the organizational goals and objectives identified in the Act. As the OPM pointed out, "The more traditional process-oriented performance elements and standards for employees and organizations started to give a more results-oriented focus, with the Federal sector embracing and adapting for its purposes evaluation tools like the Kaplan and Norton Balanced Scorecard."[114]

Many aspects of these changes in human resource management imposed by the GPRA, however, were still rooted in the position-centric approach of the 1978 Civil Service Reform Act. For this reason, the SES played a major role in the implementation process of the new law. The SES award system, indeed, continued and increased the focus on individual and organizational performance, basing it mostly on the merit pay (financial reward) system. In the end, with the GPRA a greater rigidity in personnel management was introduced, the autonomy and independence of the executive agencies were established by law, and performance measurement was imposed from the center on to all departments and agencies. In many ways, the 1993 GPRA was the natural completion of the 1978 Civil Service Reform Act, adding to the latter a more sophisticated formalization of performance management but without changing the career organization and the administrative structure.

In 1994, the Republicans won the congressional elections, and for the Clinton presidency there began a much more complex period for program implementation. The new majority demanded a reduction of activities managed by the federal government, since the Republican message was still focused on "small government," that is, on the reduction of public spending and on the regulation and taxation of private businesses. This implied a shift in the priorities of the NPR, which passed from the modernization of the administrative machinery to the re-writing of rules on business activities. The simplification of rules related to workplace or environmental security became part of the plan, as did the reinforcement of the relationship between government and protagonists from the economic-financial world. For this reason, the Code of Regulations was emended, many regulations were cancelled, and others were reduced, involving the interests present in the sector.[115]

Moreover, the OPM followed the NPR recommendation and in 1995 issued performance management and awards regulation that decentralized the design and operation of appraisal and awards system and programs and supplied broad guidelines for agencies to follow when designing their own programs, especially to deal with the "old structures, new requirements" challenge posed by the 1993 GPRA. Many agencies exploited the new flexibility to focus on organizational performance measurement and to use awards programs to recognize senior individuals achieving beyond expectations. Under the pressure of NPR, hiring also went through a process of decentralization. The reinvention had recommended giving departments and agencies authority to conduct their own recruiting and examining for all positions and the abolition of OPM's central registers and standard application forms.[116] In 1995, Congress authorized OPM to delegate competitive examining to the agencies.[117]

Last and perhaps most importantly came federal labor relations. Executive Order 12871, issued on October 1, 1993, created a national partnership council to join federal management and public unions in implementing NPR reforms. The National Partnership Council (NPC) required federal agencies to form labor-management partnerships as a means of fostering improved labor relations within the federal government. The NPC allowed for management and labor to collaborate to the mutual benefit of both parties over such issues as health, safety, and quality of work life.

Just before Clinton began his second term, the OPM circulated a draft civil service reform bill called the Federal Human Resource Management Reinvention Act of 1995.[118] However, it was harshly opposed by the unions who promised to oppose it if forwarded to Congress. In various forms, the Clinton administration and the OPM continued to submit and negotiate proposals for new legislation. Stymied on overall legislation, the next thrust focused on reforms involving the SES. The proposal went nowhere.

In January 1999, Vice-President Al Gore announced one more attempt for a legislative initiative to "improve the performance management systems of the federal workforce and to encourage a culture of high performance and labor/management collaboration."[119]

By midyear, the proposal was refused by the unions, who essentially wanted no part of the improvement package until they saw the partnership executive order (EO 12871) of 1993 enforced regarding the expansion of bargaining. The 1999 Civil Service Improvement Act was the conclusion of six long years of intense activity in workforce reform on both fronts, with very little progress on either increasing the scope of bargaining under partnership or rewriting significant portions of the CSRA. In conclusion, this administrative and legislative history of civil service reform for the 1990s showed only fragments of results: pay reform in 1990, downsizing legislation in 1994, and a few appropriation riders enabling agencies to create their own personnel systems, in part by moving to excepted service (most notably the FAA and the Internal Revenue Service (IRS)).

Toward the New Century

As the 2000 presidentia election approached, the NPR returned to the more populist tones and themes of the early 1990s. Once again, under the pressure of a Republican Congress, the main objective was that of "putting an end to the era of big government." This did in fact occur, since the NPR reduced the number of federal government bureaucrats, which from 1993 to 2001 decreased by 426,200, far more than the 252,000 promised when the NPR was started. Those individuals who worked for the program claimed that they had saved the government 136 billion dollars, more than the 108 promised at the program's beginning. In addition, they cut 78,000 managerial positions, removed 640,000 pages of regulation, closed over 2,000 regional offices, and eliminated 250 governmental programs.[120]

The program also aimed to strengthen the capacities of civil servants, particularly by increasing the discretionary powers of public managers in charge of administrative agencies. In this phase, the coordination usually carried out by the OPM diminished, in favor of greater autonomy for the agencies, which in their own turn instituted semipublic entities to accomplish specific predetermined services. Managers were being more and more encouraged to conduct their work as if they were business entrepreneurs, who had to set and meet financial objectives as well as qualitative and quantitative standards. According to the reformers, this would bring substantial improvement of services and public relations. In this sense, as Anne Laurent observed, the federal government became a genuine "business incubator," nurturing a significant number of new small business activities in the public services field, which developed within the agencies themselves, which transformed into bona fide business organizations.[121]

This implied new recommendations, such as, for example, that of transforming some agencies from providers of services to "performance-based" organizations. In other words, the White House's control over the agencies and departments increased, and the organization of work changed. Now the chief of the administrative agencies would be called CEO, just as in the large private companies, and he or she would not be subject to the rules of civil service, but instead bound by a contract, on the model of a private administrative director, and evaluated on the basis of his or her performance and the results obtained.

In terms of NPR's implementation, the GAO, in a review of September 2000 based on a survey that involved ten executive agencies, found that

> of the 72 NPR recommendations covered in our review, the 10 selected agencies considered almost 90 percent of them to be either fully or partially implemented. The agencies characterized 33 of the 72 recommendations as fully implemented (...). The agencies also considered another 30 recommendations as partially implemented because the recommended actions could not be done all at once and required time (several years in some cases) to complete them.[122]

Despite these good results in the implementation process, the evaluation of the GAO is only partially satisfying:

> NPR was one of a number of catalysts that stimulated agencies to become more effective and efficient. NPR operated along with other congressional, administration, and agency actions, all of which concurrently affected federal management reform efforts. Congress developed a statutory framework to instill a performance-based approach into the management of federal agencies, and also provided the needed authorities and resources to help agencies implement some of NPR's recommendations. However, because the recommendations lacked clear and measurable performance goals, it is difficult to assess the level of improvement that agencies achieved.[123]

In this scenario, evaluating the actual results of the NPR appears to be highly problematic.[124] To positive opinions such as those of Laurent, one can add more realistic and mixed reviews, which analyze the numerous difficulties faced by the federal government in the remodulation of the executive branch following the principles of private sector management. Critics, on the other hand, perceived in NPR an erosion of the legal bases on which the federal administration rested, as well as a weakening of the agencies and the federal government's authority, in favor of a general process of disintegration of executive power, a potential threat to the respect of democratic values.[125]

In broader terms, if, on the one hand, the introduction of new managerial techniques, the quest for efficiency, and a reorganization geared toward making government administration resemble private business entailed a depoliticization of the federal bureaucracy—rendering it always more technocratic and always less unionized—on the other hand, it produced a surreptitious politicization through the monitoring of performance, awards-based compensation, and the surveillance and checking of results. Politics set the rules, standards, and objectives of the administration, and it sought to control them through quantitative and qualitative means. To implement effectively the reform programs, to achieve more efficiency at the operational level, and to follow the private sector organizational model, personnel management and policy-making became more decentralized into agencies, and public managers got more autonomy on budget and human resource management. At the same time, however, the performance management system was used by politics to better control and direct the work of the executive branch.

George W. Bush between Neo-managerialism and National Security

An MBA President

In 2000, George W. Bush won the presidential election with a narrow margin over the Democrat and former Vice-President Al Gore.

President Bush was the first American president to hold a master's degree in business administration (Harvard University, 1975), and according to Donald Kettl, George W. Bush was "the very model of a modern MBA president."[126] Secrecy, speed, and top-down control are all qualities attributed to business management, especially by public officials who must cope with the inevitable leaks, dilatory bureaucratic processes, and a system of shared powers.[127] President Bush articulated a clear vision, set priorities, and then delegated the implementation to his vice-president and his loyal staff team. In his autobiography, *A Charge to Keep*, he put it this way: "My job is to set the agenda and tone and framework, to lay out the principles by which we operate and make decisions, and then delegate much of the process to them."[128] President Bush preferred short memos, oral briefings, and rapid meetings, and his circle of advisers remained relatively small. According to American Enterprise Institute President Christopher DeMuth, "It's a too tightly managed decision-making process. When they make decisions, a very small number of people are in the room, and it has a certain effect of constricting the range of alternatives being offered."[129]

Neither had Bush sought a broad range of outside advice: "I have no outside advice. Anybody who says they're an outside adviser of this Administration on this particular matter [the war on terror] is not telling the truth."[130]

President Bush's approach to his role as chief executive resembled that of a CEO of a corporation. He thought of himself as tough-minded and able to make decisions quickly, leaving the details up to his team. His White House staff was trained to have a tight message discipline and to avoid any unauthorized leaks. President Bush loved to present himself as a determined decision-maker: "I listen to all voices, but mine is the final decision... I'm the decider, and I decide what's best."[131] In contrast to his father or to Bill Clinton, who would agonize over important decisions, Bush decided and moved on. The detached Bush style was probably more similar to the style of President Ronald Reagan.

According to National Security Advisor Condoleezza Rice, "He least likes me to say, 'This is complex.'" Bush has described his personal approach to decision-making as intuitive: "I just think it's instinctive. I'm not a textbook player. I'm a gut player."[132] He did not believe in elaborate deliberation or explanation of his thinking to his White House staff. As he told Bob Woodward,

> I'm the commander—see, I don't need to explain—I do not need to explain why I say things. That's the interesting thing about being the president. Maybe somebody needs to explain to me why they say something, but I don't feel like I owe anybody an explanation.[133]

Former Treasury Secretary Paul O'Neill thought that the Bush White House had no serious domestic policy process. "It was a broken process, ... or rather no process at all; there seemed to be no apparatus to assess policy and deliberate effectively, to create coherent governance."[134] John Dilulio, a public administration scholar who worked in the Bush White House, said, "There is no precedent in any modern White House for what is going on in this one: a complete lack of a policy apparatus."[135]

Despite President Bush's care in recruiting an experienced and well-credentialed cabinet, he was not about to reverse the trend of the past four decades of power gravitating toward the White House.[136] Early in the Bush administration, all the major policy priorities were dominated by White House staffers rather than led by the cabinet. As one high-level White House official said, during the transition from the first to the second term:

> The Bush brand is few priorities, run out of the White House, with no interference from the Cabinet... The function of the Bush Cabinet is to provide a chorus of support for White House policies and technical expertise for implementing them.[137]

Political centralization of decision-making in the White House and a stronger managerial approach in the executive branch were the prerogatives of Bush as administrator.

Federal Workforce and Government Size

George W. Bush inherited a surplus of 128 billion dollars and a federal work-force that was 600,000 employees smaller than his father's administration had been at the end of his term. He had room to maneuver as he entered office after an economic boom under Clinton. Bush did not seem interested in further downsizing during his transition. Clinton had already harvested most of the peace dividend, represented by the smallest blended workforce headcount in recent history. By the end of his presidency, the total number of federal, con-tract, and grant employees went to a 20-year low, and Washington's workforce seemed to be moving toward the proper meshing.[138]

As a response to the unexpected 9/11 terrorist attack, he sent U.S. troops to war in Afghanistan and Iraq, and defense spending rose 30% over his first three budgets. Having started with Clinton's defense cuts, Bush pushed defense spending to 450 billion dollars in 2002, 492 billion dollars in 2003, and 531 billion dollars in 2004. Non-defense spending would rise almost 18% during the same period, as he pursued several relatively expensive domestic priorities, including the Transportation Security Administration, a new Farm Bill, edu-cation reforms, and medicare prescription drug coverage.[139]

As went the defense budget, so went the workforce trend. Between the years 2002 and 2005 alone, the Bush administration added almost 1.4 million contract and grant employees to the federal bureaucracy. With that large increase, the percentage of contract and grant employees as a share of the federal workforce also grew significantly, as the wars expanded. Whereas there were 2.3 contract and grant employees for every federal employee in 2002, the ratio became 3:1 in 2005. In terms of bureaucracy's composition, the Bush II presidency might be considered as a period of "contractorization" of the new federal workforce.

Public Appointments in the Executive Branch

Published work on the Bush administration's administrative strategy suggests that President Bush aggressively used a variety of tools, including his staffing power, to exert control over the bureaucracy. Scholars have identified distinct institutional, ideological, or personal motivations for these actions.

Bush, like other presidents, sought to expand his power in order to meet the immense expectations of the office. Against the backdrop of 9/11, he attempted "to take over the bureaucracy and take on the Congress, to concentrate on ad-ministrative steps and correspondingly downgrade legislation as the principal route for bringing about domestic change."[140]

The Bush administration exercised tight control over the selection of all subcabinet appointments. As Clay Johnson, Bush's first personnel director, said, "they (appointees) need to know that the president selected them," or when things got tough, their loyalty would be to the president rather than the secretary.[141] While this was the case, the Bush President's Personnel Office (PPO) sought to work with cabinet secretaries and top officials so that, in their words, they did it "with them, not to them."[142] In practice, the Bush personnel operation operated with a mutual veto system. Both the PPO and the agency had the right to recommend candidates for consideration and refuse candidates they did not like. Over time, the mechanisms for selecting appointees on the basis of loyalty had become more sophisticated. The Reagan administration built up institutional staff to look for candidates with conservative credentials and past evidence of activity for "movement" or Goldwater-type conservatism. The Clinton administration was careful to select New Democrats with policy views close to Clinton's own.

The Bush II administration valued loyalty to the president very highly and worked to foster it through both the selection process and their procedures for orienting political appointees. A one-page document summarizing the Bush personnel operation given out at the beginning of the administration states, "this is not a beauty contest. The goal is to pick the person who has the greatest chance of accomplishing what the principal wants done."[143]

The process emphasized picking people who would satisfy the technical requirements for the job and share the president's views. After deciding on the candidates who were most likely to accomplish the directives of the "political top," personnel officials were instructed to assess the political wisdom of the choice.

To sum up, the Bush administration personnel operation looked like the next natural development of the personnel operations that preceded it. This administration learned the lessons of past presidents, both Democrats and Republicans, exceptionally well. The personnel system was established by a group of professionals who began earlier than any other personnel official and who probably understood past presidential practice as well as any other person in his position. The Bush personnel operation succeeded in recruiting effectively for executive positions, they maintained control of subcabinet appointments, and the Office of Political Affairs used the distribution of federal jobs to the political advantage of the administration.

Location and Numbers

The Bush administration increased the number of appointees between 2000 and 2004 by 350 positions. This was a significant increase relative to the Clinton administration, but the total number of appointees was still less than the two presidents before him. The increase can partly be explained by the fact that

Clinton was in his second term. By the eighth year of his presidency, Clinton would have had a hard time both recruiting and retaining appointees, and he had had eight years to change policy and identify sympathetic career employees to fill top executive jobs. Bush also enjoyed a majority in Congress for part of his term, whereas Clinton did not during his second term. This made it more difficult for Clinton to alter the number of appointees.

With increases in appointees in the Departments of Labor and Education, the Commission on Civil Rights, the Office of Special Counsel, the National Foundation on the Arts and Humanities, and the Environmental Protection Agency, there is some evidence that the 350 appointees increase was biased toward agencies that would not naturally share Bush's views on policy. As David E. Lewis reports in his study, there was an average increase between 2000 and 2004 in the percentage of agency managers who are appointees by agency ideology. While the number and percentage of appointees increases for all types of agencies, the increases are largest for liberal agencies.[144] This appears to confirm that this Republican president aimed to achieve a better political control over liberal agencies more than already moderate or conservative agencies.

Moreover, the Bush administration made an effort to maximize the political responsiveness of the SES, as the percentage of non-career SES members increased to 9.97% of the total ranks.[145] Moreover, to advance the strategic human capital management designed by the President's Management Agenda, the G.W. Bush presidency launched a substantial reform of the SES that became part of the 2004 National Defense Authorization Act. Under the act and a subsequent executive order, agencies not certified by OMB as making real merit distinctions in rewarding SES members were given lower pay scales than certified agencies. However, these changes were scaled back after court suits.

The President's Management Agenda

Early in his administration, President Bush unveiled his "president's management agenda," aimed at revamping the federal government workforce. The agenda identified 14 management problems within the federal government, and it offered specific solutions to address each of them. Bush's agenda called for rethinking government, a reduction of middle management, and a "results-oriented," "market-based" administration. It proposed several government-wide initiatives, including the competitive sourcing and strategic management of human capital, specifically related to civil service reform.

As the first "MBA president," George W. Bush made better management and performance of the federal government a plank in his campaign platform. He acted on it early in his administration by developing a targeted agenda to improve agency-level management capacity and program-level performance and results. He maintained a consistent focus on the core elements of this agenda over the course of his entire administration. His management initiatives were run out of the OMB, and the deputy director for management reported directly to him on the progress of these initiatives. The initial agenda was developed by a small team in the OMB and implemented systematically over the entire eight-year period. His key initiatives included an agenda to improve agency management capacity, a tracking system for following the implementation of the agenda, and a program-by-program assessment process to rate the effectiveness of individual programs.

On February 28, 2001, a month following his inauguration, President Bush presented to Congress a budget plan titled "A Blueprint for New Beginnings."[146] In a section named "Government Reform," the president called for a governmental action that "empowers States, cities, and citizens to make decisions; ensures results through accountability; and promotes innovation through competition."[147] He went on to explain that "if reform is to help the Federal Government adapt to a rapidly changing world, its primary objectives must be a Government that is: Citizen-centered—not bureaucracy-centered; Results-centered—not process-oriented; and Market-based—actively promoting, not stifling, innovation and competition."[148]

Later that spring, on April 8, 2001, the president revealed more details of his proposed fiscal year 2002 budget.[149] Section 1, entitled "Improving Government Performance," promised that the administration would "reform and modernize" government on the basis of the three objectives described in *The Blueprint for New Beginnings*. It promised that in just a few months, the administration would announce a more comprehensive reform and management plan.[150] Finally, the section on "Improving Government Performance" included three sentences that were to be repeated many times throughout the president's tenure:

> Good beginnings are not the measure of success in Government or any other pursuit. What matters in the end is performance. Not just making promises, but making good on promises. This will be the standard for this Administration—from the farthest field office to the highest office in the land—as we begin the process of getting results from Government.[151]

Crafting the Strategy OMB Director Mitch Daniels started the work to finalize the details of the President's Management Agenda. On Saturday, March 15, 2001, the director convened the OMB's senior management across in the White House Conference Center. He asked them all to suggest the most important issues needing attention. The meeting generated more than 100 policy, program, and management issues.

In addition, OMB Deputy Director Sean O'Keefe called for an inventory of the top ten management recommendations by the inspectors general, the

GAO's high-risk list, and the encyclopedic listing of management problems assembled the year before when Senator Fred Thompson chaired the Senate Committee on Governmental Affairs. Director Daniels also reached outside to the National Academy of Public Administration for help, recruiting its president, Bob O'Neill, to come to the OMB on a six-month Intergovernmental Personnel Act assignment to advise him on management issues and the development of an agenda to determine them.[152]

Anticipating the release of a management agenda later that summer, in July 2001, the president issued a memorandum directing department and agency heads to designate chief operating officers, and he reestablished the PMC consisting of those officers. The PMC provided an integrating mechanism for policy implementation within agencies and across government. The Council met on a regular basis, providing an integrating mechanism for policy implementation within agencies and across government. Importantly, the PMC was conceived as a way for the departments and agencies to support the president's government-wide priorities and build a community of management leadership who could work together. The PMC had played an important role in developing standards for success for each of the five PMA initiatives. The PMC also played a key role in the selection and early implementation of 25 cross-cutting e-government projects under the PMA's expanding e-government initiative.[153]

In August 2001, the president issued his President's Management Agenda. Rather than pursuing a wide set of initiatives as his predecessor Clinton, the president focused attention on five core management problems: (1) strategic management of human capital, (2) competitive sourcing, (3) improvement of financial performance, (4) expansion of e-government, and (5) budget and performance integration. These five core management problems were targeted because they were "the most apparent deficiencies where the opportunity to improve performance is the greatest." Each of the five elements of the PMA was further defined by eight to ten "standards of success" that were measurable. The PMA focused on remedies to problems generally agreed to be serious, and the PMC committed to implement these remedies fully.[154]

The administration assigned four political appointees in the OMB and one in the OPM as government-wide leaders for each initiative, holding them personally responsible for leading their government-wide implementation. These assignments gave a clear signal to other political appointees, as well as career staff, of the administration's commitment to and strong interest in achieving management reform. The assignments also underscored the importance the president placed on disciplined, ongoing attention to these government-wide priorities. Agencies were expected to develop plans, identify responsible officials, and apply resources to achieve these improvement goals within their own organizations. The administration relied on OMB career program examiners to track agency implementation, forging a stronger link between management and budget than had been present in prior reform initiatives.

Public Personnel Management

Less than one month into his first term, President George W. Bush issued Executive Order 13203, revoking Clinton's eight-year-old executive order (EO 12871) that had established the NPC. The NPC had been operating rather successfully; but without any written or verbal justification, Bush dissolved the NPC and rescinded agency directives implementing partnerships. Unions and management expressed disappointment over the move.

It was the first in a series of actions that would result in some of the most substantive changes in civil service in 25 years.

The Chief Human Capital Officers (CHCO) Act of 2002, enacted as Title XIII of the Homeland Security Act of 2002, replaced rule-of-three hiring government-wide with category ranking and direct hires. Category ranking allowed an agency manager to select any candidate placed in a "best qualified" category, rather than selecting one of the top three scoring candidates. Direct-hire authority empowered an agency to appoint individuals to positions without adherence to certain competitive examination requirements when there was a shortage of qualified candidates or there was a critical hiring need.

The CHCO Act also enabled the heads of 24 executive departments and agencies to appoint or designate CHCOs. Each CHCO served as his or her agency's chief policy advisor on all human resource management issues and was charged with selecting, developing, training, and managing a high-quality, productive workforce. In addition, the CHCO Act set up a CHCO Council to advise and coordinate the activities of members' agencies on such matters as the modernization of human resources systems, improved quality of human resources information, and legislation affecting human resources operations and organizations. The law was significant because it established a process of decentralization of personnel management from the presidency. Indeed the system moved from a presidency-centered human resource management, established with the 1978 Civil Service Reform Act, to a more decentralized mechanism, based on agencies and departments' CHCOs. In the Bush era, management principle reaffirmed as predominant over merit principle in personnel management, due to the introduction of direct hiring and category ranking for agencies and departments, but it was a decentralized management, spread among the different administrative units and not monopolized by the Executive Office of the President.

Moreover, in April 2002, OPM released a white paper entitled "A Fresh Start for Federal Pay: The Case for Modernization."[155] The white paper examined the condition of the federal civil servants pay and job evaluation system. It was the first step to discuss the possibilities for using more up-to-date approaches for setting and adjusting pay in the federal government to improve the balance across internal, external, and individual equities. The merit system principles promised all three, but the white paper set out a strong case that the

General Schedule became market-intensive, performance-intensive, and overly dominated by internal equity.

In this vein, on the front of benefits, the OPM had already implemented a Health Insurance Premium Conversion Plan in September 2000.[156] The plan involved around 1.6 million of federal civil servants who participated in the Federal Employees Health Benefits (FEHB) program. The civil servant earmarked a portion of gross pay to be used to pay premiums for the FEHB plan coverage he chose. OPM adopted the plan on behalf of the federal executive branch. Moreover, former OPM Director Kay Coles James secured the rollout of flexible spending accounts to move the federal government into a more competitive position with the private sector.

In addition, the progressive path of the federal civil service toward family-friendly policies and practices continued with the approval of the Long-Term Care Security Act. The law was prompted by an increasingly urgent issue of helping civil servants pay for extremely costly long-term care services such as home care or care in a nursing home or assisted living facility for themselves or family members. OPM crafted with private insurance companies long-term care insurance policies for federal civil servants, retirees, and their families. Then, the Federal Long-Term Care Insurance Program was presented in 2002.[157] Despite the fact that the government did not contribute, the costs were significantly reduced because of a group policy rate and economies of scale. OPM Former Director James explained, "Our long-term care insurance program establishes the Federal Government as a pacesetter in the marketplace."[158]

The Bush administration maintained a politically centrist position: it made efforts to improve the conditions of the federal civil servants and not to dismantle them using an ideological anti-statism approach, but with the enhancement of a stronger cooperation with the private sector. The federal government acted as a coordinator and guarantor toward private insurance companies, rather than as a direct provider.

The Department of Homeland Security and the Department of Defense

In 2002, President Bush struggled to secure authority both for the new Department of Homeland Security (DHS) and the Department of Defense (DoD) to create their own personnel systems outside the traditional service system.

When the new DHS was established in the spring of 2003, it comprised 22 different agencies with 170,000 employees and a budget of 40 billion dollars.[159] It was the largest reorganization of the executive branch since the National Security Act of 1947.

The DHS legislation promised the new department the authority to create its own personnel system outside of the government-wide system under which most federal agencies and departments had operated. The aim was to improve the way workers were paid, promoted, deployed, and disciplined. Civil service rules and provisions that traditionally embraced civil servant protection were to give way to ones that supported performance and managerial flexibility and discretion. New regulations, to cover 35,000 employees, were jointly issued by the DHS and the OPM in February 2005. In 2002, OPM director Kay Cole James told a House committee, "with a mission this critical, we cannot afford a personnel system that rewards mediocrity and demoralizes high performers".[160]

In April 2003, officials from the new department, OPM, and ten representatives from three federal employee unions were brought together to begin developing proposals for new personnel policies in six core areas: classification, compensation, adverse actions, appeals, labor relations, and performance management. This design team consulted with representatives from a variety of federal agencies, state and local governments, and private organizations and reviewed publications addressing public personnel management issues.[161]

The team developed a long list of alternative proposals for personnel policy in the areas specified, including options that ranged from maintenance of current practices to dramatic departures from traditional civil service procedures.[162] Final decisions on the nature of the new system favored the most far-reaching reform ideas and were published as proposed regulations in the Federal Register on February 20, 2004. The proposed new rules for the DHS personnel system called for the establishment of new systems for job classifications, pay administration, and employee performance appraisals.[163]

The department would abandon the government-wide General Schedule classification system for white-collar employees by classifying jobs into broad occupational categories based on the type of work and skills needed on the job. A broad-banded pay structure would then be developed, with broad salary categories corresponding to work at specific levels (designated "entry or developmental," "full performance," "senior expert," and "supervisory"). Individual pay adjustments within each band would consist of market-related adjustments, locality pay supplements, and annual performance-based pay increases.

Moreover, the regulations established that the results of the individual performance appraisals were to be used to inform decisions regarding annual increases in salary. The proposed rules also significantly compressed employee rights to collective bargaining. Bargaining over wages and benefits was already denied by federal government, but in the DHS, bargaining over fundamental working conditions also was to be restricted.

The rules specifically forbade negotiation over the number and the types of employees in a given unit; the methods and means employees use to perform work; management's right to determine mission, organization, budget, and internal security practices; and management's right to hire, assign, and direct employees. The department had the authority to take any action in any of these areas without advance notice.

Final regulations outlining the new DHS personnel system, known as MAX HR, were announced on February 1, 2005. Federal employee unions strenuously opposed the new system and immediately announced a series of lawsuits against the DHS, arguing that the new collective bargaining rules violated guarantees of collective bargaining in the Homeland Security Act.

These series of union challenges and court rulings prevented the DHS from implementing the labor relations provisions of the new system.[164] While the department went ahead with performance management, appeals, and adverse actions portions of the system, it decided to hold off implementing its pay-for-performance provisions. Finally, having lost support in Congress as well, the department's fiscal year 2009 appropriations act prohibited it from spending funds to operate its provisions. In October 2008, the new system was cancelled.

Meanwhile, the personnel reforms in the DHS had led to proposals from the DoD to revise its personnel system for close to 750,000 of its civilian workers. Created under authority provided by the 2004 National Defense Authorization Act, the National Security Personnel System included provisions to limit unions' scope of bargaining and permitted the DoD to create an alternative due process system for employees subject to adverse action. Subsequently, a group of unions filed a lawsuit challenging the DoD's regulations and a federal appellate court found in their favor. The DoD then elected to apply the system only to non-unionized workers, at least initially. However, the system ultimately became very complicated while continuing to generate suspicion from some employees that it was not fair. The 2010 Defense Authorization Act repealed the new system's legal authority and required that existing regulations governing the pay-for-performance system be rescinded by January 1, 2012. That act also called for the Secretary of Defense to plan, in consultation with the OPM, for a new performance management system. The nature of that system is still unknown, but given the controversy, it is unlikely that it will be tied to compensation.

Along with the personnel reforms developed by the DHS and the DoD, the OPM and White House officials developed plans to rewrite and, hence, eviscerate civil service rules governing all federal government employees. For example, the OPM and the OMB drafted legislation (the Working for America Act, formerly known as the Civil Service Modernization Act of 2005) that would have replaced the general schedule with performance- and market-based pay government-wide. Nothing came of this bill.

A year earlier, a less ambitious piece of legislation, the Federal Workforce Flexibility Act of 2004, was passed and signed into law by President Bush. Among other provisions, it did the following: it gave agencies, with permission from the OPM and the OMB, the authority to set a higher level of pay for critical positions crucial to the agency's mission; it required agencies to establish a comprehensive management succession program to include training of employees to develop managers; and it gave agencies the authority to establish larger recruitment and relocation bonuses, and to pay retention bonuses to employees that would leave the service.

The reforms for the DHS and DoD were proposed in the name of national security; this was the political motivation that allowed the legislation to pass, even if it was short-lived. This represented a change from previous eras, when other rationales were advanced for civil service reform. For instance, even in the 1990s, Congress allowed the IRS and the FAA to develop their own personnel systems because of the urgent need for computer modernization. In the case of the DHS and DoD (and potentially across the government, as desired by the Bush II administration), the reforms proved too massive to prevail.

Implementing PMA: "Traffic Light" Scorecard and Management Legislation

The administration developed an Executive Branch Management Scorecard to track the implementation of the PMA. The scorecard employed a simple "traffic light" grading system to track the status and progress of each department and major agency. Scores for status were based on a government-wide standard for success for each initiative.[165] The standards were developed by the PMC and discussed with experts throughout government and academe, including the National Academy of Public Administration. A green status score meant that the agency had met all of the elements of the standard for success according to the plans agreed upon with the OMB; yellow meant that the agency had achieved an intermediate level of performance in all the criteria; and red meant that the agency had one or more serious flaws. When the PMA was launched, 110 of the 130 scores (26 agencies each working on five separate initiatives) were red: almost none of the agencies were satisfactorily managing their people, programs, costs, or investments in information technology.

Every 90 days, OMB program examiners reassessed each department's and agency's status and progress, and published updated scores. Not only did the OMB's deputy director for management meet regularly with agency officials to review and critique their scorecards, but also the president was reported to have discussed the scores with his cabinet members.[166] In addition, during the Bush II presidency, there were some important but little known legislative proposals to achieve government-wide management reform. Months before 9/11, the Bush administration began drafting several pieces of legislation related to the elimination or reduction of barriers to efficient government operations, through either the repeal or amendment of current law or the provision of new authority. One legislative proposal was the Freedom to Manage Act of 2001, the first bill that President Bush personally transmitted to Congress.[167] This act would have allowed management reform measures to receive expedited congressional consideration. The proposed bill established a procedure whereby heads of departments and agencies could identify statutory barriers to good management. Congress, in turn, would quickly consider those obstacles and act to remove them.

In November 2001, OMB deputy director Sean O'Keefe testified about the bill in a hearing before the House Rules Committee:

> Unfortunately, federal managers are greatly limited in how they can use financial and human resources to manage programs. They lack much of the discretion given to their private sector counterparts to do what it takes to get the job done. Red tape still hinders efficient operation of government organizations, excessive control and approval mechanisms afflict bureaucratic processes.[168]

A second legislative proposal was the Managerial Flexibility Act of 2001, which would have provided federal managers with tools and flexibility in areas such as personnel, budgeting, and property management and disposal. The personnel flexibilities included provisions addressing SES performance and compensation, personnel demonstration authorities, government-wide buyout authority, early-out amendments, recruitment and retention incentives, and hiring flexibilities. Budgeting for results provisions would have provided for full funding of federal retiree costs, full charging of costs for support services, capital acquisition, and hazardous waste cleanup. Property disposal provisions would allow agencies to use the proceeds from property sales or leases.

Each of the government-wide management reform legislative proposals—the Freedom to Manage Act and the Managerial Flexibility Act—quickly died in Congress. Despite their introduction by Senator Fred Thompson in the Senate (S.1612 and S.1613), the measures received little support. Members of both parties had concerns about ceding any legislative power to the White House. Many viewed the fast track process as an unprecedented grab for power by the executive branch. The proposals also met thorough opposition from the two largest federal labor groups. The American Federation of Government Employees described one of the bills as "a grab bag of changes which provides higher salaries and lower accountability for the most highly paid federal executives."[169] In the end, the two bills failed.

Another act, known informally as the Working for America Act, further described the types of reforms the Bush administration would have liked to institute for the federal civil service; however, it met a similar demise as the other Bush II–era measures. A lesson from the Bush II years is that civil service reform cannot succeed if one makes an enemy of the unions.

Nonetheless, the administration's push for greater freedom to manage did not cease with these bills. Several provisions of the Managerial Flexibility Act found their way into subsequent legislative proposals. Indeed, as we have seen, the administration's proposed legislation creating the U.S. DHS included provisions for revamping federal civil service rules, as did legislation authorizing the DoD to create a National Security Personnel System.

Continuity and Change

The Bush II presidency presented some continuities both with the past Republican presidencies of Ronald Reagan and his father, and with the Democratic one of Bill Clinton. Compared with the former Republican presidents, and Reagan in particular, George W. Bush appeared more interested in making the machine work, rather than concentrated on trying to dismantle it and to pursue a small government approach. As he stated in the incipit of his agenda,

> We must have a government that thinks differently, so we need to recruit talented and imaginative people to public service. We can do this by reforming the civil service with a few simple measures. We'll establish a meaningful system to measure performance. Create awards for employees who surpass expectations. Tie pay increases to results. With a system of rewards and accountability, we can promote a culture of achievement throughout the Federal Government.[170]

Bush's discourse was still permeated by neo-liberal rhetoric. As president, he promoted some contracting-out policies, and he attempted to curb the civil service unions for the sake of pursing his policy objectives, but his approach appeared more technocratic than that of his Republican predecessors. Indeed, at the administrative level, he had been an "MBA President," very interested in management and personnel policy rather than in reduction in force or cutting costs. In terms of public appointments, he was more like Reagan than his father had been, using an aggressive posture on spoil systems and toward the merit principle.

With the reforms of DHS and DoD he proved to be very keen on achieving increased political control over federal bureaucracy and on promoting management principle over merit one. Indeed, he fully used the space left by the 1978 CSRA to politicize the SES, in which he achieved more than past presidents had. Moreover, the Bush administration showed to prefer decentralized performance management to the OPM's monopoly, giving more autonomy to agencies and department in managing human resources.

Both Bush II and Clinton placed similar attention on improving program performance and obtaining results. While the Clinton reform effort undertook the initial implementation of the GPRA, which created a new supply of performance information, the Bush administration systematically attempted to use that information to improve agencies' performance and increase accountability of their managers. Both had similar shifts in implementation strategy, starting with top-down recommendations and initiatives, then shifting to more of a support role where they worked with senior agency leaders to develop initiatives and performance targets jointly. This led to greater ownership by agency-level political appointees.

Yet Bush and Clinton were different in their scope. Clinton's performance review produced more than 1,200 recommendations. Clinton generated an inflation of recommendations and some of them were too idealist and naive. This approach produced some failures in reorganizing the federal civil service. However, the Clinton effort continued to generate initiatives and recommendations during the entire eight-year period. It issued more than 100 reports and publications. In contrast, Bush's "President's Management Agenda" focused on a few main ideas that represented long-standing and well-known management challenges. The Bush administration narrowly focused on the implementation of these core elements for its entire eight years, and it added or deleted relatively few items to or from its management agenda.

The two presidencies differed in managing their respective staffs. Clinton's NPR formed on its own a team of temporary dedicated staff and agency-based teams, while the Bush administration relied on OMB's permanent career staff as well as permanent staff in the departments and agencies.

In terms of strategy, the NPR attempted to directly engage civil servants. It did this through its awards program, its reinvention lab initiative, and meetings. The Bush administration, on the other hand, systematically engaged agency political leaders in much more of a top-down, chain of command manner, briefing them on the top policy priorities of the President's Management Agenda.

The two presidents differed from each other even in labor/management approaches. The NPR made an extensive effort to bargain with federal employee unions via labor–management partnership councils in each agency. In contrast, as we also have seen, an early Bush administration directive curtailed their role and sought to expose the delivery of government services to competition with the private sector.

In broader terms, Bush's agenda for administrative reform was government-wide and less detailed in its aims than Clinton's program, but it was more technocratic and probably more sophisticated in the implementation process.

Notes

1 Paul D. Moreno, *The Bureaucrat Kings: The Origins and Underpinnings of America's Bureaucratic State* (Santa Barbara, CA: Praeger, 2017), 128.
2 James Q. Wilson, *The Politics of Regulation* (New York: Basic Books, 1980).
3 National Journal, "Bureaucrats Under Fire," September 30, 1978, p. 1540.
4 U.S. Congress, House Committee on House Administration, *Campaign 1976. Vol. 1, Part 1, Jimmy Carter, committee print, 95th Cong., 2nd sess.* (Washington, DC: GPO, 1978), 581.
5 R. P. Seyb, "Reform as Reaffirmation: Jimmy Carter's Executive Branch Reorganization Effort," *Presidential Studies Quarterly* 31 (2001): 104–121.

6 For a reconstruction of the origins of the neo-managerial theories in the 1970s, see Laurence E. Lynn Jr, *Public Management New and Old* (London: Routledge, 2006).

7 See Gabriel Kolko, *The Triumph of Conservatism* (New York: Free Press, 1963); James M. Landis, *Report on Regulatory Agencies to the President-Elect* (Washington, DC: Government Printing Office, 1960).

8 James E. Carter, *Why Not the Best?* (Washington, DC: Broadman Press, 1977), 147.

9 U.S. Congress, Senate, Committee on Government Affairs, *Nomination of John P. White to be the Deputy Director of the Office of Management and Budget*, Hearings, 96th Cong. 1st Session, Government Printing Office, Washington, 1979, 28.

10 Michael J. Hogan, *A Cross of Iron* (Cambridge: Cambridge University Press 1998), 44.

11 Stephen P. Waring, *Taylorism Transformed* (Chapel Hill: University of North Carolina Press, 1991).

12 Moe, *Administrative Renewal* (Lanham, MD: University Press of America, 2003), 99.

13 U.S. Library of Congress, Congressional Research Service, *The Carter Reorganization Effort: A Review and Assessment*, CRS, Rept. 80-172G (Washington, DC: CRS, 1980).

14 Reorganization Act of 1977 P.L. 95-17; 91 Stat. 29.

15 Peri Arnold, *Making the Managerial Presidency* (Lawrence: University Press of Kansas, 1986).

16 Patricia Ingraham and Carolyn Ban, *Legislating Bureaucratic Change. The Civil Service Reform Act of 1978* (Albany: State University of New York Press, 1984).

17 J. P. McGrath, "The Senior Executive Service: Morale and Staffing Problems. A Brief Overview," *Congressional Research Service Report*, Washington, DC, 1987.

18 Reorganization Plan No. 1, 43 F.R. 19807, 92 Stat. 3781, March 9, 1978.

19 The board would take over all the appeals functions that the commission had exercised, except classification appeals which remained to OPM. The board would protect merit systems by two methods: (a) in the manner of an administrative court, hearing and deciding cases in which federal officials and employees are charged with violating merit system rules and procedures; (b) annually, or more often, reporting on signification actions of OPM.

20 The term "whistleblowers" denotes those civil servants who denounce recognizable malpractices and cases of corruption in their offices.

21 Reorganization Plan No. 2, 43 F.R. 36037, 92 Stat. 3783, May 23, 1978.

22 Robert Maranto and David Schultz, *A Short History of the United States Civil Service* (Lanham, MD: University Press of America, 1991), 131.

23 For a comprehensive analysis on performance management introduced by CSRA 1978, see Ingraham and Ban, *Legislating Bureaucratic Change.*

24 J. L. Perry, "The Civil Service Reform Act of 1978: A 30-Year Retrospective and a Look Ahead," *Review of Public Personnel Administration* 28, no. 3 (Sept. 2008): 200–204.

25 Sar A. Levitan and Alexandra Noden. *Working for the Sovereign: Employee Relations in the Federal Government* (Baltimore, MD: Johns Hopkins University Press, 1983), 111–113.

26 As underlined by Maranto and Schultz, *A Short History,* 149–161.

27 Personnel Management Project, Volume 1 Final Staff Report in the President's Reorganization Project, December 1977, Section 4 "Improving Opportunities for Women and Minorities," pp. 81–103.

28 See Lawrence C Howard, "Civil Service Reform: A Minority and Woman's Perspective," *Public Administration Review* 38, no. 4 (1978): 305–309.

29 Levitan and Noden, *Working for the Sovereign,* 7–8.

30 Ethics in Government Act 1978, Pub. L. 95–521, titles I–V, Oct. 26, 1978, 92 Stat. 1824–1867.

31 Grace Commission, *President's Private Sector Survey on Cost Control: A Report to the President* (Washington DC: GPO, 1984).

32 Grace Commission Report, I-1.

33 President's Private Sector Survey on Cost Control, *War on Waste* (New York: Macmillan, 1984), 1.

34 President's Private Sector Survey on Cost Control, *War on Waste*, 3.

35 Grace Commission Report, II-1.

36 Grace Commission Report, IV-2.

37 Grace Commission Report, IV-3.

38 Grace Commission, 1, Letter of transmission to the President.

39 Grace Commission Report, II-3.

40 Grace Commission Report, II-19.

41 Grace Commission Report, III-4.

42 S. D. Zink, *Guide to the Presidential Advisory Commissions 1973–84* (Alexandria, VA: Chadwyck-Healey, Inc., 1985), 456–475. Office of Management and Budget, *Management of the United States Government Fiscal Year 1988* (Washington, DC: GPO, 1988).

43 Arnold, *Making the Managerial Presidency*, 375.

44 On this point, see James R. Locher, III, "Taking Stock of Goldwater-Nichols," *Joint Force Quarterly*, Institute for National Strategic Studies National Defense University, 12 (1996): 10–17.

45 The Supreme Court decision INS vs. Chandha of 1977 had a significant impact on deliberation in Congress. The Supreme Court ruled that legislative vetoes, including those attached to the reorganization authority, were unconstitutional.

46 See U.S. Library of Congress, Congressional Research Service, *The President's Reorganization Authority: Review and Analysis*, by Roland C. Moe, CRS, RL30876, Washington, March 8, 2001.

47 Charles L. Heatherly, *Mandate for Leadership: Policy Management in a Conservative Administration* (Washington DC: The Heritage Foundation, 1981).

48 Walker Wallace and Michael Reopel, "Strategies for Governance: Transition and Domestic Policymaking in the Reagan Administration," *Presidential Studies Quarterly* 16, no. 4 (1986): 734–742.

49 Dom Bonafede, "Reagan and His Kitchen Cabinet are Bound by Friendship and Ideology," *National Journal* 13, no. 5 (1981): 609.

50 Dick Kirschten, "You Say You Want a sub-Cabinet Post? Clear it with Marty, Dick, Lyn or Fred," *National Journal* 4 (Apr. 1981), 564.

51 Ingraham, Patricia W. "Toward More Systematic Consideration of Policy Design." *Policy Studies Journal* 15, no.4 (1987): 611.

52 As highlighted by Calvin G. Mackenzie, *The In and Outers* (Baltimore, MD: John Hopkins University Press, 1987).

53 GAO, "Effects of Presidential Transition on the SES," letter to representative Patricia Schroeder, FPCD-82-29, 23 March 1982.

54 Mark W. Huddleston, *The Government's Managers* (New York: Priority Press, 1987).

55 Patricia Ingraham, "Building Bridges or Destroying Them: The President, The Appointees and the Bureaucracy," *Public Administration Review* 47, no. 5 (1987): 425–435.

56 Kirschten, "You Say You Want," 735.

57 Department of Commerce, Bureau of Statistics, *Statistical Abstract of the United States: 1989*, 318.

58 H.R.6410—Paperwork Reduction Act of 1980, P.L. 96-511, 94 STAT. 2812.

59 On this point, see David Savoie, *Thatcher, Reagan, and Mulroney: In Search of a New Bureaucracy* (Pittsburgh, PA: University of Pittsburgh Press, 1994).

60 J. L. Perry, B. A. Petrakis, and T. K. Miller, "Federal Merit Pay, Round II: An Analysis of the Performance Management and Recognition System," *Public Administration Review* 49, no. 1 (Jan.–Feb. 1989): 29–37.

61 National Research Council, *Pay for Performance: Evaluating Performance Appraisal and Merit Pay* (Washington, DC: National Academies Press, 1991).

62 Committee on Post Office and Civil Service House of Representatives, *Reauthorization of the Performance Management and Recognition System* (Washington, DC: GPO, 1989).

63 G. B. Lewis, "Progress Towards Racial and Sexual Equality in the Federal Service?" *Public Administration Review* 48, no. 3 (May/June 1988): 701.

64 R. W. Hurd and J. K. Kriesky, "The Rise and Demise of PATCO Reconstructed," *Industrial and Labor Relations Review* 40, no. 1 (1986): 115.

65 Hurd and Kriesky, "The Rise and Demise," 121.

66 Herbert Roof Northrup and Amie D. Thornton, *The Federal Government as Employer: The Federal Labor Relations Authority and the PATCO Challenge* (Philadelphia: The Wharton School, University of Pennsylvania, 1985), 16–21.

67 See Terry M. Moe, "The Politicized Presidency," in *The New Direction in American Politics,* eds. (Washington, DC: The Brooking Institution, 1985).

68 James P. Pfiffner, "Establishing the Bush Presidency," *Public Administration Review* 50, no. 1 (1990): 64–73.

69 Maranto and Schultz, *A Short History,* 184.

70 *National Journal,* "A Gathering of Friends," 10 June 1989, 1402–1403.

71 Robert Maranto, "Comparing the Clinton, Bush and Reagan transition in the Bureaucracy: Views from Bureaucrats," *Midwest Political Science Association Meeting,* Chicago, IL, 1995.

72 On this point, see John Podhoretz, *Hell of a Ride: Backstage at the White House Follies, 1989–1993* (New York: Simon and Schuster, 1993).

73 Maranto, "Comparing the Clinton."

74 Maranto, "Comparing the Clinton."

75 J. Haveman, "Senior Civil Servants Face New Rules with Pay Hike," *Washington Post,* 21 October 1989, A8.

76 Haveman, "Senior Civil Servants."

77 P. B. Petersen, "Total Quality Management and the Deming Approach to Quality Management," *Journal of Management History,* 5 (1999): 468–488.

78 M. E. Milakovich, "Total Quality Management in the Public Sector," *National Productivity Review* 10, no. 2 (1991): 195–213.

79 For a more ample picture of liberalization and privatization, see B. H. Milward, "Implications of Contracting Out: New Roles for the Hollow State," in *New Paradigms for Government: Issues for the Changing Public Service,* eds. (San Francisco, CA: Jossey Bass, 1995), 41–62.

80 M. Doud, "President Vetoes a Bill and Makes Threat on a Second," *New York Times,* 16 June 1990, A1.

81 Emmanuel Savas, *Privatization and Public Private Partnership* (New York: Seven Bridges, 2000).

82 Robert F. Durant, *Building the Compensatory State* (Abingdon and New York: Routledge, 2019), pos. 6149.

83 Durant, *Building,* pos. 6122.

84 National Performance Review, *From Red Tape to Results: Creating a Government that Works Better and Costs Less* (Washington, DC: U.S. Government Printing Office, 1993), 48.

85 David Osborne and Ted Gaebler, *Reinventing Government: How the Entrepreneurial Spirit is Transforming the Public Sector* (New York: Plume, 1992).

86 David Osborne and Peter Plastrik, *Banishing Bureaucracy: The Five Strategies for Reinventing Government* (Reading, MA: Wesley Addison, 1997).

87 John Dilulio, "Recovering the Public Management Variable: Lessons from Schools, Prisons, and Armies," *Public Administration Review* 49, no. 2 (1989): 127–133.

88 Michael Barzelay and Babak J. Armajani, *Breaking Through Bureaucracy: A New Vision for Managing in Government* (Berkeley: University of California Press, 1992), 127.

89 Osborne and Gaebler, *Reinventing Government,* 1992.

90 National Performance Review, *From Red Tape to Results,* 3.

91 National Performance Review, *From Red Tape to Results,* 8.

92 *History of the National Partnership for Reinventing Government Accomplishments,* Washington DC, 1993 – 2000.

93 G. Calvin Mackenzie and Robert Shogan, *Obstacle Course* (New York: Twentieth-Century Fund, 1996).

94 James P. Pfiffner, *The Strategic Presidency. Hitting the Ground Running* (Lawrence: University of Kansas Press, 1996), 169.

95 David A. Schultz and Robert Maranto, *The Politics of Civil Service Reform* (New York: Peter Lang, 1998), 202.

96 Robert Maranto, "Exploring the Clinton Transition: Views from the Career Civil Service," *American Political Science Association Meeting,* Washington, DC, 1993.

97 S. Barr, "Un-Hatched Workers Practice Their Politics," *Washington Post,* 26 August 1996, A11.

98 Charles Peters, *How Washington Really Works* (Reading, PA: Addison-Wesley, 1992).

99 Thomas J. Peters and Robert H. Waterman, *In Search of Excellence: Lessons from America's Best Run Companies* (New York: Warner, 1992).

100 J. A. Champy and M. M. Hammer, *Reengineering the Corporation: A Manifesto for Business Revolution* (New York: Harper Business), 1993.

101 See Barzelay and Armajani, *Breaking through Bureaucracy*; also Christopher Hood, *The Art of the State* (Oxford: Oxford University Press, 2000).

102 W. J. Clinton, "Remarks by the President," 3 March 1993.

103 Stephen Cohen and William Eimicke, *The New Effective Public Manager: Achieving Success in a Changing Government* (San Francisco, CA: Jossey-Bass, 1995), 137.

104 Clinton, "Remarks."

105 Clinton, "Remarks."

106 J. Kamensky, "A Brief History of the National Performance Review," *National Performance Review Library,* Washington, DC, 1997, 3.

107 Kamensky, "A Brief History," 3.

108 On this point, see Spencer Zifcak, *New Managerialism: Administrative Reform in Whitehall and Canberra* (Buckingham: Open University Press, 1994).

109 Arnold, *The History,* 370.

110 National Performance Review, *From Red Tape to Results.*

111 For a critique of this model, see Ronald C. Moe, "The Reinventing Government Exercise," *Public Administration Review* 54 (1994): 111–122.

112 S. Barr, "Gore's Team Turn to Making Reinvention Deliver," *Washington Post,* 3 March 1998, A15.

113 Government Performance and Results Act (GPRA) 1993, P.L. 103-62 (107 Stat. 285).

114 OPM, *Biography of an Ideal: A History of the Federal Civil Service* (Washington, DC: U.S. Civil Service Commission, 2012), 301.

115 See the National Performance Review, *Common Sense Government* (Washington, DC: GPO, 1995).

116 The OPM elaborated a one-size-fits-all application form, the SF-171.

117 Public Law 104-52 (1995).

118 The OPM considered the Act very important at that time: "The Office of Personnel Management's (OPM's) priorities for the coming year will center on human resource management reforms that will enable the Federal Government to meet the challenges of downsizing, increased use of technology, delayering, decentralization, improved labor-management relationships, and other changes that are reinventing the Federal work force. The passage of the Federal Human Resource Management Reinvention Act of 1995 is central to OPM's plans for reform. Many of its provisions will increase the opportunities for Federal agencies to use broadbanding, more demonstration projects, and performance-based pay plans, such as team incentives and goal-sharing. All of these tools are needed to lead Federal human resource management into the twenty-first century." See OPM, *The Regulatory Plan and Unified Agenda of Federal Regulations* (Washington DC: GPO, 1995).

119 Al Gore, *National Partnership for Reinventing Government*, Thursday, January 14, 1999. Available here: https://govinfo.library.unt.edu/npr/library/news/011499. html (accessed 17th July 2020).

120 U.S. Office of Management and Budget, *Government-wide Performance Plan* (Washington DC: Government Printing Office, 2000).

121 Anne Laurent, *Entrepreneurial Government: Bureaucrats as Businesspeople* (Washington, Dc: PWC, 2000).

122 GAO, *Reinventing Government: Status of NPR recommendations at Ten Federal Agencies*, GGD-00-145: Published: September 21, 2000. Publicly Released: Oct 12, 2000, Washington, DC: GAO, 4.

123 GAO, *Reinventing Government,* 2000, 18.

124 See J. R. Thompson, "Reinvention as Reform: Assessing the National Performance Review," *Public Administration Review* 60 (Nov.–Dec. 2000): 508–521.

125 Larry Terry, "Administrative Leadership, Neo-managerialism and the Public Management Movement," *Public Administration Review* 58 (May–June 1998): 194–200.

126 Donald Kettl, *Team Bush: Leadership Lessons from the Bush White House* (New York: McGraw Hill, 2003), 31.

127 James P. Pfiffner, "The First MBA President: George W. Bush as Public Administrator," *Public Administration Review* 67, no. 1 (2007): 6–20.

128 M. Allen, "Management Style Shows Weaknesses," *Washington Post*, 2 June, 2004; quoted in Pfiffner, "First MBA President," 7.

129 Ron Suskind, "Faith, Certainty, and the Presidency of George W. Bush," *New York Times Magazine*, 17 October, 2004.

130 N. Lemann, "Without a Doubt," *The New Yorker*, 14–26 October, 2002, 158; quoted in Pfiffner, "First MBA President," 7.

131 White House, "President Nominated Rob Portman as OMB Director and Susan Schwab for USTR," 18 April, 2006.

132 Robert Woodward, *Bush at War* (New York: Simon and Schuster, 2002), 144.

133 Woodward, *Bush at War,* 145–146.

134 Ron Suskind, *The Price of Loyalty: George W. Bush, the White House, and the Education of Paul O'Neill* (New York: Simon and Schuster), 97.

135 Quoted in Pfiffner, "The First MBA President," 8.

136 Jonathan D. Breul and John M. Kamensky, "Federal Government Reform: Lessons from Clinton's "Reinventing Government" and Bush's "Management Agenda" Initiatives," *Public Administration Review* 68, no. 6 (2008): 1009–1026.

137 J. VandeHei and G. Kessler, "President to Consider Changes for New Term," *Washington Post*, 5 November, 2004.

138 Paul C. Light, *The True Size of Government* (New York: Volcker Alliance, 2017), 7.

139 Numbers from Light, *True Size*.

140 Richard Nathan, *The Plot that Failed: Nixon and the Administrative Presidency* (New York: John Wiley and Sons, 1975), 8.

141 Clay Johnson interviewed by D. E. Lewis, 25 October 2006. Quoted in Colin Provost and Paul Teske, eds., *President George W. Bush's influence over Bureaucracy and Policy* (New York: Palgrave Macmillan, 2009).

142 Clay Johnson, "The 2000–2001 Presidential Transition: Planning, Goals and Reality," in *The White House World*, eds. Martha Joynt Kumar and Terry Sullivan (College Station: Texas A&M University Press, 2003), 311–317.

143 Reported by D. E. Lewis, "Personnel Is Policy: George W. Bush's Managerial Presidency," in *President George W. Bush's Influence*, eds. C. Provost and P. Teske (New York: Palgrave Macmillan, 2009), 27.

144 Lewis, "Personnel Is Policy."

145 See Robert F. Durant, *Building the Compensatory State: An Intellectual History and Theory of American Administrative Reform* (London: Routledge, 2019), Kindle Ed., pos. 6408.

146 G. W. Bush, *Blueprint for New Beginnings* (Washington, DC: Government Printing Office, 2001), 3.

147 G. W. Bush, *Blueprint,* 179–181.

148 G. W. Bush, *Blueprint,* 179.

149 *Budget of the United States,* Fiscal Year (Washington DC: Office for Management and Budget, 2002).

150 *Budget of the United States,* 11.

151 *Budget of the United States,* 11

152 Breul and Kamensky, "Federal Government Reform."

153 See President Bush's Memorandum for Heads of Executive Departments and Agencies, July 11 2001. Accessed 2 July 2020: https://georgewbush-whitehouse.archives.gov/news/releases/2001/07/20010711-5.html

154 President's Management Agenda, Fiscal Year 2002, accessed 2 July 2020: https://georgewbush-whitehouse.archives.gov/omb/budget/fy2002/mgmt.pdf

155 OPM, *A Fresh Start for Federal Pay: The Case for Modernization,* 19 April, 2002. The paper is available here: https://ourpublicservice.org/publications/opm-a-fresh-start-for-federal-pay-the-case-for-modernization/

156 See OPM, *Health Insurance Premium Conversion Plan,* GPO, Federal Register/Vol. 65, No. 139/Wednesday, July 19, 2000/Rules and Regulations.

157 The program was established in 2002 as a result of an act of Congress, the Long-Term Care Security Act of 2000 (Public Law 106-265)

158 OMB, *Biography of an Ideal.*

159 Pfiffner, "First MBA President," 16.

160 Katherine C. Naff and Meredith A. Newman, "Symposium: Federal Civil Service Reform: Another Legacy of 9/11?" *Review of Public Personnel Administration,* 24, no. 3 (2004): 197.

161 U.S. General Accounting Office, *DHS Personnel System Design Effort Provide for Collaboration and Employee Participation* (Washington, DC: US Government Printing Office, 2003).

162 U.S. Department of Homeland Security and Office of Personnel Management, *Human Resources Management System: Design Team Review of Current Practices* (Washington, DC: GPO, 2003).

163 U.S. Federal Register (2004), *Department of Homeland Security Human Resources Management System. Proposed Rule,* 8030-5347.

164 Judge Rosemary M. Collyer, a George W. Bush appointee of the U.S. District Court of Columbia, ruled that the department's regulation violated the Homeland Security Act because they did not ensure collective bargaining rights for federal employees. See *National Employees Union et al. v. Michael Chertoff,* Secretary, DHS, et al. 2005. The federal government appealed to the U.S. Court of Appeal for the

District of Columbia circuit. With a unanimous decision, the Court of Appeal not only upheld the lower court's decision but also expanded it by ruling that the DHS had inappropriately restricted the scope of bargaining. See *National Treasury Employees Union et al. v. Michael Chertoff*, Secretary, DHS and Linda M. Springer, Director of the Office of Personnel Management, 2006.

165 US Office for Management and Budget, *President's Management Agenda* (Washington, DC: GPO, 2001).

166 See J. D. Breul, "Three Bush Administration Management Reform Initiatives: The President's Management Agenda, Freedom to Manage Legislative Proposals, and the Program Assessment Rating Tool," *Public Administration Review* 67, no. 1 (2007): 21–26.

167 G. W. Bush, "Message to the Congress Transmitting the Proposed Freedom to Manage Act 2001," *Weekly Compilation of Presidential Documents* 37, no. 42 (2001): 1505–1506.

168 S. O' Keefe, Statement before the Senate Budget Committee, 7 February, 2002.

169 Quoted in Breul, "Three Bush Administration Management Reform Initiatives," 23.

170 OMB, *The President's Management Agenda* (Washington, DC: GPO, 2001), 11.

Bibliography

Arnold, Peri. *Making the Managerial Presidency*. Lawrence: University Press of Kansas, 1986.

Balogh, Brian, Joanna Grisinger, and Philip Zelikow. *Making Democracy Work: A Brief History of Twentieth Century Federal Executive Reorganization*. Charlottesville: University of Virginia Center of Public Affairs, 2002.

Barr, S. "Un-hatched Workers Practice Their Politics." *Washington Post*, 26 August 1996, A11.

———. "Gore's Team Turn to Making Reinvention Deliver." *Washington Post*, 3 March 1998, A15.

Barzelay, Michael, and Babak J. Armajani. *Breaking through Bureaucracy: A New Vision for Managing in Government*. Berkeley: University of California Press, 1992.

Berry, Jeffrey M. *The Interest Group Society*. Boston, MA: Little Brown, 1984.

Bonafede, Dom. "Reagan and His Kitchen Cabinet are Bound by Friendship and Ideology." *National Journal* 13, no. 5 (1981): 609.

Brauer, Carl M. *Presidential Transitions: Eisenhower through Reagan*. Oxford and New York: Oxford University Press, 1986.

Breul, Jonathan D. "Three Bush Administration Management Reform Initiatives: The President's Management Agenda, Freedom to Manage Legislative Proposals, and the Program Assessment Rating Tool." *Public Administration Review* 67, no. 1 (2007): 21–26.

Breul, Jonathan D., and John M. Kamensky. "Federal Government Reform: Lessons from Clinton's "Reinventing Government" and Bush's "Management Agenda" Initiatives." *Public Administration Review* 68, no. 6 (2008): 1009–1026.

Budget of the United States, Fiscal Year. Washington, DC: Office for Management and Budget, 2002.

Bush, George W. *Blueprint for New Beginnings*. Washington, DC: Government Printing Office, 2001.

———. "Message to the Congress Transmitting the Proposed Freedom to Manage Act 2001." *Weekly Compilation of Presidential Documents* 37, no. 42 (2001): 1505–1506.

Carter, James E. *Why Not the Best?* Washington, DC: Broadman Press, 1977.

Champy, J. A., and M. M. Hammer, *Reengineering the Corporation: A Manifesto for Business Revolution.* New York: Harper Business, 1993.

Clinton, W. J. Announcing the Initiative to Streamline Government, "Remarks by the President," Washington DC, 3 March 1993 (https://govinfo.library.unt.edu/npr/library/speeches/030393.html accessed 9/11/2020).

Cohen, Stephen, and William Eimicke. *The New Effective Public Manager: Achieving Success in a Changing Government.* San Francisco, CA: Jossey-Bass, 1995.

Committee on Post Office and Civil Service House of Representatives. *Reauthorization of the Performance Management and Recognition System.* Washington, DC: GPO, 1989.

Crenson, Matthew, and Francis Rourke. "By Way of Conclusion: American Bureaucracy since World War II." In *The New American State,* edited by Louis Galambos, 137–177. Baltimore, MD: Johns Hopkins University Press, 1987.

Department of Commerce, Bureau of Statistics. *Statistical Abstract of the United States: 1989,* 318.

Dilulio, John. "Recovering the Public Management Variable: Lessons from Schools, Prisons, and Armies." *Public Administration Review* 49, no. 2 (1989): 127–133.

Doud, M. "President Vetoes a Bill and Makes Threat on a Second." *New York Times,* 16 June 1990, A1.

Durant, Robert F. *Building the Compensatory State.* Abingdon and New York: Routledge, 2019.

Ferejohn John A., and Larry D. Kramer. "Independent Judges, Dependent Judiciary: Institutionalizing Judicial Restraint." *NYU Law Review* 77 (2002): 962–1009.

———. "Minnowbrook II: Changing Epochs of Public Administration." *Public Administration Review* 49, no. 2 (1989): 95–100.

GAO. *Reinventing Government: Status of NPR recommendations at Ten Federal Agencies,* GGD-00–145: Published: 21 September, 2000. Publicly Released: October 12, 2000, Washington, DC: GAO.

Gore, Al. *National Partnership for Reinventing Government,* Thursday, January 14, 1999. Available at https://govinfo.library.unt.edu/npr/library/news/011499.html.

Government Performance and Results Act (GPRA) 1993, P.L. 103–62 (107 Stat. 285).

Grace Commission. *President's Private Sector Survey on Cost Control: A Report to the President.* Washington, DC: GPO, 1984.

Graham, Otis. *Toward a Planned Society: From Roosevelt to Nixon.* Oxford: Oxford University Press, 1977.

Guy, M. E. "Minnowbrook II: Conclusions." *Public Administration Review* 49, no. 2 (1989): 219–220.

Hamburger, Philip. *Is Administrative Law Unlawful?* Chicago, IL: University of Chicago Press, 2014.

Haveman, J. "Senior Civil Servants Face New Rules with Pay Hike." *Washington Post,* 21 October 1989, A8.

Heatherly, Charles L. *Mandate for Leadership: Policy Management in a Conservative Administration.* Washington DC: The Heritage Foundation, 1981.

Kamensky, John. *History of the National Partnership for Reinventing Government Accomplishments.* Washington DC, 1999 (https://govinfo.library.unt.edu/npr/whoweare/history2.html accessed 9/11/2020.)

Hodgson, Godfrey. *America in Our Time: From World War II to Nixon, What Happened and Why.* New York: Vintage Books, 1978.

Hogan, Michael J. *A Cross of Iron.* Cambridge: Cambridge University Press, 1998.

Hood, Christopher. *The Art of the State.* Oxford: Oxford University Press, 2000.

Huddleston, Mark W. *The Government's Managers.* New York: Priority Press, 1987.

Hurd, Richard, and Jill Kriesky. "The Rise and Demise of PATCO Reconstructed." *Industrial and Labor Relations Review* 40, no. 1 (1986): 115–122.

Ingraham, Patricia. "Building Bridges or Destroying Them: The President, The Appointees and The Bureaucracy." *Public Administration Review* 47, no. 5 (1987): 425–435.

Ingraham, Patricia, and Carolyn Ban. *Legislating Bureaucratic Change. The Civil Service Reform Act of 1978.* Albany: State University of New York Press, 1984.

Ingraham, Patricia, and David H. Rosenbloom. "The New Public Personnel and the New Public Service." *Public Administration Review* 49, no. 2 (1989): 116–126.

Johnson, Clay. "The 2000–2001 Presidential Transition: Planning, Goals and Reality." In *The White House World*, edited by Martha Joynt Kumar and Terry Sullivan, 311–317. College Station: Texas A&M University Press, 2003.

Kamensky, J. "A Brief History of the National Performance Review." *National Performance Review Library*, Washington, DC, 1997.

Kane, B. "Post Office Privatization Comes to Binghamton, N.Y." *Labor Notes* 43 (July 1990): 3.

Karl, Barry. *The Uneasy State: The United States from 1915 to 1945.* Chicago, IL: The University of Chicago Press, 1983.

Kettl, Donald. *Team Bush: Leadership Lessons from the Bush White House.* New York: McGraw Hill, 2003.

Kirschten, Dick. "You Say You Want a Cabinet Post? Clear it with Marty, Dick, Lyn or Fred." *National Journal* 4 (Apr. 1981), 564.

Kolko, Gabriel. *The Triumph of Conservatism.* New York: Free Press, 1963.

Landis, James M. *Report on Regulatory Agencies to the President-Elect.* Washington, DC: US Government Printing Office, 1960.

Laurent, Anne. *Entrepreneurial Government: Bureaucrats as Businesspeople.* Washington, DC: PWC, 2000.

Lemann, Nicholas. "Without a Doubt," *The New Yorker*, 14–26 October, 2002, 158–159.

Levitan, Sar A., and Alexandra Noden. *Working for the Sovereign: Employee Relations in the Federal Government.* Baltimore, MD: Johns Hopkins University Press, 1983.

Lewis, David E. "Personnel Is Policy: George W. Bush's Managerial Presidency." In *President George W. Bush's Influence over Bureaucracy and Policy: Extraordinary Times, Extraordinary Powers*, edited by Colin Provost and Paul Teske, 19–40. New York: Palgrave Macmillan, 2009.

Lewis, G. B. "Progress Toward Racial and Sexual Equality in the Federal Civil Service?" *Public Administration Review* 48 (1988): 700–707.

Light, Paul C. *The True Size of Government.* New York: Volcker Alliance, 2017.

Locher III, James R. "Taking Stock of Goldwater-Nichols." *Joint Force Quarterly*, Institute for National Strategic Studies National Defense University, no. 12 (1996): 10–17.

Lowi, Theodore J. *The End of Liberalism: The Second Republic of the United States*, 40th anniversary edition. New York: Norton, 2009.

Lynn Jr., Laurence E. *Public Management New and Old.* London: Routledge, 2006.

MacKenzie, G. Calvin. *The Politics of Presidential Appointments.* New York: Free Press, 1981.

————. *The In and Outers*. Baltimore, MD: John Hopkins University Press, 1987.

Mackenzie, G. Calvin, and Robert Shogan. *Obstacle Course*. New York: Twentieth-Century Fund, 1996.

Maranto, Robert. "Exploring the Clinton Transition: Views from the Career Civil Service." *American Political Science Association Meeting*, Washington, DC, 1993.

Maranto, Robert. "Comparing the Clinton, Bush and Reagan transition in the Bureaucracy: Views from Bureaucrats." *Midwest Political Science Association Meeting*, Chicago, IL, 1995.

Maranto, Robert, and David Schultz. *A Short History of the United States Civil Service*. Lanham, MD: University Press of America, 1991.

McFarland, Carl. "Landis' Report: The Voice of One Crying in the Wilderness." *Virginia Law Review* 47 (1961): 392–416.

McGrath, J. P. "The Senior Executive Service: Morale and Staffing Problems. A brief Overview." *Congressional Research Service Report*, Washington, DC, 1987.

Milakovich, M. E. "Total Quality Management in the Public Sector." *National Productivity Review* 10, no. 2 (1991): 195–213.

Milkis, Sidney M. *The President and the Parties*. Oxford: Oxford University Press, 1993.

————. "Remaking Government Institutions in the 1970s: Participatory Democracy and the Triumph of Administrative Politics." *Journal of Policy History* 10 (1998): 51–74.

Milward, B. H. "Implications of Contracting Out: New Roles for the Hollow State." In *New Paradigms for Government: Issues for the Changing Public Service*, edited by Patricia W. Ingraham and Barbara S. Romzek, 41–62. San Francisco, CA: Jossey Bass, 1995.

Moe, Ronald C. "The Reinventing Government Exercise." *Public Administration Review* 54 (1994): 111–122.

————. *Administrative Renewal*. Lanham, MD: University Press of America, 2003.

Moe, Terry M. "The Politicized Presidency." In *The New Direction in American Politics*, edited by John E. Chubb and Paul E. Peterson. Washington, DC: The Brookings Institution, 1985.

Moreno, Paul D. *The Bureaucrat Kings: The Origins and Underpinnings of America's Bureaucratic State*. Santa Barbara, CA: Praeger, 2017.

Nathan, Richard. *The Plot that Failed: Nixon and the Administrative Presidency*. New York: John Wiley and Sons, 1975.

————. *The Administrative Presidency*. New York: MacMillan, 1983.

Naff Katherine C. and Newman Meredith A. "Symposium: Federal Civil Service Reform: Another Legacy of 9/11?" *Review of Public Personnel Administration* 24, no. 3 (2004): 191–201.

National Performance Review. *From Red Tape to Results: Creating a Government that Works Better and Costs Less*. Washington, DC: U.S. Government Printing Office, 1993.

National Performance Review. *Common Sense Government: Works Better and Costs Less*. Washington, DC: GPO, 1995.

National Research Council. *Pay for Performance: Evaluating Performance Appraisal and Merit Pay*. Washington, DC: National Academies Press, 1991.

National Security Act, Public Law 235 of July 26, 1947; 61 STAT. 4.

Niskanen, William. *Bureaucracy and Representative Government*. Chicago, IL: Aldine-Atherton, 1971.

Northrup, Herbert Roof, and Amie D. Thornton. *The Federal Government as Employer: The Federal Labor Relations Authority and the PATCO Challenge*. Philadelphia: The Wharton School, University of Pennsylvania, 1985.

Office for Personnel Management, 2012.

Office of Management and Budget. *Management of the United States Government Fiscal Year 1988*. Washington, DC: GPO, 1988.

OPM. *The Regulatory Plan and Unified Agenda of Federal Regulations*. Washington, DC: GPO, 1995.

OPM. *Health Insurance Premium Conversion Plan*. Washington, DC: GPO, Federal Register/Vol. 65, No. 139/Wednesday, July 19, 2000/Rules and Regulations.

OPM. *A Fresh Start for Federal Pay: The Case for Modernization*, 19 April 2002. https://ourpublicservice.org/publications/opm-a-fresh-start-for-federal-pay-the-case-for-modernization/

Osborne, David, and Ted Gaebler. *Reinventing Government: How the Entrepreneurial Spirit is Transforming the Public Sector*. New York: Plume, 1992.

Osborne, David, and Peter Plastrik. *Banishing Bureaucracy: The Five Strategies for Reinventing Government*. Reading, MA: Wesley Addison, 1997.

Performance Rating Act of 1950, Sept. 30, 1950, chap. 1123, 64 Stat. 1098.

Perry, J. L. "The Civil Service Reform Act of 1978: A 30-Year Retrospective and a Look Ahead." *Review of Public Personnel Administration* 28, no. 3 (Sept. 2008): 200–204.

Perry, J. L., B. A. Petrakis, and T. K. Miller. "Federal Merit Pay, Round II: An Analysis of the Performance Management and Recognition System." *Public Administration Review* 49, no. 1 (Jan.–Feb. 1989): 29–37.

Peters, Charles. *How Washington Really Works*. Reading, PA: Addison-Wesley, 1992.

Peters, Thomas J., and Robert H. Waterman. *In Search of Excellence: Lessons from America's Best Run Companies*. New York: Warner, 1992.

Petersen, P. B. "Total Quality Management and the Deming Approach to Quality Management." *Journal of Management History* 5 (1999): 468–488.

Pfiffner, James P. "Establishing the Bush Presidency." *Public Administration Review* 50, no. 1 (1990): 64–73.

———. *The Strategic Presidency. Hitting the Ground Running*. Lawrence: University of Kansas Press, 1996.

———. "The First MBA President: George W. Bush as Public Administrator." *Public Administration Review* 67, no. 1 (2007): 6–20.

Podhoretz, John. *Hell of a Ride: Backstage at the White House Follies, 1989–1993*. New York: Simon and Schuster, 1993.

President's Private Sector Survey on Cost Control. *War on Waste*. New York: Macmillan, 1984.

Provost, Colin, and Paul Teske, eds. *President George W. Bush's influence over Bureaucracy and Policy*. New York: Palgrave Macmillan, 2009.

Rabin, Jack. *Handbook of Public Personnel Administration*. New York: Marcel Dekker, 1995.

Rosenbloom, David H. *Federal Service and the Constitution*. Washington, DC: Georgetown University Press, 2014.

Savas, Emmanuel. *Privatization and Public Private Partnership*. New York: Seven Bridges, 2000.

Savoie, David. *Thatcher, Reagan, and Mulroney: In Search of a New Bureaucracy*. Pittsburgh, PA: University of Pittsburgh Press, 1994.

Schultz, David A., and Robert Maranto. *The Politics of Civil Service Reform*. New York: Peter Lang, 1998.

Seyb, R. P. "Reform as Reaffirmation: Jimmy Carter's Executive Branch Reorganization Effort." *Presidential Studies Quarterly* 31 (2001): 104–121.

Suskind, Ron. "Faith, Certainty, and the Presidency of George W. Bush." *New York Times Magazine*, 17 October 2004.

Suskind, Ron. *The Price of Loyalty: George W. Bush, the White House, and the Education of Paul O'Neill*. New York: Simon and Schuster, 2004.

Terry, Larry D. "Administrative Leadership, Neo-managerialism and the Public Management Movement." *Public Administration Review* 58 (May/June 1998): 194–200.

Thompson, J. R. "Reinvention as Reform: Assessing the National Performance Review." *Public Administration Review* 60 (Nov/Dec 2000): 508–521.

Thompson, Vincent A. *Without Sympathy or Enthusiasm: The Problem of Administrative Compassion*. Tuscaloosa: University of Alabama Press, 1979.

U.S. Congress, House Committee on House Administration. *Campaign 1976. Vol. 1, Part 1, Jimmy Carter, committee print, 95th Cong., 2nd sess*. Washington, DC: GPO, 1978.

U.S. Congress, Senate, Committee on Government Affairs. *Nomination of John P. White to be the Deputy Director of the Office of Management and Budget*. Hearings, 96th Cong. 1st Session. Washington, DC: Government Printing Office, 1979.

U.S. Department of Homeland Security and Office of Personnel Management. *Human Resources Management System: Design Team Review of Current Practices*. Washington, DC: GPO, 2003.

U.S. Federal Register. *Department of Homeland Security Human Resources Management System. Proposed Rule, 8030-5347, 2004*.

U.S. General Accounting Office. *DHS Personnel System Design Effort Provide for Collaboration and Employee Participation*. Washington, DC: US Government Printing Office, 2003.

U.S. Library of Congress, Congressional Research Service. *The Carter Reorganization Effort: A Review and Assessment*, CRS, Rept. 80–172G. Washington, DC: CRS, 1980.

U.S. Library of Congress, Congressional Research Service. *The President's Reorganization Authority: Review and Analysis*, by Roland C. Moe, CRS, RL30876, Washington, DC, March 8, 2001.

U.S. Office of Management and Budget. *Government-wide Performance Plan*. Washington, DC: Government Printing Office, 2000.

U.S. Office of Management and Budget. *President's Management Agenda*. Washington, DC: Government Printing Office, 2001.

U.S. Personnel Management Office. *Biography of an Ideal: A History of the Federal Civil Service*. Washington, DC: U.S. Civil Service Commission, 2012.

VandeHei, J., and G. Kessler. "President to Consider Changes for New Term." *Washington Post*, 5 November 2004.

Van Riper, Paul. *History of the United States Civil Service*, New York: Row, Peterson, and Co., 1958.

Vogel, David. "The New Social Regulation." In *Regulation in Perspective: Historical Essays*, edited by Thomas K. McCraw, 155–185. Cambridge, MA: Harvard University Press, 1981.

———. "The Public Interest Movement and the American Reform Tradition." *Political Science Quarterly* 95, no. 4 (1981): 607–627.

Waldo, Dwight. *The Administrative State*. New York: Ronald Press, 1948.

———. "Public Administration in a Time of Revolution." In *Classics of Public Administration*, edited by Jay M. Shafritz, 310–317. Oak Park, IL: Moore Publishing, 1978.

Wallace, Walker, and Michael Reopel. "Strategies for Governance: Transition and Domestic Policymaking in the Reagan Administration." *Presidential Studies Quarterly* 16, no. 4 (1986): 734–742.

Waring, Stephen P. *Taylorism Transformed.* Chapel Hill: University of North Carolina Press, 1991.

Weaver, Paul H. "Regulation, Social Policy and Class Conflict." *Public Interest* 50 (1978): 45–63.

Wilson, James Q. *The Politics of Regulation.* New York: Basic Books, 1980.

Woodward, Robert. *Bush at War.* New York: Simon and Schuster, 2002.

Zifcak, Spencer. *New Managerialism: Administrative Reform in Whitehall and Canberra.* Buckingham: Open University Press, 1994.

Zink, S. D. *Guide to the Presidential Advisory Commissions 1973–84.* Alexandria, VA: Chadwyck-Healey, 1985.

CONCLUSION

Continuity and Change in the U.S. Federal Civil Service

Reforming the U.S. Civil Service

The concluding chapter does well to reaffirm the fundamental points of a given historical arc, and in the present case, to seek a precise understanding of the continuities and changes which have characterized the postwar U.S. federal civil service.

A few final considerations can be formulated regarding the two fundamental aspects of the U.S. civil service history scrutinized in this book. They concern the politics of the reorganization of the executive branch, progressively affirmed since the first years of the twentieth century, and the reforms of the federal civil service: both developed along parallel lines, following the evolution of the relationship between politics and public administration, and of that between merit and management.

As we have seen, the decade that followed the war aimed to establish order and to consolidate the new Administrative State. The New Deal legislation was not repealed, executive agencies remained in place, and the national security apparatus steadily grew. At the civil service level, the merit system was further strengthened and civil servants enjoyed new rights and benefits, particularly in pay and personnel management. Most of the reforms aimed to reorganize, and not to dismantle, the federal bureaucracy, reducing overlapping and multiplied functions of the agencies established in the war period, and providing a more rational organization to the executive branch; new departments established for managing welfare policies were created during the 1950s, and the federal government was opened to experts and scientists. On these points, there was a solid continuity between the Democrat Truman and the Republican Eisenhower. Moreover, Eisenhower attempted to forge a new administrative élite through the introduction of "Schedule C," composed of confidential or policy-determining positions which bridged politics and administration, paving the way to the creation of a Senior Civil Service on the British model. We can consider the 15 years after the World War II as an era of "pax burocratica," with moderate ideological conflicts within both political and administrative environments, and of diffuse trust in government. This special condition was exploited by the presidents to institutionalize the reinforcement of the White House offices begun by Franklin Delano Roosevelt and to consolidate the new bureaucratic organization within the federal executive branch.

A second wave of change gained momentum in the early 1960s, when the bureaucratic development was no mere continuation of the trends established before that time. New sociopolitical developments, such as the civil rights movement, economic growth, and the demand for welfare expansion, produced a shift in the objects of federal expenditure from defense to domestic programs. In this context, administrative reorganizations and civil service reforms aimed to make public administration more representative of minorities and to open it to new societal interests, to further reinforce the role of the presidency in policy-making, to increase rights (particularly unionism) and benefits for professional civil servants, and to use more sophisticated analytical techniques for policy evaluation.

The presidencies of John Fitzgerald Kennedy and Lyndon Johnson empowered the federal civil service, leading to the apex of the power and prestige of Washington's bureaucracy. Kennedy gave the right to the federal civil servants to organize their unions in order to bargain with the federal government about their contracts, and he established new polices for pluralizing the civil service and for promoting diversity and equal opportunities. This trend was strengthened by his successor Lyndon Johnson, who pursued a nondiscriminatory and inclusive approach in the recruiting procedure of the civil service. Moreover, the Kennedy administration raised civil servants' pay, revamped the performance management system, and increased the centralization of personnel management (exams and training) within the Civil Service Commission (CSC). Johnson went on to implement new training programs for women and ethnic minorities, and he attempted to increase the level of the competences of the new civil servants, directing recruiting toward more technical roles. In the same wake, new techniques of performance budgeting were introduced by the Johnson administration, in order to achieve better control of policy outcomes. In addition, and in contrast to the trend established by the New Deal, the new administrative agencies established in the 1960s primarily concentrated on social issues and less on economic regulation.

The presidency of Richard Nixon can be considered the final part of this era for several reasons: like his predecessors, Nixon maintained the administrative structures he inherited; he launched a series of administrative reforms to undermine the constitutive role of federal agencies and to "presidentialize" them; he strengthened White House offices and personnel; he improved the pay conditions of civil servants. Moreover, as a Republican he did not embrace a frontal confrontation against big government, but he pursued the strategy of "administrative presidency," acting on the implementation of existing laws through regulations, to circumvent a Democratic Congress hostile to his agenda. At the same time, Congress counterbalanced the presidency by imposing continuity on anti-discrimination and equal opportunities policies in the federal government. Unlike his predecessor, however, Nixon played much more aggressively with political appointments, aiming to increase presidential control of the professional bureaucracy. He tried to impose a politicization of the highest rank on the civil service, weakening the merit system. Nixon's administrative presidency approach, and civil service politicization, was cut short by his resignation after impeachment in 1974, but each of his successors has amplified its use because of the increase in legislative polarization, and they have done so by typically couching their efforts as agency administrative reforms enhancing economy and efficiency.

Although the 1970s have been perceived as a decade of profound crisis, the roots of this malaise already appeared in the mid-1960s when a vocal mass of Americans, both from the left and from the right, believed that America's commercial republic had transformed into a plutocracy of elites that ran the world to the detriment of citizens. These elites had created bureaucracies of nameless, faceless bureaucrats guided by scientism. Administrative systems were difficult to navigate, geared toward marginalizing citizens, and insufficiently grounded in social equity; and, at the same time, they were perceived as too bureaucratic and adverse to business. Public trust in government further waned during the 1970s, first stimulated by the forced resignation of President Nixon due to the Watergate scandal. Nor did the end of the gold standard, the introduction of floating exchange rates, and the use of the U.S. dollars as the world's major reserve currency help, by buttressing inflationary forces and prompting international backlash. Next came the two Arab oil embargoes (1973 and 1979), the first during the Nixon presidency and the second during the Carter presidency (1977–1981). Both created gasoline shortages for automobiles, raised energy costs enormously, and helped produce double-digit inflation and unemployment that Keynesian economic theory said was impossible.

As a response to this scenario, the third phase of the postwar civil service history developed from the mid-1970s through the end of the 1990s, in which reorganization efforts sought to provide an answer to citizens' disaffection toward the administrative state and its élites. The American ruling class found the answer to this crisis in the neoliberal paradigm that promised to reduce both the sway of the public sector and the regulation of financial markets, as well as to open government sectors to economic competition and to apply private sector financial and managerial mechanisms to the public sector. This period was characterized by the redefinition of the boundaries of the federal government through a spate of contracting-out measures and privatizations. It also saw the advent of a new managerialism that promoted entrepreneurial culture within the governmental apparatus and that favored the production of public services modeled on those of the business market. The federal bureaucracy itself was urged to assume the shape of private companies, and civil servants aimed to transform themselves into public business managers with budgetary responsibility, defined planning objectives, and personnel performance to monitor.

Viewing these facts with an historian's eyes, we can perceive a certain homogeneity in the phase spanning the Rooseveltian administrative reforms to Carter's introduction of the 1978 Civil Service Reform Act. These decades witnessed a growing consolidation of the administrative state, a marked increase in federal administration offices and personnel, an increasing centrality of the presidency in managing the executive branch, and a progressive expansion of the rights and benefits of professional civil servants. In this sense, Carter's Civil Service Reform Act can be seen as a decisive rupture, which, in responding to the late 1960s–early 1970s crisis of political legitimacy, offered itself as the springboard toward a new epoch. It nurtured a new paradigm, which primarily aspired to reduce the economical interventionism of the government, and, in conjunction, to improve the efficiency of bureaucratic organization. There thus was a shift from the apex of welfare-based development, reached with the institution of the programs of the Great Society and the 1960s–1970s reign of Keynesism, to the neo-liberal and neo-managerial paradigm installed first by Jimmy Carter and Ronald Reagan, and then implemented by George H. W. Bush, Bill Clinton, and George W. Bush.

As noted above, from the end of the 1970s, the campaign against "big government," "red tape," and wasteful expenditures would continue through the end of the century. In this sense, the American contribution was fundamental, especially because of the cultural influence that the United States exerted over the rest of the Western world. At the technical and practical levels, the avant-garde was represented by the Australian and New Zealand governments, and then by the United Kingdom of Margaret Thatcher.[1]

In administrative terms, this cultural change produced the next round of reforms, a response that Donald Kettl aptly calls the "competition prescription," the epitome of market rationality. For minimal-state proponents, this market-modeled version of administrative reforms was called the New Public Management (NPM). NPM proponents argued that metrics—market competition, performance measurement, outcomes-based administration, and citizen satisfaction scores—should override bureaucratic procedures as accountability mechanisms. Thus, in contrast to the "maximum feasible participation" of Lyndon Johnson's War on Poverty, NPM proponents saw the rationality of markets and quasi-market administrative structures as the mechanism for citizen participation. Its intellectual foundations were microeconomics, public choice theory, and transaction cost analysis. In an age of neoliberal economics prompting rule-based economic globalization in a new "information age," the NPM fit neatly into the political zeitgeist and informed the Reagan Revolution of the 1980s.[2] Moreover, it continued in various iterations into the presidencies of Republican George H. W. Bush (1989–1993), Democrat Bill Clinton (1993–2001), and, later, Republican George W. Bush (2001–2009).

Indeed, the passage from the Republican administrations of Reagan and Bush to Clinton's Democratic one did not undercut the essential philosophy of administrative reformism. In some ways, Clinton's "reinventing government" was a sort of NPM-lite. Like Reagan, Clinton stressed debureaucratization and decentralization of authority within agencies, giving states greater flexibility in administering programs and focusing on customer service and partnering. He also embraced the practice of making agencies more entrepreneurial, by letting programs opt into becoming reinvention laboratories to encourage innovation. To be sure, there persisted some differences, for example, between Reagan's inclination to use outside advisers from the business world—as was the case with the Grace Commission—and Clinton's preference for stimulating career civil servants' capacity for self-reform. Contrary to Reagan, "Reinventing Government" eschewed deep budget cuts to agencies and wholesale personnel cuts that could cripple agencies.

The Republican George W. Bush followed the path traced by Clinton, placing emphasis on management, performance evaluation, and pay and benefits modernization, combining it with new national security policies and institutions and assuming a more aggressive posture on political appointments, maximizing the political responsiveness of the Senior Executive Service (SES).

In terms of political appointments, the postwar period was marked by an oscillating pattern. The 1883 Pendleton Act was an undoubted turning point for the "spoils system." From that time forth, in fact, the number of political appointments in federal administration declined, and in tandem there was an increase of civil service careers based on the merit principle. This trend predominated during the first three decades of the twentieth century, when the technocratic culture of the Progressives had conquered the political classes and the highest spheres of the American State. In this era, the merit principle for the selection of federal bureaucrats seemed to clearly prevail over the democratic principle of the spoils system. Nonetheless, the following historical phase confirmed that the number of politically appointed civil servants tends to increase in times of emergency: this was the case during the two World Wars, and the first two Franklin Roosevelt administrations set up to combat the Great Depression, with appointments more or less ideologically determined by the president's own orientation. In this second case, the political-ideological control over appointments appeared to be stronger for those presidents who cast themselves as "outsiders" to the two major political parties and the systems of Washington power, as demonstrated by Franklin Delano Roosevelt, Richard Nixon, and Ronald Reagan.

A Stronger Institution? More Strengths than Weaknesses

In its historical evolution, the U.S. civil service changed from its status as a merely instrumental element of democratic politics as it was before World War I into being an integral and essential part of these same politics.[3] In this sense, the history of the civil service mirrors the history of the United States. The civil service expanded when there were wars to be fought; it shrunk when they were over, while maintaining most of the transformations that had occurred; it became the blood of the administrative state, fundamental for its operational functioning; it learned from private sector management practices; it showed how flexible it could be in its relationship with political elites and, above all, to let itself become part of the American élites.

Indeed, the postwar history of the U.S. civil service showed us the consolidation and the evolution of new élites, the administrative élites. An administrative élite forged by the creation of the New Deal Agencies, the administrative bodies of World War II, the executive reorganizations of the three decades which followed the postwar era, the "Schedule C" class established by Eisenhower, the increasingly intense series of training programs, the ethnic pluralization and diversification of civil servants' background from the 1960s on, the SES created with the 1978 reform, and the neo-managerial policies implemented in the past few decades of the century.

Despite its changing and flexible relationship with politics and the persistence of the spoils system as part of the American tradition, the merit system resisted through time and a new élite flourished. The size and complexity of government tasks have increased form the end of the World War II, and the technical expertise to handle them has become an added source of power for professional civil servants. Moreover, the progressive devolution of more autonomy, in terms of budgeting, organization, and personnel policies, to agencies and public managers during the postwar era increased the influence of the federal civil service on policy-making process.

In short, it seems evident that the twenty-first-century U.S. civil service is more important and central for the American political system than it was at the beginning of the twentieth century.

There were two fundamental turning points in the civil service postwar history. The first took place in the immediate postwar period, when the new administrative agencies and offices, created first by the New Deal and then by the war, were maintained and rationalized. In fact, with the Truman and Eisenhower presidencies, a process of decentralization started in favor of the administrative agencies, while the merit system prevailed over the spoils system. In this context, career civil servants gradually became an independent source of decision-making power.

The second turning point was the response to the crisis of the seventies that led to the 1978 Civil Service Reform Act. The reform established the SES, formalizing the top grades of the administrative pyramid, and paved the way for the import of managerial techniques from the private sector. This change provided the springboard for the reforms of the following 30 years, shaping a managerial bureaucracy freer to manage budgets, organization, and policy objectives.

Yet the 1978 Civil Service Reform Act (CSRA) showed two major inconsistencies, never completely resolved by subsequent developments.

The first one was the conflict between the desire for greater political responsiveness and the desire for greater managerial capability and independence. Traditionally, political leaders have been frustrated by their inability to control the bureaucracy. Major portions of the SES were designed to give political appointees greater control over career executives. The stated intent of SES, however, was to increase management competence and job flexibility at the highest levels. This implies some measure of career independence and concentration on management problems, rather than increased attention to political directives. As a consequence, it grew the specialization of the federal civil servants in the policy field of their agency or department, without a wide rotation of the offices. Career bureaucrats became more fossilized into their administrative unit and they assumed a more technocratic posture.[4] In the end, the aim to politicize the federal civil service paradoxically produced a broader depoliticization of the administrative élite, particularly in the class of the career civil servants, focused on management techniques rather than on policy objectives.

The second was the conflict between the concept of a management cadre with a sense of identity and *esprit de corps* and the concept of competition to increase productivity. The SES, clearly modeled after the British Higher Administrative Class, a group with a distinct élite identity, was intended to create a team of generalist managers. The members of this same group, however, competed against one another for a relatively small pot of money for bonuses and rank awards. This process, which pitted managers against each other, was intended to increase and reward productivity but clearly undermined the birth of a stronger "institutional bond." In conclusion, an administrative élite was created in structural, economical, and legal terms with the reform, but not in cultural and institutional ones. Compactness, homogeneity, flexibility, and generalism were still missing in the top-level federal civil servants.

Furthermore, it emerged that administrative reorganizations, born of presidential initiative and voted for by the Congress, gradually lost strength during the 1970s and became formally exhausted in the mid-1980s, due to the growing polarization of the political parties. In order for reorganization reforms to be effectively implemented, there must be some agreement on the goals of reform, and Congress, federal employees, and other key stakeholders must be involved. Because of growing political polarization, these conditions became increasingly difficult to attain.

A Layering of Patronage, Merit and Management

In the field of civil service manpower, merit and management had lived side by side in government, in a kind of undeclared truce during the early decades of the twentieth century. During the 1930s, however, the contradiction began to come out in the open. And personnel management, through executive offices controlled by the presidency, gained ground over merit, guaranteed by an independent CSC. By the Roosevelt era and afterward, the argument about merit vs. management raged for nearly half a century in civil service personnel policy.[5]

Merit was the longtime battle cry of the Progressive-era reformers and the middle class, seeking a political system without corruption and spoils. Civil servants should be free from any political taint. Instead, they should be expert professionals who were hired, compensated, and promoted without partisan considerations. Civil service reform had been a mass movement leading up to its enactment at the federal level (for only a fraction of federal employees) in the 1883 Pendleton Act and widespread enactment in states and localities. CSCs were viewed as the best protectors of the merit system. Yet at the same time, there occurred the rise of the management class. Large corporations were no longer run by owners and boards of directors. Instead, the American solution was for a professionally trained class of managers who would make all important decisions regarding the operations of the corporation. The rise of management as an idea was a kind of endorsement of the new American political economy. Managers were the new heroes, a new class of supermen, the men who would make tough decisions based on the facts. All power would be vested in them and their decisions would affect all others in the hierarchy below them. Everybody had to pull in the direction indicated by the manager. Given the dominance and idolatry of business in the American political economy, the common perspective has been that government needed more businesslike practices. Transposing business administration to public administration was presumed to be valid and preferred. Government needed to be made as efficient as business. In this context, it was essential to give the president the managerial powers to run the executive branch like a corporate CEO, including the powers of budgeting, personnel, and planning.

The idea of the primacy of management considerations over merit persisted and eventually won out after the 1970s, in part because the basic elements of a merit system had become such a deeply established institution and value that it could not be easily erased, certainly not endangered by an executive-centric personnel agency. The concept that the permanent workforce of any governmental unit be merit-based had rooted deeply into the DNA of American political culture. Nonetheless, American society and values increasingly came to defer to the managerial paradigm, whether those senior managers were in the private or public sectors.

For the first few decades of the controversy, merit prevailed over management. Then, as the federal government became increasingly cumbersome in its operations and effectiveness, the tide turned. Management as the central principle of government human resources systems finally triumphed in 1978, with the approval of the CSRA. It abolished the U.S. Civil Service Commission and replaced it (largely) with the Office of Personnel Management (OPM). By the time of the 1978 CSRA, the one constant in all the reform ideas was to further improve public management without the need for major organizational change. As such, management prevailed over merit—although with the strong caveat that merit is alive and well, despite being within an institutional structure oriented to personnel management. Yet at the same time, in the postwar civil service, the merit principle had prevailed over political patronage, which in turn resisted in a more limited form for top-level political executives in the development of a professional bureaucracy.

As Michael Nelson pointed out, "the evolution of American bureaucracy has been marked by one ironic failure after another, the "grand irony" of which is that repeated efforts to bring government under political branch control have enhanced the power of bureaucracy."[6] This view was already anticipated by Herbert Kaufman in 1956:

> For though the mechanisms of neutral competence were remarkably successful in reducing the influence of political parties on the administrative hierarchy, they did not necessarily increase the President's control over administration. (...) The components of the "neutral" bureaucracy, by virtue of their expertness and information and alliances, have become independent sources of decision-making power.[7]

Kaufman theorized that American governmental history reflected a constant swinging pendulum among the values of neutral competence, representativeness, and executive leadership. Representativeness, through the spoils system managed by the parties, dominated most of the eighteenth century; neutral competence held sway for most of the twentieth century, with the introduction of the merit principle and the action of the CSC; while reformers (the Brownlow Committee) of Franklin Delano Roosevelt's age, and afterward, sought to elevate executive leadership in the field of civil service personnel management over neutral competence. Their views did not prevail until the passage and the subsequent implementation of the 1978 CSRA, which abolished the CSC and created the OPM, and the development of the neo-managerial paradigm in public administration.

In this sense, the U.S. civil service is a layering of political patronage (appointees), merit principle (recruiting on the base of neutral competence), and management (the search for efficient organization to accomplish political aims).

In the last century, Americans reduced the space of patronage in favor of merit and management in the civil service. They affirmed their desire to make merit and management be a part of their democracy. This development made the civil service a more stable, influential, and powerful institution. Despite some inconsistencies and peculiarities of the American administrative system, which we have already analyzed, there has been an overall strengthening of the professional administrative élite. At the beginning of the twenty-first century, the federal civil service was far more important for American politics than it was one century before. And today, merit and above all management are far more important compared to a century ago. For these reasons, the history of the civil service matters a great deal, for understanding the present political system of the United States.

Notes

1 On Thatcher's civil service reforms, see Lorenzo Castellani, *The Rise of Managerial Bureaucracy. Reforming the British Civil Service* (New York and London: Palgrave Macmillan, 2018).
2 As pointed out by Durant, Robert F. *Building the Compensatory State: An Intellectual History and Theory of American Administrative Reform* (London: Routledge, 2019).
3 As also noted by Brian J. Cook, *Bureaucracy and Self-Government: Reconsidering the Role of Public Administration in American Politics* (Baltimore, MD: John Hopkins University Press, 2014).
4 In the early 1990s, only 23% of career civil servants had served other than their current agency or department. See Joel D. Aberbach and Bert A. Rockman, *In the Web of Politics. Three Decades of the US Federal Executive* (Washington, DC: The Brookings Institution), 2000, 76.
5 On personnel management, see Mordecai Lee, *A Presidential Civil Service. FDR's Liaison Office and Personnel Management* (Tuscaloosa: University of Alabama Press, 2016); and Norma Ricucci, Katherine C. Naff, Madinah F. Hamidullah, *Personnel Management in Government. Politics and Process*, 8th ed. (London: Routledge, 2020).
6 Michael Nelson, "A Short, Ironic History of Bureaucracy," *The Journal of Politics* 44 (1982): 774.
7 Herbert Kaufman, "Emerging conflicts in the Doctrines of Public Administration," *The American Political Science Review* 50, no. 4 (1956): 1070.

Bibliography

Aberbach, Joel D., and Rockman Bert A. *In the Web of Politics. Three Decades of the US Federal Executive*. Washington, DC: The Brookings Institution, 2000.
Castellani, Lorenzo. *The Rise of Managerial Bureaucracy. Reforming the British Civil Service*. London and New York: Palgrave Macmillan, 2018.
Cook, B. J. *Bureaucracy and Self-Government: Reconsidering the Role of Public Administration in American Politics*. Baltimore, MD: John Hopkins University Press, 2014.
Durant, Robert F. *Building the Compensatory State: An Intellectual History and Theory of American Administrative Reform*. London: Routledge, 2019.
Kaufman, Herbert. "Emerging Conflicts in the Doctrines of Public Administration." *The American Political Science Review* 50, no. 4 (1956): 1057–1073.

Lee, Mordecai. *A presidential Civil Service. FDR's Liaison Office and Personnel Management.* Tuscaloosa: University of Alabama Press, 2016.

Nelson, Michael. "A Short, Ironic History of Bureaucracy." *The Journal of Politics* 44 (1982): 747–778.

Ricucci, Norma, Katherine C. Naff, and Madinah F. Hamidullah, *Personnel Management in Government. Politics and Process,* 8th ed. London: Routledge, 2020.

Spicer, Michael W. *Public Administration and the State.* Tuscaloosa: University of Alabama Press, 2001.

INDEX

Note: Page numbers followed by "n" refer to end notes.

Made in the USA
Middletown, DE
04 August 2022